Routledge Revivals

Ethnomethodological Studies of Work

First published in 1986, this collection of essays brings together ethno-methodological studies from key academics of the discipline, including the renowned scholar Harold Garfinkel who established and developed the field.

In addition to four case studies, the volume begins and ends with two essays which discuss some of the theory employed by ethnomethodologists. The essays in this collection look at a range of areas, from truck wheel accidents and their regulation, to martial arts and alchemy and provide concise and insightful examples of the ways in which ethnomethodology can be applied to a number of settings and subjects.

This work will be of interest to those studying ethnomethodology and sociology.

Ethnomethodological Studies of Work

Edited by
Harold Garfinkel

Routledge
Taylor & Francis Group

First published in 1986
by Routledge

This edition first published in 2017 by Routledge
2 Park Square, Milton Park, Abingdon, Oxon, OX14 4RN
and by Routledge
711 Third Avenue, New York, NY 10017

Publisher's Note
The publisher has gone to great lengths to ensure the quality of this reprint but points
out that some imperfections in the original copies may be apparent.

Disclaimer
The publisher has made every effort to trace copyright holders and welcomes
correspondence from those they have been unable to contact.

A Library of Congress record exists under LC control number: 85025695

ISBN 13: 978-1-138-71659-9 (hbk)
ISBN 13: 978-1-315-17875-2 (ebk)
ISBN 13: 978-1-138-71670-4 (pbk)

Directions in Ethnomethodology and Conversation Analysis

Series Editors: Andrew Carlin, Manchester Metropolitan University, UK and K. Neil Jenkings, Newcastle University, UK.

Ethnomethodology and Conversation Analysis are cognate approaches to the study of social action that together comprise a major perspective within the contemporary human sciences. Ethnomethodology focuses upon the production of situated and ordered social action of all kinds, whilst Conversation Analysis has a more specific focus on the production and organisation of talk-in-interaction. Of course, given that so much social action is conducted in and through talk, there are substantive as well theoretical continuities between the two approaches. Focusing on social activities as situated human productions, these approaches seek to analyse the intelligibility and accountability of social activities 'from within' those activities themselves, using methods that can be analysed and described. Such methods amount to aptitudes, skills, knowledge and competencies that members of society use, rely upon and take for granted in conducting their affairs across the whole range of social life.

As a result of the methodological rewards consequent upon their unique analytic approach and attention to the detailed orderliness of social life, Ethnomethodology and Conversation Analysis have ramified across a wide range of human science disciplines throughout the world, including anthropology, social psychology, linguistics, communication studies and social studies of science and technology.

This series is dedicated to publishing the latest work in these two fields, including research monographs, edited collections and theoretical treatises. As such, its volumes are essential reading for those concerned with the study of human conduct and aptitudes, the (re)production of social orderliness and the methods and aspirations of the social sciences.

The Academic Presentation
Situated Talk in Action
Johanna Rendle-Short

Institutional Interaction
Studies of Talk at Work
Ilkka Arminen

Ethnomethodological Studies of Work
Edited by Harold Garfinkel

Ethnomethodological studies of work

Edited by **Harold Garfinkel**

ROUTLEDGE
Taylor & Francis Group

London and New York

First published in 1986
by Routledge
2 Park Square, Milton Park, Abingdon, Oxon, OX14 4RN

Published in the USA by Routledge & in assocation with
Methuen Inc. 270 Madison Ave, New York NY 10016

Reprinted 1995, 1998, 2001

Transferred to Digital Printing 2005

Routledge is an imprint of the Taylor & Francis Group

Set in Linotron Times 10 on 11pt
by Intype London Ltd

Library of Congress Cataloging in Publication Data
Main entry under title:

Ethnomethodological studies of work.

(Studies in ethnomethodology)
Includes index.
Contents: Sociological indication and the visibility
criterion of real world social theorizing / M. D. Baccus
Multipiece truck wheel accidents and their regulations
/ M. D. Baccus Kung Fu / George D. Girton [etc.]
1. Work—Addresses, essays, lectures. 2. Sociology
Methodology—Addresses, essays, lectures.
3. Ethnomethodology—Addresses, essays, lectures.
I. Garfinkel, Harold. II. Series.
HD4904.E84 1986 306'.36 85-25695

British Library CIP Data also available

ISBN 0-7100-9664-X (pbk)
ISBN 0-415-11965-0 (hbk)

Contents

Introduction

Ethnomethodological studies of work began in 1972 with Harvey Sacks's observation that the local production of social order existed as an orderliness of conversational practices upon whose existence all previous studies depended, but missed. David Sudnow had tried to extend the relevance of Sacks's observation about conversational practices to the work of professional jazz ensembles but was able to do so only with ethnographic materials. Subsequently he made it cogent for the locally produced organizational things of single person improvisational jazz-piano playing and improvised touch typing. Taking up Sacks's observation, Sudnow and I used ethnographically documented conjectures about university lecturing in introductory chemistry to sketch topical initiatives in studies of work. After that graduate students and faculty at various universities in the United States, England, and Canada, as an evolving group, in seminars and through their empirical studies, developed these beginnings into a research program. The studies in this volume are founded on, continue, and depend upon the work of a large company of colleagues.

Soon after our studies began it was evident from the availability of empirical specifics that there exists a locally produced order of work's things; that they make up a massive domain of organizational phenomena; that classic studies of work, without remedy or alternative, depend upon the existence of these phenomena, make use of the domain, and ignore it. It was soon evident, too, *that* that domain is ignored is not a fault of classic studies but is among its identifying practices. It is as well a condition under which classic studies are able and permitted coherently to continue. Further, *that* the domain is ignored is a systematically produced feature of ordinary society and accompanies ordinary society's locally produced orderlinesses and their natural accountability as identifying details of ordinary society's production and accountability. *That* the domain is ignored is a systematically produced feature of ordinary society's practical objectivity, its observability, its recognition, its understanding, or its analysis.

It is the achievement of the company of colleagues that their studies now compose a corpus, and, affiliated to that corpus, a serious current situation of inquiry. For researchers with interests in the achieved production and accountability of the phenomena of order in and as ordinary society these provide access to an immense technical domain of organizational phenomena. These phenomena were not suspected until these studies established their existence, provided the methods to study them, and provided what methods and their accompanying phenomena of relevance, evidence, adequate description, observability, empiricism, validity, structure, object coherence, details, and the rest could be.

1 Sociological indication and the visibility criterion of real world social theorizing

M. D. Baccus

Peter Winch, in his book *The Idea of a Social Science*[1] discusses the nature of social regularity in terms of the rules for deciding the equivalency of events. Since regularity is understood as the recurrence of similar events its analysis is thought to be a problem of identity judgment. This problem is to be met with the provision of some rule with which to specify the criteria of such a judgment. Only one rule is to be associable with an equivalency. The rule, it seems, is particular to an inquiry and so judgments of identity are to be made with respect to that one rule prevailing over some specific inquiry. It may be that this 'one rule' provision arises from the notion that a given set of conditions holds for the determination of the validity of some measure, experimental result, or decision about the appropriateness of some data. For whatever reason, the one rule thus refers to the existence of a *formulation* of a given set of conditions and not to the situated work of doing an inquiry.

The problem of the nature of rules arises. Winch refers to the feature of informed looking which a rule presupposes in order for it to direct anything. Winch, however, confounds the issue by introducing a regressive argument about the social context of the observer's looking and the communication system (shared with his colleagues in science) presupposed in that looking. This is a false issue of objectivity in that the looker cannot be separated from his fellows, given Winch's notion of context, in order to look 'objectively' at them or the object of study. There is no way he can be logically extricated from his colleagues into a position of objective purity for he knows how to look only via his association with them. This membership can be referred to as the contextual necessity of an investigation, remembering that our original problem was one of deciding equivalencies.

1

To make judgments about institutions, or other social phenomena which display 'regularities,' then, the criteria and concepts in use must be understood 'in relation to the rules governing sociological investigation,'[2] in general and as a practice. Winch states that a problem ensues in that the phenomena under study, as well as the investigator's activities, are themselves subject to rules – the 'social rules' holding within the phenomenon, and which, in fact, produce its accountable regularities. This can be referred to as the docile subject issue, for instead of lighting upon the constitution of the phenomenon by investigatory practices, Winch takes the phenomenon as given and as having an objective existence (in this case, what it is accountably about) unaltered by constructive analytic theorizing. However, in that social phenomena are subject to social rules, according to Winch, he does recognize what might be called the pre-eminence of the phenomenal rules. It is, says Winch, those rules which hold *within* the phenomenon and not those of the investigation as a scientific enterprise which are of primary importance in deciding equivalencies; 'the same thing' equivalency is to be decided by those rules presiding over the social phenomenon *as recognized by its practitioners* and not as brought to the scene by investigators. There is a set of interphenomenal criteria which determine equivalencies, and specifically with respect to the structure of *that* social setting. These criteria are not directly answerable to those of the investigator's rules. The issue, then, is that the investigator cannot have a simply 'objective' relation with his object of study: he is both a member of a contextual necessity (as investigator) and his object of study has its own internal rules of the equivalency of its events.

Social investigation is not, therefore, analogous to that in the natural sciences. External accounts, no matter how logically adequate, are insufficient: 'more reflective understanding must necessarily presuppose . . . the participant's unreflective understanding.'[3] That is, the investigator must first have some idea of the internal workings of a social phenomenon (in its naturally available way) before he can go on to make statements about the phenomon from his point of view as an investigator. He thus must have some practitioner's knowledge about his object, knowledge which is 'unreflective' because it is in natural use by members of the production of the phenomenon. The investigator's concept of a phenomenon, which is informed primarily by investigatory practices and rules rather than from the phenomenon itself, still must rest on an understanding of those natural use concepts at work in his subject. Investigatory concepts must be answerable to the requirements of those intrinsic to the subject. This raises the issue of what constructs are and also of the 'integrity' of phenomena.

Theoretic constructs may not be the investigator's also (if they are naturally available to parties to the phenomenon), but they also may not be easily and naturally observable without 'knowing how to look' as the analyst's enterprise. A constructive analytic account formulating non-vernacular accounts but utilizing vernacular concepts as its elements gains in observability (and so in reliability, objectivity, reasonableness – in real worldliness) while preserving the analyst's technical enterprise of producing accountably non-vernacular accounts which make social phenomena their docile objects of study. In that Winch is providing for the integrity of phenomena he may also be providing for a stronger sense of the observability of their features. If phenomena have conceptual rights of their own, and those concepts are natural use notions and, so, practical visibles (with strong visibility for members engaged in producing the phenomenon), then the investigator's constructs gain visibility by being formulated by appropriating those strongly visible natural use concepts as real-world talk. Social theorizing about real-worldly phenomena can thus capture an aura of observability, and avoid a speculative or metaphysical tone by trading on the strong sense of the observability of real-world activities.

But there is a question to be raised here. Does this assume that real-worldly practical actions are a) unreflectively engaged in because of the unremarkableness of methods of production and accounting practices; b) are 'unreflective' because they are directed to producing some practical achievement to thus preclude reflective inquiry during the course of this production; or c) that because it is a *practical* production its elements are all highly observable ones ('practical' here having to do with accountably observable)? What constructive analytic accounts make social phenomena out to be trades on this unreflectiveness and seizes on it as a resource for the analyst's enterprise.

The criteria of real-world social theorizing

Accounts of social phenomena are accomplished in such a way as to constitute their objects of discourse as real-worldly, that is, as actual, objectively extant phenomena. To say that there are criteria for real-world social theorizing is to say that accounts of social phenomena provide those elements which assure the real-worldly character of its objects, whether they be events, actions, properties, structures, ideal types, concepts, or constructs. The 'objects' of social accounts are thus things to be found in the real world; above all they are recognizable as things that are or happen in the real world. The criteria should not be thought of as necessities to be met by the account but as elements which, in being provided by the account, *are* the account. They are the criteria which establish the worldly reality of the objects of discourse of the account. One such criterion is that of visibility.

Winch hits on interphenomenal integrity as a way of making social theorizing more appropriate to its objects (though he is pursuing a solution to the problem of generalization in social theory) in that it takes into account the properties, or structures, relations, etc., of social phenomena within themselves. The judgments of equivalency, the fundamental problem of regularity in social research, is to be based on these phenomenal properties. That phenomena have rights of their own is not a new idea, but the extension of this notion to an operational requirement for the legitimacy of social theorizing is. If identity judgments are to be valid and appropriate to some phenomenon, given phenomenal integrity, then the 'rules' to which Winch refers are those of everyday social theorizing and investigation is a set of practices which explicitly accommodates these as not only legitimate but as primary operations of investigation. But the ultimate effect of interphenomenal integrity is not merely a careful or principled concern with 'real' properties, as opposed to only abstractive ones; it is, rather, a recognition and an explicit assurance of the strong visibility of the features of social phenomena.

Central to the notion of interphenomenal integrity is that what is looked at has properties internal to it which must be taken into account; moreover, the very selection of phenomena and the looking itself are to provide for phenomenal integrity. The rules which Winch refers to as holding within the phenomenon are 'unreflective' but are observable as a natural account of the production of the phenomenon and are known by the investigator as a party to such social productions. Those properties which are to be treated as integrous are those properties which a member knows about, but this also means that they are visible (are naturally available) and accountably so. Adherence to operations of social theorizing which preserve interphenomenal integrity makes that theorizing more 'real' in that it enhances, and relies on, the strong visibility of these properties by emphasizing the very properties which are naturally available to members, either actually observationally or imaginably so. Note that observational availability refers to the accountable features of a phenomenon. These are used as elements of the theorizing, they are the 'data' from which the account (analytic or practical) is produced and to which it, the account, is reflexively referential.

Imagined availability of those accountable features is the standard means by which social theorizing is checked for its accuracy, reliability (given the aid of statistical measures), validity, and the rest; the elements, in that they are those naturally available ones, practically visible to members, are also the stuff from which the essential *reasonableness* of a social account is decided. That 'reasonableness' relies on the indexicality of the account as an essentially vague referencing device which allows the imagined availability of properties and features of the phenomenon. The accomplishment of an analytic account is that it is removed from the phenomenon in such a way that 'cases,' or analytic instances of the events of a phenomenon, are now things to be measured *against the account* and not against each other as in the production of the account, or, as in deciding the equivalency of events or actions. Nor are cases matched to an account to find *its* adequacy; accounts are read to find the *adequacy of the case* and as *an instance of the account*. Thus cases are read in or out of relevance with respect to the adequacy of the account to delineate their cogent features; and, each case is relevant only as one of a *collection* of instances which are *adequately equivalent*, that is, made so by collecting naturally available properties into some accountable unit which stands as a 'case.'

That the realness of social accounts is enhanced by preserving inter phenomenal integrity and done so by emphasizing naturally available and highly visible properties of social phenomena, is of interest here only in so far as it points up the provision of a visibility criterion for social accounts. Our concern is with what that visibility criterion is and how it is accomplished.

The visibility criterion: Social objects in the world

The visibility criterion of social theorizing has to do with the requirement of real-worldly objects being visible in some way. One notion of visibility is that real-worldly objects have to 'reside' somewhere in the world where one could go looking to find them. This residence is not a 'place' in the real world, but is the *constituted sense* of an object as accountably locatable in the world, either physically or through knowing how to look via some technical operation. That location assures it various properties, one of which is its 'objective' visibility. We are not, however, concerned here with deciding the objective existence of social objects, nor are we interested in the distinction Husserl makes, as a traditional problem in philosophy, between the ideal object and the real or experiential one. We are only concerned with the way real-worldly talk gets done and are indifferent to the question of whether its objects are imagined, observable, or analytic, just so that they are real-worldly and accountably so. More narrowly, we are interested here in the problem of constituting social objects and the practices in analytic social theorizing which constitute them as real-worldly social objects.

That visibility is a 'criterion' for the real-worldliness of social objects is to say that social objects, the objects of analytic social theorizing, are constituted so as to provide for their visibility via *some means*. One such 'means' is the establishment of sign-reading and indication as an account of their visibility to analysis, i.e., those analytic practices of social theorizing engaged in by investigators which produce visible topics of analysis are accountably seen as 'indication' or sign-reading practices. It should be noted that in focusing on sign-reading practices and indication as a means for satisfying the visibility criterion, we are concerned here with the methods of *referencing* social objects via analytic devices and so are dealing exclusively with the problem of reference where the properties and structures of social objects are indicated because they cannot be seen directly – for whatever reason. This point will be raised again in the discussion of the 'essentially unseen' but it is important to keep in mind that we are dealing here only with the problem of reference of an unseen and not of observables in the ordinary or mundane sense. The accomplishment of sign-reading discussed here is that the visibility criterion of real worldly social theorizing can be met for the objects of theorizing which are unseeable, *nevertheless*, and the fact that they are unseeable does not exclude them from being accountably real-worldly objects.

We will first take up the question of signs and sign-reading as a natural and adequate account of a way of satisfying the visibility criterion. Then we will look at what indication might be for sociological inquiry.

Signs and sign-reading

'Sign' is ordinarily defined as representation, a token, an omen, a trace, or vestige. But the central implication (which it shares with its synonyms such as signal, index, icon, and symbol) is of pointing to, indicating, standing for, setting up for, or being as good as, something else. A term common to definitions of sign is 'token' – very suggestive for us because its original sense was not of partial fulfilment, mere semblance, or presentation, but was 'to show.' Signs, as things, in a very real sense 'show' their referent; they are the visibility elements of the existence of their referent objects and go to constitute their accountable features. The kind of signs with which we are here concerned are 'acommunicable,' in that they are not linguistic or behavioral but are of the same nature as those physical signs 'read' in everyday practical natural theorizing about events or states in the real world. For example, the analysis of physical evidence is the practical 'reading' of such signs for their significance in constructing indicated events or situation not seen directly. A linguistic or quasi-linguistic account of these signs, the prevalent analysis of signs, and their uses is inadequate to explicate their character as practical objects and the contingencies of their use.

The nature of sign-reading practices will not be gotten at, however, by a principled definition of 'sign.' Acquiescence to the notion of the sign as a thing to be read is the acceptance of a natural account of sign-reading which will ignore the central issue of sign-reading as a method of inquiry. That issue is that the injunctive use of such a natural account assures not just the successes of sign-reading but the very existence of that which is 'read' as evidenced by the 'sign.' The invocation of the natural account of sign and referent *as part of sign-reading practices* provides for the methodological reliability, the rationale and the rationality of the activities which go to constitute sign-reading practices of natural theorizing. This invocation carries with it a laying-out of accountable parts, the definitional elements, which are created by virtue of the activity of sign-reading as providing for the natural account; at a minimum those elements consist of the sign itself, an interpreter and a referent.

We are interested in these parts only in so far as their existence implies that sign-reading is a mediated taking account, that the sign 'stands between' interpreter and object, and that the object is known 'through' the sign. The successes of sign-reading center on this issue of mediation because it establishes simultaneously the unseen in the real world, now available and interpretable, and the evidence with which to discern its structure and its events. Mediation is the theoretic pivot of the natural account of sign-reading. It is the device which allows for the unseen to exist on the other side of the operation of producing sign/referent and which allows it to be 'seen.' Sign-reading as a method of inquiry, either analytic or mundane, depends on this structural–analytic split, this referencing of the unseeable by the immediate via mediation. The practices of such inquiry take on the mediation account, the indexicality of sign to referent, as a methodological

7

sanction; practitioners know their practical enterprise through and as this account.

Sign-reading as a method of referencing the essentially unseen

What the unseen consists of in real-world natural theorizing, in the practical accountability of the world, is a structure isomorphic to the accomplished accountable world, a projection of the known, of the taken-for-granted structures. The unseen as constructed from sign-reading holds no surprises, not only in the sense that it was constructed common-sensically, but because it is *essentially* unseeable, that is, unobservability is an essential feature of the construction. In the way that omens show what is afoot behind mundane reality, it remains that it is only the 'omens' which are ever seen. Yet they 'reference' the unseen and are used to constitute its structure.

Sign-reading practices clearly display the reflexivity of object and method, of what is known as embedded in how it is known. The positing of sign/referent in the real world creates an evidence-formulation dicotomy, where the unseen is formulated as a whole, a reasonable model whose features are now documentable via the indexicality of the sign. It is the reflexivity of knowing the ways of the unseen through signs, where the unseen is recognized from a 'knowledge' of sign production (that is, the production of evidences as a kind of residue of events) as part of the natural world. This knowledge is member's knowledge of the production of real world structures and their accountability through natural theorizing.

The primary understanding of mediation is that the 'sign' is not the thing itself, that is, it is not identical to the thing it references and is essentially separate from it. The mediation account is not, however, a consequence of the separation in time and space of sign and referent or, more importantly, of the availability of the referent to observation, as it would have sign-reading to be. Rather, the essential separation is a result of natural theorizing about the production of those residues of worldly events which are taken to be signs. This is the essential separation of an acommunicable sign (those with which we are concerned here) from its referent. Moreover, signs as abstracted visibility elements of the unseen, their referent, gives to mediation the sense of a separation not of things, of sign and referent, but a separation of *observability* and *the formulated construction* which the unseen is. That is the accomplishment of the natural account of signs.

Mundane acommunicable signs, those bits of physical evidences of events in the world we rely on in everyday natural theorizing, are taken as fortuitous to that theorizing about the unseen; analytic signs, indicators, measures, are systematically provided for in sociology and in and as constructive analytic theorizing. Mundane signs may be 'found' in the world because they are a kind of residue of events, but the sense of foundness of analytic signs resides not in their circumstantial occurence but in their fortuitous support in constituting a natural analytic construction. The fortuitous 'finding' of analytic signs is rather a concern with the producibility of such sign events. The initial finding of an indicator as a fortuitous event (with respect to its consequentiality for the bit of theorizing being done) is of little consequence as compared to the pre-eminent concern with operations which *assure* the existence of systematically provided for, objectively available, and reliable analytic signs. The foundness of indicators, once the construction has been formed as a constructive analytic formulation of the unseen, phases into a sense of good indexicality to the construct; more importantly, they are seeable now as stable indices which are *reliable features of the construction*. The production of analytic signs, or indicators, is the sign-reading practice of using signs as a way of providing for this sign-reading in a reflexive production of the reading of the read.

Sign-reading as an adequate account of a means of satisfying the visibility criterion

It has been proposed here that the visibility criterion of social theorizing is a *feature* of real-worldly social accounts rather than a criterion that has to be met by these accounts. In the same way that sign-reading is a natural account of the production of an unseen, as a reflexively constituted object, sign-reading can be taken as an account of one means whereby the visibility criterion can be met by constituting social objects as worldly phenomena which are accountably visible. Yet there is no criterion and there is no unseen. What then are we talking about? We are referring to the work of 'indication' as the *constitution* of the accountable features of the accomplishment that is constructive–analytic, real-worldly, social theorizing. We have discussed the 'visibility criterion' of real-worldly social objects but now we can speak of the criterion as an *accomplishment* of social accounts in that those accounts provide for objects of analysis which have the property of visibility, as real-worldly objects. 'Sign-reading practices,' with an unseen referenced by signs, as a means of meeting the visibility criterion, can now be seen as *an account* which constitutes the

9

objects of social theorizing as real-worldly in that it accounts for its theoretic constructions as objects referentiable via signs. Note that we are talking about social theorizing as an *accounting practice* and are not concerned with the nature of the 'real world' nor the reality of its phenomena – objects, events, or the like. There is no dispute here with the practices of natural and constructive analytic social theorizing. Rather, it is the *accomplishment* of such theorizing with respect to indication which is being considered. Of particular interest to us is what indication, as the constitution of measures, indices, and indicators, is for sociology.

Sociological indication

David Willer and Murray Webster, in a paper entitled 'Theoretical Constructs and Observables',[4] make the distinction between 'observables,' descriptive terms drawn from everyday social experience, and 'theoretical constructs,' which are 'abstract properties of particular persons, places or events.' Furthermore, 'the construct is not the same as the observable features of any particular event or object, nor is it simply an abstract representation of an observable.'[5] It was proposed above that the 'realness' of social accounts is enhanced by preserving the interphenomenal integrity of social phenomena and done so by emphasizing their naturally available and highly visible properties. Stating that the visibility criterion must be met, and can be done so by trading on highly visible properties of social phenomena, is not to point out the same distinction between 'observables' and 'constructs' as that made by Willer and Webster. Our concern with visibility is not one of the distinction between the mundane and analytic taxionomic features of social phenomena. Satisfaction of the visibility criterion is not a problem of 'observables' versus 'constructs.' *Both* Willer and Webster's 'observables' and 'theoretic constructs' meet the visibility criterion because both are a product of natural theorizing. 'Visibility' in this paper refers to the *availability* of the accountable features of social phenomena to natural theorizing *as* social theorizing done in and as constructive analytic accounts.

If theoretic constructs are the stuff of which constructive analytic accounts are made, we have yet to define what relationship we propose to exist between the nature of those theoretic constructs and 'indication' in social theorizing. Also, if we are to retain the expedient of sign-reading as *an account* of indication, then what could the 'unseen' be for such a thing as the analysis of quantitative data? To address these questions it is first necessary to discuss what is posited here as 'indication.'

Indication occurs in sociological theorizing wherever the natural account of that work specifies that indices, indicators and measures are produced and used. Lazarsfeld[6] speaks of selecting indicators which are the appropriate, valid, and reliable measures of some conceptual dimension, as observable (and thus measurable) events, which have not an absolute relation with the thing they reference but a probabilistic one. Indicators are of necessity observables if they are 'variables.' They are observables as simple occurrences (events, quantities, rates, behaviors, etc.) or as contrived responses (expressed attitudes, choices, reasonings, etc.). Though Lazarsfeld was referring to their 'statistical' characteristics, indicators have a 'probabilistic' relationship with what they reference because there is no way of providing for an account of the construct, as an analytic formulation, such that *it* also provides for, as one of its features, the perfect accountability of its indicators to itself as referent. That is the sense of their probabilistic nature, formulatively *or* statistically. This is why we must speak of the visibility of the elements of theoretic constructs as *availability to natural theorizing* rather than of their simple *observability* as events or things in the world.

An example of indication will be helpful. Peter Blau, in his paper 'Structural Effects,'[7] seeks to demonstrate the external constraint effect a group value has on individual behavior in groups of caseworkers in a public assistance agency. The problem is how to avoid individual, idiosyncratic behavior and beliefs and get to the behavior affected by the existence of a group value. It is the fundamental problem in sociology of accounting for aggregate social 'structures' (such as group values) which are independent of individual behavior (as a formulation it is independent of the worldly phenomena it accounts for), while still nevertheless having to deal in the behavior of individuals. We will not go into a lengthy discussion of Blau's article, interesting as it is, but will focus only on the element of indication in the work.

Blau used as a measure of the orientation of workers to their clients a single strong survey item: should the amount of assistance to clients be increased? This item correlated highest with other measures of orientation to clients and was chosen as the single, strongest measure of the attitude of the individual toward clients. Caseworkers in Blau's study were organized into small groups of five or six with a supervisor over each group. The primary question at issue in the study was: 'Does the prevalence of pro-client values in a group affect the performance of duties of its members independently of the individual's own attitude to clients?'[8] In order to define the 'prevalence' of a positive orientation toward clients in a work group, the 'amount of assistance' measure was used to tally the number of members having a positive attitude; groups with a majority of members in favor of increased assistance were defined as having a positive orientation, *as a group*, toward their clients.

This positive orientation, or prevalence of favorable attitudes toward clients, was taken as the 'external constraint' on all members of the group to offer clients more assistance, as defined by casework duties, regardless of their personal attitude toward assistance. The 'structural effect' is the presence, or demonstration, of this constraint.[9] It is the working of a social value on individual behavior, a prevalent value which exerts 'social constraints upon patterns of conduct that are independent of the influence exerted by the internalized orientation'[10] of individuals. Those internalized orientations are attitudes and values held by an individual which affect his behavior.

The point is to show that the association between the group value or norm and patterns of behavior of group members is *independent* of an individual's personal orientation. For Blau's study the empirical demonstration of external constraint, or the 'structural effect,' would be made if he could show that the association between the prevalence of positive orientation and group patterns of client assistance is independent of group members' personal orientation toward assistance. Two findings from cross-tabulations of his survey data were: (1) that workers with pro-client attitudes (as measured by the increased assistance measure) were more service-oriented toward their clients, and (2) the major finding of the paper, that 'regardless of their own attitudes, members of groups in which pro-client values prevailed [i.e., where there was a majority of pro-client members] were more apt to be oriented toward casework service than members of groups with other values [i.e., with a minority of pro-client members].'[11] Note that this means that *both* pro-client and non-pro-client individuals were more service-oriented in the groups with the positive orientation value than in those without it.

We are proposing that Blau's study is an example of the use of 'indication' in a constructive analytic formulation which is an empirical demonstration of the existence of an unobservable, social constraint, which is an attribute of a social collective and as such is a theoretic construct. Let us look to Figure 1.1 for a schematized representation of Blau's study as an example of indication in constructive analytic social theorizing. It can be seen from the explanatory notes that we are proposing that the 'increased assistance' survey item was used by Blau as an indicator, or measure, of the group attribute 'positive orientation toward clients'[12] and as such referenced the group attribute which

The Survey Items   **The Theoretic Construct**

the indicators

the referent
and what is
indicated

The structural   the unobservable
"name" for   "process"

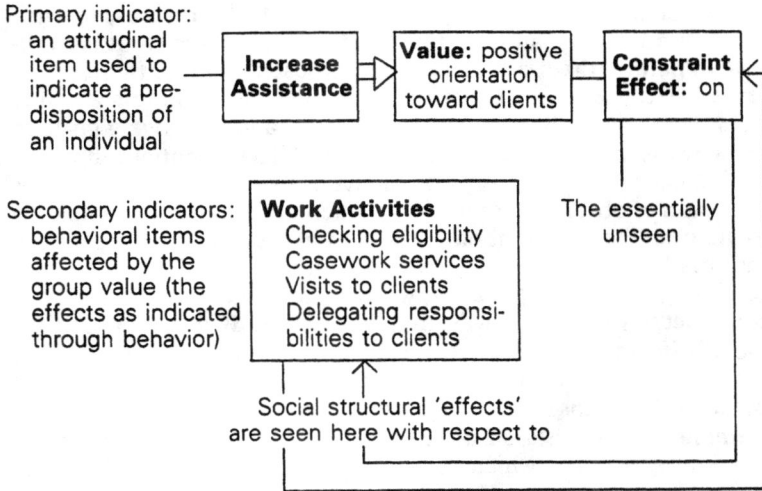

Primary indicator:
  an attitudinal
  item used to   **Increase**   **Value:** positive   **Constraint**
  indicate a pre-   **Assistance**   orientation   **Effect:** on
  disposition of   toward clients
  an individual

Secondary indicators: **Work Activities**   The essentially
  behavioral items   Checking eligibility   unseen
  affected by the   Casework services
  group value (the   Visits to clients
  effects as indicated   Delegating responsi-
  through behavior)   bilities to clients

Social structural 'effects'
are seen here with respect to

FIGURE I.I   Blau's 'structural effects' as an example of indication in
constructive analytic social theorizing

affected the social constraint. The structural *name* for this theoretic construct is 'group value;' the corresponding *process* is referred to as the 'constraint effect' or 'structural effect' empirically demonstrated. The construct, group value as constraint, is essentially unseen, that is, unobservable because it is a theoretic formulation of a phenomenon. Its primary indicator is the increased assistance measure; as an indicator it is a measure which goes to *define the presence* of the positive value as extant in the world. It is an indicator of the group value because *it was assumed as an indicator of individual orientation* toward clients and those individuals make up the caseworker groups.

But this is not the only indicator of the structural effect. Structural constraint is displayable only with reference to the work activities which are taken to be the empirical evidence of orien-

13

tation to casework service. Note that the increased assistance measure, as an expression of an attitude, is an indicator of individual orientation but that behavioral survey items, those listed under work activities, are reflexively indicative to the construct 'constraint' because of their availability to natural theorizing about the nature of *the consistency of attitudes and behavior*. The inconsistency, as displayed in the cross-tabulations of group membership, personal orientation, and casework activities within groups, is the theoretic key to the construct social constraint; the display of primary and secondary indicators, as visibility elements of the unseen constraint, are not just a display of observables, or variables, used as indicators of the construct. They are what is available to natural theorizing about the 'unobserved' constraint, unobserved because it is a constructive analytic formulation which is referenced via 'indicators' and 'measures' and reflexively gives to those measures their sense of 'indicator.' The essential reflexivity of indication in constructive analytic social theorizing is this provision of observables which are taken up as items now available to natural theorizing about how they were produced within an essentially unseeable enterprise. It may be argued that we are confusing an unobservable, worldly process with a theoretic construct, in the same way that Willer and Webster argued for the distinction between observable events and constructs. But note that Blau was after an 'empirical' demonstration of a social 'structure' which is an 'attribute of social collectivities.' This 'demonstration' rests on the display of *observable features* within a theoretic account which reflexively provides for those features' *comprehensibility as indicators* of the construct and the construct as seeable through them. Remember that we proposed that the 'visibility criterion' was not one of the simple observability of things in the world but is the *availability to natural theorizing* of those elements which are taken to indicate the construct *as a formulation of* how they were produced as the residues of some unobservable process. That the formulation which is the construct cannot provide for the perfect accountability, or perfect correspondence, of its indicators to itself *as one of the features of itself as a formulation* means that 'indication' must be the natural account of what is going on in the satisfaction of the visibility criterion – the criterion that to be real-worldly theorizing the objects of analysis must be demonstrable as objectively extant in the world. The visibility criterion is met by providing 'indicators'; 'indication' is a feature of the natural account of the theorist's enterprise; the criterion of visibility is *not a necessity to be met by the account*, but, in *being provided by the account, is the account*. That is, the real-worldly character of social accounts are not established by meeting some criteria of the worldliness of their objects of analysis; the criteria reside in and through the account as features of that account and not as criteria of the acceptability of worldly events or objects to theorizing. That is why 'indication' is only a natural account of the theoretic enterprise of producing constructive analytic formulations of essentially unseeable objects of analysis made 'visible' through indicators, measures and indices. The constructive analytic theoretician's real accomplishment is not finding indicators to reference an unobservable but is the establishment of that unobservable and those indicators as 'real' objects in the world via theorizing which is accountably, and *made* accountably, 'indication.'

Data and theoretic constructs in sociological indication

So far we have been speaking of attitudes, behavior, and group values as indicators and referents. But what of 'quantitative data' and 'theoretic constructs'? What are indicators as data and what is the construct as empirically demonstrated by that data? In order to understand how data is used as the empirical content of a constructive analytic theoretic construct we must first quickly review what has just been proposed about the nature of 'indication.'

Blau's study as an example of sociological indication consists of the following. Indicators (the survey items) and value (the group attribute) are being constituted as sign and referent, where the referent is, here, something already known as a formulatable: group value, a naturally available observable, and now substantiable in analytic detail via statistical values of its elements (i.e., the individual attitudes and behaviors and their frequencies). The analytic account proposes the value as an attribute of a group and a piece of social structure which consequently affects individual behavior. But *as a theoretic construct* it is unobservable directly as an operative element, as a process. The constraining effect of the group value was a formulation for what was going on in the group, as an attribute of that social collectivity, but the formulation *as an account* – or an accountable feature of what the group was about – is unobservable except reflexively to features *situatedly available in that setting*. The constructs of constructive analytic accounts, like 'values' and 'structural constraint,' are essentially unobservable because they are formulations and as such do not *in themselves* reference observable elements of a social production. They are descriptive formulations but they are so without providing *as one of their features*, worldly observational referents. They can be made *sensable* by such practices as exampling where stories can be told as accompanying the theoretic account. But this is only an accounting device to make the construct lively. These observational citations are not acceptable as an essential feature of a constructive analytic formulation because such a formulation systematically provides for its *strong indexicality* with respect to observables and that is its primary accomplishment. Cases, with their observables, can be measured against the account but the account is indifferent to the occasioned properties of cases.

To remedy the unobservability of theoretic constructs as formulations, 'indicators' are constructed. Blau's problem was how to get at social structural constraint as an attribute of a social collectivity, the group, through individuals as cases – the assumption being that the structural effects must rest, somehow, in individual behavior so that the individual is taken as the case – while avoiding individual predilections and behaviors as solely attributes of the individual. The collective attribute must be demonstrable through individual attributes which are taken to be more than the expression of the individual's private, isolatable orientation. The private orientation assumption is an artifact, for sociological constructive analysis, of taking the individual as the case unit with unit attributes constituted in accounting formulations of individual behavior as the topic and as made accountable via reasons, motivations, attitudes, orientations, etc., as the explanative account of individual behavior as isolatable and integrous *to the unit* of analysis, i.e., the 'individual.' This sense of the integrity of the attributes of the case unit which is seen as affected by association with other 'case units,' i.e., the social effect seen, was used as a resource in the Blau study implicitly to display the 'social structural effect' through the 'inconsistency' of the answer to the increased assistance question as an attitude and attribute of the individual, and the casework activities as behaviors naturally available as pro- or less pro-client in character. The artifactual nature of the private orientation, or pre-social character if you will, rests in the confounding of accountable features – of the individual as an accountable unit with characteristics *isolatable to that unit* inherent to a *level of analysis*. When the individual is taken as the unit of analysis of the naturally available 'social' or 'collective attribute' phenomenon, constructive analytic theorizing must constitute the *process* of that production of the social attribute, an essentially unseeable given this type of analysis, through such things as indicators.

Attributes of individuals, as the case unit, are taken as data furnishing the 'empirical' or observable stuff to which a formulation of that social process is made analytically indexical. The construct may be unobservable but the indicators are not. The behaviors of the caseworkers as individual attributes can be taken as 'effects' (of social constraint) only with respect to the group attribute (the constraining group value) *as a formulation* reflexively accounting for those behaviors as effects, as data, and so as an empirical demonstration of the existence of the process of which the construct is a formulation. Blau goes on to reason about the social process in terms of such things as sanctioning activities in the group, but this reasoning only makes the process *sensible*; it does not empirically *display* the process as an observable. Only the data does that; that is, the data as indicators of the effect produced on the individuals and measurable through the survey question – and, it might be noted, through only *one* survey administration: not even the accountable feature of time was needed to display the effects of a process here.

In Blau's study the data had a very special relation to the construct because of the implicit reliance on the perceived discrepancy between the assumed integrity of attitude and behavior of an individual. More generally, data need not have this property of a confounding of levels of analysis to be used to indicate a theoretic construct. Constructs are 'unobservable' because they have to be indexical to their constitutive elements in order to be something more than their sum or description. But a construct, as a formulation about real-worldly phenomena, can be made 'visible' through indicators which make the construct's features, as talk about the real world, available to natural theorizing, and thus reasonable as worldly structures. This availability is the *imagined* availability of accountable features of the phenomenon (such as the consistency of attitude and behavior) of which the formulation stands as an account. The construct's features (as an account about the real world) are *indicated* by variables taken as indicators, measures, indices, and as data. The observable constitutive elements of the construct in constructive analytic social theorizing is this data, these indicators, which are indicative of the construct but are not equivalent to it, *display* its accountable features but are only simple 'observables,' *provide its visibility elements* as real events, actions, attitudes, etc., but are, in the end, cases to which the account is indifferent for its successes: the construct is indexical to the data which reflexively gives it life and only imaginably indexical to worldly things.

Indication as constructive analytic social theorizing

We have just proposed that a construct, an essentially unseen and unobservable which is a formulaic account about the social world, is made 'visible' through the data, the variables, measures, and indicators, as a formulation about real-worldly phenomena. *That visibility is the availability. of the data to natural theorizing about its production, and hence about its worldly character.* What relation, then, does the construct have to real-worldly phenomena, to real-world events? It has none. A constructive analytic theoretic construct has a relation only to the data providing its empirically demonstrable existence as *world-sensible,* as *real-worldly,* but that data is not the world's events; it is rather the material reflexively constitutive of the construct as a piece of constructive analytic social theorizing. Constructive analytic data does not stand to the theoretic construct as the world stands to analysis: data, as constituted and constituting of its theoretic referent (that is, *any* explanation of the data) is comprehensible *only* with respect to the theoretic occasionality of *its production and its use.* Its production, via 'method,' is reflexive to its comprehensibility, i.e., 'theory.' That is why the construct is made 'visible' *in, as,* and *through* the data and through such things as 'indicators,' correlation coefficients, or even simple cross-tabulation frequencies as in Blau's example. The data is sensible only through natural theorizing about its production, i.e., sensible only through *theorizing which is method.* The reflexivity of theory and method in constructive analysis is such that data is essentially theory-provided, that is, it does not exist independent of a theory of its natural production and as collectable in the world. Theoretic accounts, referred to as 'theory,' are merely formulations which give to the data its meaning, though the natural account is usually that the data provides the basis for the theory as an explanation of it. Theoretic formulations are indexical to real-world settings as occasions of their occurrence only because of what they take from, or impart to, those settings *as data.* 'Indexical' here means not to stand as an incomplete account, indefinite because it cannot be fully elaborated, but to inform what is to be found there via the account which rests on data as its constitutive element. The 'there' is the data collectable from it, which stands as 'it,' the real-world setting.

Why then is the construct 'indifferent to,' or indexical to, its cases; why does it stand as something more than its particular cases, transcendental to their constitutive sense? Because they only 'indicate' the construct; that is, the natural account of indication provides for signs, referents and mediation. It does not provide for reflexive constitution. Nor does it provide for the essential reflexivity of theory and method. Cases and data, indicators and measures have only a 'probabilistic' relation with their constructs because the natural account of indication makes them signs. The referent may be made 'visible' via those signs, but it is only 'indicated' by them: the referent is not identical to the sign. Yet 'visibility' is natural theorizing about the production of such signs, as data; it is, more simply, natural theorizing about the world. When we speak of the visibility criterion as having been met we refer to the accomplishment of an analytic account which *as a feature of the account* provides for the objective worldliness of its objects of discourse. For constructive analytic social theorizing 'indication' is the provision of the real-worldly character of theoretic constructs.

Notes

1 Routledge & Kegan Paul, London, 1958, pp. 83–91.
2 *Ibid.*, p. 87.
3 *Ibid.*, p. 89.
4 *American Sociological Review*, vol. 35, no. 4 (August 1970), pp. 748–57.
5 *Ibid.*, p. 748.
6 'Evidence and Inference in Social Research,' *Daedalus*, vol. 87, no. 4, pp. 99–130.
7 *American Sociological Review*, vol. 25, no. 2 (April 1960), pp. 178–93.
8 *Ibid.*, pp. 180–1.
9 Structural effects are, as noted by Blau, a 'special type of the "contextual propositions" of Paul Lazarsfeld.' See 'Problems in Methodology,' in Merton, R. K. *et al*, *Sociology Today*, Basic Books, New York, 1959, pp. 69–73.
10 *ASR*, vol. 25, no. 2, p. 179.
11 *Ibid.*, p. 181.
12 We are emphasizing the *positive* group attribute because the study sought to demonstrate *its* effect on group behavior.

2 Multipiece truck wheel accidents and their regulation

M. D. Baccus

Description

A multipiece truck wheel, referred to here as multipiece rims, consists of a rim base over which a truck tire is mounted, and a wheel center which is bolted onto the axle of the vehicle. The wheel center can be either a disc which is welded or riveted to the wheel base or a spoke center which is bolted to the wheel base. A truck tire is held in place on the wheel base by an interference fit of the tire bead against the flanges of the rim base. It is the flange mechanism that determines the type of rim, multi- or single-piece. Single-piece rims are of the same design as passenger car wheels, a single wheel base over the flanges of which is forced the tire bead, or inner lip of the tire. Multipiece rims consist of a design whereby one flange is in effect removable. Instead of a simple interference fit, the separable flange pieces form an interlocking fit under pressure of the tire inflation. Single-piece rims take tubeless truck tires, multipiece rims utilize tubes. Truck tires are inflated to a 90–120 psi range, depending on the specific tire. Thus, the flange assembly is placed under 90–120 lb per square inch pressure which effects a 'clamping' force on the interlocking rim parts; this clamping force is approximately 40,000, or 20 tons for a wheel assembly at 90 psi.

The arrangement of what we will call here for ease of description a removable flange, allows for a simpler tire-to-wheel assembly requiring less physical force to mount the tire and less complicated tools to do it. There are several variations on removing one flange of the wheel base and a number of designs for the interlocking of the parts making up that flange. The removable flange consists of one or more parts which are referred to as a side ring, the flange surface in a multipiece assembly, and a lock ring which provides the 'locking' mechanism for the removable flange arrangement. Two-piece rims consist of a wheel base and a side ring; three-piece rims consist of a wheel base, a side ring and a lock ring which holds the side ring in place. Side rings in two-piece rims are often referred to informally as lock rings or locking rings so that, generally, any removable flange part is referred to as a lock ring. One variation of the removable flange consists of a 'split wheel' rim which, instead of having a ring assembly, effects the flange removal by splitting the wheel base in half at its central circumference so that the locking mechanism takes place not at the outer edge of the rim but at the inner circumference of the wheel over which the tire is mounted.

Side rings can be split or a closed circle. Split rings have a closure 'spring' to them so that they maintain a circle when not in the wheel assembly. Rings that are 'sprung' are those which have lost their integrity as effective parts either by fatigue cracking within the ring or from being bent out of shape from too much use or mishandling. The non-split ring is one which has to be slipped over the wheel base without the give allowed by a gap in split rings. They form a slightly looser fit over the rim as a result, although they are designed to form a secure flange area in the same way a split ring does. The multipiece rims are designed so as to hold together loosely while under no pressure. Once the tire is pressurized, the locking effect of the rim parts comes into effect as they are held together under approximately 40,000 of pressure until that situation is altered. Generally speaking there are two types of circumstances which alter this locking effect: (1) part failure and (2) improper 'seating' of the side/lock ring(s). Part failure comes about through fatigue cracking of the components or damaging incidents while the wheel is in service. Improper seating of the ring(s) results from a number of circumstances.

A blow-out with a sudden loss of air pressure but continued load exerted on the tire and wheel assembly can force apart the rim components. A tire run on lower than normal pressure can have in effect an unseated ring in that it is not ideally aligned for proper locking; airing up of the tire exerts pressure on the misaligned parts. Servicing of the tires and rim requires that all air pressure be evacuated from the tire before disassembly is attempted; premature disassembly unseats the ring(s), allowing them to break apart under pressure. Proper alignment of the rim components prior to airing up is required for the locking effect to take place: bent parts or insufficient snapping in of the ring(s) does not allow for proper seating. The effect of part failure and improper seating is the same: the ring(s) fly apart from the wheel base and the wheel base itself lifts off the ground. This is referred to as a 'rim separation.' The force of the separation depends on the amount of pressure behind the components, i.e., whatever part of the normal 40,000 of air pressure is in the truck tire at the time of the separation. Because of the forces involved rim separations are often referred to as 'explosive separations.'

The regulatory problem

On October 2 1978 the Insurance Institute for Highway Safety issued a press release announcing action the Institute had taken in posing the multipiece wheel as a source of needless and avoidable danger on the road and in the workplace because of its explosive potential. A press statement by William Haddon Jr, MD, president of IIHS, issued on that day outlined an argument of the danger inherent in their design and a remedy of the situation. A petition was filed with the Department of Transportation, NHTSA, for a proposed new standard in effect to ban such wheels from future manufacture by requiring that under blow-out and run flat conditions the wheel and tire stay together rather than fly apart. On June 14 1978 the Institute had petitioned the NHTSA to initiate a safety defect investigation of these wheels. That petition pointed to the occurrence of a 'substantial number' of separations, which had occurred over the years, and the existence of a safer alternative, the single-piece rim already being manufactured. A further point was made regarding the ineffectiveness of any attempt to eliminate the problem through education of tire maintenance people alone because they comprise only part of the population at risk who have been injured. Two 'tests,' or demonstrations of explosions of wheel components were filmed and presented to the press that day. One, a simulated roadside tire change, showed the effect of a lock ring disengagement on a dummy placed over the wheel; impact speed of the ring was estimated at 100 mph. A second test simulated an on-the-vehicle inflation of a soft tire on a camper. A 75 mph disengagement speed was estimated for the loose lock ring striking a child-sized dummy placed in the ring's path. (This simulation closely resembled an actual injury case.)

The case that brought the issue to the Institute's attention involved an eighteen-year-old auto mechanic who was killed by a rim separately shortly after he had mounted and inflated a truck tire using a safety cage. His mother wrote to the Institute asking whether there was any better means to protect young workers in this area. (The worker in question suffered a head impact from a wheel separation in July of 1976. The explosion occurred as he was moving the wheel from the safety cage; he had one week's experience.) Such individual and unsolicited complaints are a major source of preliminary information on product problems and start a search for similar instances of fatalities, injuries, or 'near misses' which are gathered up as evidence of a possible defect condition in the product. There is a piece of commonsense reasoning which is prevalent in consumer attitudes toward products which is often shared by agencies in the safety field; that is, that the instance of even one or a few cases is enough evidence that a defect or unreasonably dangerous condition exists in that product. A case in point is car fires: it is commonly expressed that *any* instance of fire due to collision, especially rear-end collisions, is 'enough' to show that an unreasonable condition exists, that any automaker that puts such a car on the road should be sued for negligence in the design of the auto. A similar argument was used here by the IIHS in that because separations are *possible* the design is unacceptable.

It is doubtful that one letter started the investigatory process by the Institute because there were a number of prior safety defect investigations by NHTSA involving multipiece rims. These investigations were cited by the Institute in its petition for a defect investigation of the *entire* set of such wheels made by all manufacturers and of all designs. The most significant of these defect campaigns was the Chevrolet GMC 3/4 ton truck with a Kelsey-Hayes 15 × 5.50 three-piece wheel. The wheel was offered by GM as factory-installed equipment on the trucks so that NHTSA pursued GM rather than Kelsey-Hayes under its defect determination procedure. GM contested the original defect finding that the wheels were subject to cracking, fractures and in-service failures without warning. GM countered that the failures were due to overloading by vehicle owners and resisted notifying vehicle owners of the presence of a defect. NHTSA pursued GM in a series of federal court cases, collectively known as the 'Wheels Case,' which resulted in much more consequential issues than that of the recall of 123,170 truck wheels. The 'Wheels Cases' resulted in the establishment of a legally enforced criterion of a 'significant' or 'large' number of failures whose existence constituted a *prima facie* case of the presence of a defect. GM and NHTSA, after GM's failure to find relief in the courts, entered into a consent order under which GM agreed to notify original owners of the finding and to replace the wheels free of charge. The original safety defect determination was filed by NHTSA on November 4 1970; the consent order ending the matter occurred five years later, on November 6 1975.

Another early investigation involved the RH5° wheel manufactured by Firestone, Budd and Kelsey-Hays. (These rims were two-piece and joined at their center in the interior of the wheel.) The Utah Industrial Commission instigated an inquiry and proposed to hold hearings on the wheel with the intent of outlawing these wheels in the state of Utah, meaning not only sales of the wheel in the state but any service of them as well. The NHTSA investigation was begun October 6 1969 and established that the 'hidden' nature of the locking area made it impossible to inspect proper seating from outside the wheel. Separations could occur at any time, during inflation or deflation of the tire or in service on the road. Corrosion stress cracks were found in fourteen accident cases. NHTSA resolved the investigation by holding that the primary cause was lack of information about proper assembly procedures by shop personnel. The rim manufacturers decided to discontinue production of these wheels so that no new vehicles would be provided with them, and it was thought that natural attrition would eliminate them from the road. Some 26 million were produced in all and it was estimated that at least 15 million were still in service when the investigation was dropped.

Another case in which improper procedures was cited as the major cause was a defect investigation of the Goodyear KB, KW and KWX two-piece wheels initiated on April 16 1970. Thirty-four cases in Goodyear's litigation files were examined and it was determined that twenty-nine of these involved improper assembly. The wheel consisted of a split base and a solid continuous side ring. As with the RH5° wheel, Goodyear discontinued this model through an agreement with NHTSA.

Two approaches can be distinguished in these cases, one which locates fault in the product itself and the other which fixes the blame on inadequate maintenance procedures. Product faults in NHTSA defect findings are assigned to instances where an item fails in service, even if that failure was due to consumer misuse, so long as that misuse is judged to have been foreseeable by the manufacturer. Conceivably, a defect could be found for not properly or adequately warning a consumer about features of the product, although no such recall has in fact been ordered on this basis primarily. The maintenance fault finding in the multipiece wheels cases is due to a number of circumstances which do not surround the normal consumer product cases. There were nearly 30 million registered trucks on the road in 1977; the defect involves equipment used by an enormous segment of the transportation industry encompassing trucking, public transport (city and school buses) as well as other equipment and agricultural uses; a ban would place the burden on the *owners* of vehicles rather than the manufacturers of the wheels; in turn a safety defect recall would place the burden on the manufacturer for replacing the wheels free of charge on 90 per cent of the trucks and buses using them on the road; the activity involved in setting up the accident situation in a majority of cases is performed by professional service personnel in locatable establishments. These are all *informal* considerations. Unlike the Kelsey-Hays wheel which may or may not have suffered fatigue cracking under overloading conditions by the user of the vehicles (campers and RVs), accidents involving multipiece rim separations are routinely described in terms of some action taken by a repairman in servicing the tire. Pursuing the maintenance line of reasoning, NHTSA had supported the proposed promulgation of a shop standard by OSHA which would require the mandatory use of safety cages and training of personnel. NHTSA also distributed assembly information to service personnel; manufacturers of the wheels and their professional association have distributed charts, pamphlets, and training films.

The Insurance Institute, in accordance with a longstanding preference for environment over a person-centered safety approach, argued in its defect investigation petition that training would not solve the problem. It points up NHTSA's own findings in the RH5° case that proper safety procedures are such that only properly equipped shops can meet them, meaning only the larger establishments routinely doing this servicing. The instructions the manufacturers insist are sufficient for proper handling are not given to everyone who could possibly be involved with servicing and no warnings of the danger present are furnished on the wheels themselves. A remarkable feature (and a somewhat contradictory one) of the accident record of these wheels is that experienced personnel appear to have a higher proportion of injuries than inexperienced workers. These observations were presented in a memorandum during the investigation but did not constitute reasons for a defect finding, which was avoided in part by discontinuance of the RH5° rim production.

The Institute argued that further instruction or training would have little impact on reducing the number of separations. Experienced personnel are injured routinely and separations in-service on the road cannot be eliminated by procedures alone. By their very design nature, assembly of the rims is difficult and prone to error. A prevalent problem is mismatching of components. Use of worn or damaged components will continue either through ignorance of the danger or for financial necessity. A large number of the RH5° and Goodyear K series (both discontinued) rims are still on the road: Firestone continued small productions of the components of the RH5° merely to forestall used, damaged rings from being the only replacement parts available. A single-piece, drop-center wheel is in existence and furnishes a safe alternative to the multipiece type. (However, some recent indications of problems with the single piece rim have been observed by OSHA in that bead damage – or destruction of the integrity of the lip edge of tire forming the seal with the rim – is a prevalent problem causing explosive blow-outs in the bead area during inflation.) The institute did not specify in its defect investigation petition what measures NHTSA should take, only that an expeditious and 'permanent' removal from the road be accomplished.

The October 2 1978 petition to NHTSA for the initiation of rulemaking (i.e. standards setting) was for introduction of a performance standard forbidding wheel component and tire separations under run-flat conditions and controlled deflation as well as retention of all components in blowouts. The first petition was designed to deal with units already on the road under the defect provisions, the rulemaking petition sought to stop production of the multipiece rim by setting a standard only, it is assumed, a single-piece rim can meet. This assumption by the Institute was drawn from discussions of a sudden deflation performance test proposed by NHTSA itself as part of FMVSS 120 (tire selection and rims for motor vehicles other than passenger cars) first suggested in 1971. A similar test is required of passenger car tires and has been since 1968. Included in the docket materials on the proposed test in 1970 was a statement by Ford Motor Company: 'We know of no multipiece rim design that can be guaranteed to meet such a requirement.' That is, it was their opinion that no such rim design could be guaranteed to retain the tire and when component parts under the test conditions of the blow-out of a tire under load at 60 mph, followed by a controlled deceleration of the vehicle. NHTSA dropped the test requirement giving the reason that a pressure loss could separate the wheel components, or, that the rim could not pass such a test. The Insurance Institute was, in effect, asking NHTSA to rescind its earlier decisions and remove the design from service through its safety defect and its standards setting powers. The response by NHTSA on the defect investigation petition was outlined in a letter to Haddon by Joan Claybrook, Administrator of NHTSA, on September 29 1978. A review of past decisions was made and an examination of data collected during those investigations as well as the data furnished by Haddon in his petition for rulemaking: descriptions of 202 reported cases of separations dating from 1959 through 1980. The defect investigations of the RH5° and K type wheels which had been closed in 1974 were reopened. (A defect investigation can be reopened at any time, even after a recall.) An engineering analysis and solicitation of information from the public and from the manufacturers (through information-gathering powers) was undertaken in order to examine whether recall action was warranted. The petition was thus granted, within a limited scope. At the same time rulemaking procedures (i.e. standards setting) was started. A further action by NHTSA at this time was to urge OSHA to develop a shop standard for multipiece rim servicings as NHTSA had done earlier in 1974 as part of measures taken to relieve the safety problem. Additional reports of incidents, requested by Claybrook, were forwarded by the Institute to NHTSA on November 1 1978. They consisted of thirty-nine worker compensation board data from Florida, Kentucky and North Dakota dating from 1957 to 1978.

NHTSA issued an advance notice of proposed rulemaking on March 5 1979 (44:12072 Fed. Reg.). The rule would amend Standard 120, adding a new performance level for separation in sudden deflation and run-flat conditions. NHTSA stated that although it had recommended that OSHA develop an appropriate shop standard in 1974, OSHA had yet to do so. The agency further stated 'it is not clear to this agency that the issuance of a standard by OSHA would with certainty solve the problem.' (44: 12073 Fed. Reg.). NHTSA by this time had gathered 439 cases of explosive separations since 1957, 120 of these being reported in the five years between 1975 and 1979. (The Institute filed a total of 241 case descriptions with NHTSA involving 46 deaths and 166 serious injuries.) The additional cases were extracted from wheel manufacturer litigation and other routine records filed in the winter of 1978. The total case file at that time supported 71 deaths and 234 separations with serious injuries. In March of 1979 the Institute forwarded a list of 89 additional cases coming from the Worker Compensation Boards of California, Maryland, Ohio, New York, Puerto Rico and Washington. They represented an additional 20 deaths and 72 injuries. That brought the known cases to a total of over 500 cases representing over 90 deaths and 300 injuries.

Regulatory action

NHTSA took no action on the proposed rulemaking other than to receive comments. An informal decision was made not to pursue the matter further, although the IIHS petition has not been formally denied, a move that would officially close the case. Inactivity on a proposed rule or even a safety defect investigation which could lead to a recall is common and can in fact place the question in limbo for a number of years. Industry and government sources contacted have suggested that the matter will be left to die quietly.

On April 24 1979 OSHA set forth its notice of proposed rule-making (44: 24252 FR) on multipiece rim servicing. OSHA's version of the impetus for establishing a standard for this work, one that existed only in the construction industry (Sect. 1926.600), was that interest in a standard was generated by an internal report of 'Hazards Not Covered By A Standard' from a field office in Louisville, Kentucky, and a similar one shortly afterward from the Columbus, Ohio office. No date was given for issuance of the reports. Petitions for promulgation of a standard were submitted to OSHA by the Rubber Manufacturers Association (RMA) and Firestone Tire and Rubber Company in 1976. The suggestion that OSHA should promulgate a standard which was made as part of NHTSA's solution to multipiece rim problems in 1974 had the status of a 'recommendation' by NHTSA, not a formal petition. The manufacturers of multipiece rims and tire manufacturers, in the case of Firestone and Goodyear, also rim makers, have consistently urged the proper training and maintenance theory as a solution to problems with the rims. It is unclear why the petitions for promulgation of a standard were made in 1976. They could have been made at the request of Firestone, because of foresee-able problems with their RH5° wheel. The tactic of requesting, recommending, and urging a training solution to the problem was pursued throughout by manufacturers, especially when NHTSA opened its 1978 investigation.

OSHA described the problem as one centering around the inflation process:

> accidents are most likely to occur while a tire that has just been mounted on a rim is being inflated or immediately after it has been inflated. (44: 242523 Fed. Reg.). Accidents that have caused the greatest number of injuries appear to have been due to improper mounting, use of damaged parts, or mismatch of component parts. Accidents may also occur because of overinflating the tire or striking the lock rings or rims with a hammer.

A review of the various available data sets used by NHTSA and OSHA in assessing the problem gave as a 'lower limit on accident exposure' as 13 to 18 per cent fatalities, 63 to 67 per cent injury cases and the remainder property and non-injury instances of separations. Cases that fall under OSHA jurisdiction, i.e. work-related, showed that 53 per cent occurred while a tire was being mounted/demounted, 31 per cent while the wheel was being installed/removed from a vehicle, and 16 per cent when the wheel was being moved or handled in some way, such as storing, checking air pressure, etc. Two per cent of the separations occurred while the wheel was in a safety cage.

The issues OSHA proposed as relevant and requested comments on were: (1) whether training is an effective method to reduce accidents; (2) whether a restraining device should be required from the time of inflation to the time of installing a wheel; (3) what restraining devices are available and whether strength requirements for them should be set; (4) whether hydraulic lift devices are adequate *ad hoc* protective devices; (5) when rim components should be removed from service; (6) whether wall charts should be merely made available or posted; (7) whether warning labels should be incorporated into the wheel assembly; (8) whether inflation of a wheel on a vehicle should be allowed. These proposed standards would apply only to those workplaces covered by Part 1910 of the OSHA codes.

Regarding the training issue, it was stated that charts are essential for understanding safe operating practices. As part of the training provision OSHA solicited information and comments on appropriate materials for proper training. 'The adequacy of material on the charts as an effective training aid and availability of additional sources of information must both be assessed for establishment of training requirements.' (44: 24253-4 Fed. Reg.) OSHA received *no* comments or information from any interested parties to the proposed standard on the adequacy or content of the charts. This is not surprising since the majority of comments or information offered in standards setting is from industry sources with relatively fewer comments from special interest groups outside of industry.

The question of restraining device use from the time the tire is inflated to the time vehicle weight is put on the wheel assembly, i.e., the wheel is on the vehicle and ready for service, was brought up but OSHA did not consider such restraint feasible and declined to propose it as a requirement in the forthcoming standard. The question of what types of restraining devices were available, commonly used, and considered as safe as the restraining cage was put to solicit comments. Also, 'of concern to OSHA are those types of devices that should not be used or those specific circumstances under which their use should be prohibited'. (44: 24254 Fed. Reg.) As part of the question of restraining devices, establishment of strength requirements for the devices was thought to be essential as well as the possibility of a national standard for such devices based on design specifications and structural requirements currently in use by manufacturers of the devices.

The proposed standard would require training of workers because 'the need for training is substantiated by a review of accident cases in which there appears to be a lack of knowledge of safe operating practices' and because a majority of those petitioning for a standard requested such training be built into, and in fact form the major part of, the standard. The proposal does not, however, specify the *contents* of the training but simply requires continued proficiency in the practices of servicing the wheels. The standard is thus stated in performance terms, placing the burden on the employer for adequately meeting that performance standard for his employees. OSHA considers that 'employees are adequately trained if they have thorough knowledge of and can apply the information contained in the DOT wall charts and this OSHA regulation'. (44: 24255 Fed. Reg.)

At the same time, 'safe operating procedures' are defined and every employer would be required to train his employees in these procedures. Safe practice generally includes completing deflating a tire on a vehicle before trying to remove the wheel from the vehicle; use of a rubber lubricant on the tire bead to reduce sliding friction of rim pieces on the bead, pre-inflating a tire to 10 psig outside of a safety cage in order to set the ring prior to placing the wheel assembly on end in the cage, checking to make sure the pieces are properly seated and locked before removing the wheel from the cage, completely deflating the tire if they are not and starting over. On the last point, 'under no circumstances shall any attempt be made to adjust the seating of the side and lock ring(s) by hammering, striking or forcing the components while the tire is inflated, so as to avoid any violent separation.' (44: 24256 Fed. Reg.)

The problem of separations of just inflated wheels while being moved from the safety cage or placed in storage is addressed by proposing that the wheels be placed so that the trajectory path of a lock ring will not coincide with any part of the service area where other personnel might be located. The population at risk was calculated to be approximately 322,000 persons in 102,500 workplaces (those under OSHA jurisdiction). The regulatory assessment of the impact of the standard resulted in an estimated $8,342,000 capital costs for compliance but with no significant impacts on productivity, employment, materials, energy, or market structure. The cost of a required safety cage was pegged at $134 per cage; approximately 77,700 establishments would have to purchase one to comply. The cost of training 'should not exceed an hour of employee time plus corresponding instructor time.' (44: 24257 Fed. Reg.)

The final standard, published on January 29 1980 and taking

effect from April 28 1980 showed some changes. The use of a restraining device capable of withstanding 1.5 times the force of an explosive separation while restraining wheel parts is required but not otherwise specified as to design. Preliminary airing of the tire is reduced to 3 psi rather than 10 psi, the higher level being judged (and commented on) as being too dangerous. OSHA found that there was 'no practical method available to restrain wheel components while tires installed on vehicles are inflated or between the inflation of a demounted wheel and the time the wheel is installed on a vehicle.' (45: 6710–11.) The final standard requires use of a restraining device only during inflation. Only those tools listed in rim manuals (furnished by manufacturers) are to be used for servicing the wheels. Tires are not to be inflated on the vehicle if they have been driven underinflated by 80 per cent or less of their recommended pressure. Thus a tire which has lost 20 per cent or more of its air pressure cannot be aired on the vehicle but must be deflated, reassembled, and aired then. Deflation must be accomplished by removing the valve core. The final standard regarding seating of the ring requires that 'no attempt shall be made to correct the seating of side and lock rings by hammering, striking or forcing the components while the tire is pressurized.' 1910.177 (f)(8.)

Some comments were received regarding restraining devices and *ad hoc* restraining methods. It was requested that a close specification of a restraining device such as a cage not be made so as to leave the door open for innovation in devices. As to acceptable practices, numerous *ad hoc* methods were commented on: the use of hydraulic lifts as a capping device (i.e., lowering the lift bar over the tire), placing wheels under the frame of a car or truck while airing, chains wrapped around wheel components. These comments were directed to OSHA not only as recommendations but also by way of requesting a review of certain industry practices so as to solicit OSHA reaction to these field practices in a pre-standard and informal way. The topic of various field practices arose in comments and also in informal exchanges among OHSA personnel and outside parties. OSHA personnel are, of course, cogniscent of the details of field practice in any given industry over whose workplaces they have jurisdiction. The raising of the issue of specific practices at the comment stage by industry or other interested parties is a way of getting feedback on important or common practices within the industry *prior* to standard finalization as well as a way of proposing an industry 'stand' on any features brought up as part of the proposed standard content. OSHA is responsive to industry comment in the sense that standards, at least those dealing with mechanical safety procedures, are compromises in specification. The multipiece rim standard is a classic case of formalizing good industry practice (i.e., in the sense of sound practice) with a minimum of specification.

OSHA's approach here is one of establishing a performance safety standard. That entails a top-down logic of generality such that individual or specific practices are subsumed under a covering performance criterion. For example, the restraining device can be, in practice, of any design so long as it meets the 1.5 containment safety margin criterion for withstanding explosive separations. The informal formulation is that so long as it works (within the criterion) it is acceptable. If the method does not contain an exploding assembly then it is not acceptable (and is therefore citable) under the standard. The 'compromise' inherent in this method of specification is one of leaving existing or even *ad hoc* practice in effect and untouched *just so long as they work*. Evidence of its not working, in the safety field at least, is the presence of injury-producing accidents.

'Sound practice' is defined in this absence-of-accidents terms also. Note that it is the absence of *injury-producing* accidents which is the determining factor (although near-misses do carry some weight in defining unsafe conditions, it is unclear how much weight they carry in defining safe *practice* as such). Practices or conditions are, however, citable under a standard if they are *known* to lead to accidents or do not meet the general performance criterion (here – elsewhere they could be design criterion) by way of the laws of physics or capabilities of materials. For instance, wrapping a light-weight chain around a wheel (or a heavy-weight chain insufficiently wrapped) would not meet the containment specification because the chain material or the configuration could not withstand the force of an explosive separation. In fact, such a device, when its restraining capabilities are over-reached by the force of the separation, becomes one of the missiles projected by the explosion.

Accident data

Accident data submitted to NHTSA and OSHA as substantiating evidence of the existence of a problem furnish the consequential particulars for a jurisdictional reading of the data as accident events with specifically relevant properties (see Appendix 1). The short summaries of the accidents offer short descriptions which serve to signal the relevance of the event, at a minimum, but also offer directed comments regarding the elements of the accident cause – which can be 'inferred,' filled in, or imagined, given the small amount of information. A jurisdictional reading of these summaries requires only the fact of a separation event for NHTSA, given their failure of performance principle which does not require a cause or knowledge of how a part is defective, only that it fails and its failure affects traffic safety. OSHA on the other hand must read the account as a workplace event. The summary accounts are loosely designed to furnish this information as their purpose but it is a mild rather than a strongly purposeful feature of the accounts that they give the 'right' information for agency interest because they give additional, or seemingly gratuitous, information along with what is needed to make the case that they are highly consequential incidents to be counted toward defining what has to be repaired through a safety standard or other recourse. The 'gratuitous' information includes a posing of the situation as offering either (1) an entirely unexpected or (2) an expected, accident event.

The unexpectedness of the accident event is posed by furnishing enough information so that one sees the event as unreasonable in its very appearance as a consequence in a situation as a normal setting, i.e., normally arranged, normally stable in its expectations. The expectedness of the event, on the other hand, is furnished in many workplace accidents by adding information suggesting improper or faulty practice. The accident event is thus made 'expectable,' given the (lack of) precaution or incorrect practice which is inferrable from the information when the question 'how?' is asked of the event. The severity of the injury in these events is so commonplace that the information re injuries when a group of cases is taken at once does not have the effect of gratuitous information re *degree* of injury, as a way of making the cases thus more important. Indeed the summaries center on injury as the dominant feature of the accident, yet the summaries are analyzed not for this degree of injury but for identifiable cause as an administrative search and as posing the set as a body of data showing the point being made, e.g., that the multipiece rim is inherently and irreparably defective in the design, given that such things could happen.

The repair strategies for these accidents are based on jurisdictionally bound and readable interpretations of the accident accounts, not as data but as account. The fact that injuries have occurred is not the essential feature of the accounts. NHTSA's repair can only consist of elimination of this type of wheel assembly either by banning their further manufacture and, as an extreme measure, recalling those already on the road. This is, of course, due to the powers defined for NHTSA under the Highway Traffic Safety Act of 1966. That this is the form of their only possible remedy action was relied on by the Insurance Institute in that they sought complete removal of the wheel from the road. The accident accounts, given this remedy possibility, are read for the mere *occurrence* of an accident as a demonstration of a failure in performance, one of the criteria under which NHTSA can find a defect. The number of such failures is unimportant. In a very peculiar sense, one is enough in the NHTSA safety defect-finding procedure. It is arguable that even the *possibility*, as theorized from some demonstration of events, is enough to find a defect. NHTSA need not locate a reason for the performance failure, only demonstrate that there is one. Who the accidents happen to is of importance in NHTSA's decision-making. The driving public and any other persons that use the highway are of primary importance. Those working on vehicles are of lesser importance as a jurisdictional delimitation. That only relatively few of the multi-piece rim failures affected vehicles in service on the highway or passers-by was probably a consideration in NHTSA's alternative to their only repair recourse, to leave the matter in limbo, neither denying the petition and thereby having to give reasons for it, which might be an embarrassment, nor taking any other formal action which would move the issue further forward.

OSHA's remedy is, of course, a workplace-centered one. That the accident occurred is of secondary importance to *how* they are thought to have occurred. OSHA's reading of accident accounts for indicators of how it happened furnished the basis for arguing its own jurisdictionally tied form of remedy.

There are two sources of argument which reason about the imagined remedy for this type of industrial accident. One source is an argument from the manufacturers of the wheels, the other is a rather common approach taken by OSHA-type agencies in assessing accident prevention. The manufacturers' argument is similar but not identical with OSHA's.

A report entitled 'Multipiece and Singlepiece Rims: The Risk Associated with their Unique Design Characteristics, Phase III' (June 1980), prepared by Failure Analysis Associates, Palo Alto, California, poses a risk assessment approach to judging the multi-piece rim. This type of analysis is currently in vogue as a way of 'putting it into perspective,' that is, of finding a broader context within which to pose the accident rate of the particular product so as to juxtapose the product's accident rate with more common hazards in the environment to which we are all subject. An addition to this approach consists of adding a 'cost per fatality averted' figure which summarizes the costs of eliminating the hazard under consideration in a per life saved figure, a total cost of removing the hazard divided by number of fatalities which have occurred due to this hazard. The Failure Analysis Associates report, initiated at the request of a law firm representing the National Wheel and Rim Association, trade association of rim manufacturers, poses the risk of a multipiece rim failure in terms of truck tire service frequencies and miles of travel by the trucking industry. The results of their analysis were: one fatality per 6 million tire servicings; one fatality per 26.7×10^{12} miles of truck travel. The report is, of course, an argument in defense of the threatened recall by NHTSA of all multipiece rims. A recall would in fact involve in excess of 50 million truck wheels. The cost of averting one fatality of this type was pegged at $136,000,000 by FAA. This cost of recalling multipiece rims is contrasted with other safety measures that the Department of Transportation has calculated, such as mandatory safety belt usage which would cost $506 per fatality forestalled.

Of interest here is that part of the argument which poses the OSHA servicing standard as a remedy for the multipiece rim problem.

Failure Analysis Associates analyzed all of the 422 injury producing multipiece rim wheel maintenance-related accidents to determine whether, given the circumstances described in the accident reports, the procedures prescribed in the OSHA Standard would have prevented the accidents. . . . The analysis focused only on the impact of those non-judgmental, rote work rules provided for in the OSHA Standard which demand nothing more than routine execution of a fixed procedure to produce a safe rim assembly. (pp. 28–29)

FAA's finding was that 76 per cent of the fatalities and 71 per cent of the injuries were/are preventable by following the OHSA 'rote' work rules. The report goes on further to say: 'The simplicity of these minimal OSHA requirements, and the extent of their potential impact, lead to the conclusion that the primary cause of multipiece rim accident(s) is disregard of safety procedures in the workplace.' (p. 30) Extending the OHSA provisions further to include all they encompass, training, and checking for damaged rims, affords greater impact so that of the 422 accidents identified as 'servicing pressurized separation accidents,' i.e., all servicing accidents and not those on the road, 'FAA did not find any that would definitely have occurred under a fully implemented OSHA Standard' (i.e., the one proposed). FAA stated further that moving vehicle separations 'most . . . probably involve some form of improper mounting of the tire in the workshop. Thus it is posed that moving separations could be eliminated by adhering to the

OHSA Standard and that the entire problem, in effect, can be eliminated through workplace procedure repair. FAA goes on to furnish some specific truck fleet data to support this contention by using accident rates for fleets adhering to California OSHA standards.

This argument might seem a wholly self-serving device if it were not for the fact that labor statistics and research offices use a similar approach in assessing accident data. In a December 1978 report, Research Bulletin No. 4 of the California Department of Industrial Relations, 'California Fabricated Structural Metal Products Industry: Analysis of Work Injuries and Illnesses,' analyzed six months of accident data for 1976 in this particular industry, 1,351 reports. These cases were coded for their 'preventability' according to the following process. Reports were read by the research analysts and by a staff safety engineer with expertise in determining whether the circumstances described in the report involved a safety or health order. Cases were classified into four categories, two of which were 'preventable' categories. Category One, injuries or illnesses 'which need not have occurred had there been compliance with an existing State safety or health order,' generally, California's General Industry Safety Orders (GISO), Category Two, preventable by safety and health training, including materials handling, safety protective equipment, etc. However, this category also serves as the catchall for incidents where *no* safety order violation could be inferred from the description. Thus, those areas of practice not covered directly by safety orders are subsumed under 'training' here. Category Three, accidents not preventable by either compliance with safety order or training. These injuries occurred as 'random events' that were judged not preventable under orders or training. Category Four, insufficient information to classify further. The findings of this report are close to those of the Failure Analysis Associates report: only 4.3 per cent of the 1,351 injuries (fifty-eight cases) were found to be *un*preventable by compliance with existing orders or through training. FAA avoided this 'left-over' effect by distributing cases with insufficient information by apportioning them over categories defining known circumstances. Thus, while FAA 'accounted' for 100 per cent of their accidents as cause by improper servicing practices, the California Department of Industrial Relations 'accounted' for 95.7 per cent of their cases as preventable by compliance with existing safety orders or proper training. It will be remembered that instances of no safety order violations were classified under the training category so that training in effect took up the slack in determining 'preventability.'

In the field

Theorizing in the field about the cause of accidents centers on details of procedure with tools, the nature of the parts and experience of service personnel. Those features which are pointed to as causal features of an accident situation, not necessarily an accident itself, consist mainly of skipped or ignored steps. This is similar to OSHA's approach in that it is things *missing* which are pointed to as setting up an accident and which are posed as constituting the stuff of a safe work setting. Things *done* are pointed out only in so far as they represent 'dumb' moves on the part of service personnel; they are, of course, dumb in proportion to how far away from effective practice they are observed to be, i.e., they are superfluous or in fact cause of an accident.

Within the category of things missing are overriding safety devices such as safety cases and air check extensions (OSHA missing features) and overlooked details of practice such as not bothering to lubricate the tire bead, lack of knowledge or care in mismatching rim parts, leaning over the wheel while airing. These types of practice omissions are cited by service personnel in the field as a series of specific answers to the question, 'What are the problems in multipiece rim servicing?' They are ideal features of good or proper practice in the sense that they are things that can and should be done in the shop. Yet they are contingent safe practice features. They are ideal items of practice in the sense that although they are correct and pointed to as reasons for accidents, they are in fact contingent on where and how wheel servicing must in fact be done. Fifty to 90 per cent of wheel servicing, depending on the shop, is done in the field. That means the parts at hand must be reused as a practical necessity, such things as lubricating the tire bead are often a nicety, safety cages are nonexistent.

There is also, of course, the lore of the parts themselves. These are the things known about particular manufacturer's wheels: The three-piece rim has a lightweight lock ring which is said to be easily broken (sprung or stress cracked); the center interlock Ford rim, no longer in wide use, is universally known in the field as the 'suicide rim;' Firestone and Goodyear rims are nearly identical and will 'work' but in fact are not properly interchangeable. These features, like the omitted practice items, are posed as causal particulars when the question 'How do multipiece rim accidents happen?' is posed. They are findable in the same way that missing items are findable and become part of the explicit topic lists of 'things' sayable about the multipiece rim. In that they are sayable about the rim and especially that part lore is experience-related they are especially available to be summoned up as causally relevant to accident circumstances.

The assessment of 'dumb' actions is a professionally informed one. For example, the airing up of a partially deflated tire while it is on the vehicle is known to be a risky procedure by truck tire personnel, but such an action is only inadvertently dumb when truck drivers or gas station employees do it, or owners of recreation vehicles, campers and motor homes. Hitting an inflated wheel assembly with a sledge hammer is perceivably dumb in that trained personnel cannot find a legitimate motivation for doing such a thing. That is, such an activity cannot be found in their list of recognized, and thus legitimate, service steps, nor as a substitute for any of these steps as a way of effecting the same result as one of their steps. We will later speak of 'conditions' in the service process, that is, interim goal states in the accomplishment of assembling and installing a truck wheel. By 'steps' here we mean steps recognized by service personnel as things they have to do in order to make up the work of accomplishing the overall assembly. Such steps make up the refinements of their work and are, of course, remarkable only when one would ask 'What do you do next?' Thus, 'dumb' actions do not coincide with these 'steps.' Some can be seen as motivated shortcutting, for example, the airing up of a tire on the vehicle. But others pose a mystery for professional personnel in that the action cannot be seen as an effective substitute for any legitimate steps or for a string of them.

These improprieties are contextual assessments. That is, seeing actions as improper in some fashion, either as shortcutting or as an illegitimate action, is seeable only within a context of looking. That context is made up of the existing schema of the account of what the enterprise – here truck tire servicing – is about and of what it consists. This is its reasoned and reasonable account. Use of a sledgehammer on an inflated wheel does not fit into the account as a legitimate item with the existing list. The reasonable account doesn't offer any points at which this fit can be made nor does it offer a net of understanding, a broad interpretation of parts of the account whereby sledging an inflated wheel can even conceivably fit in. The reasonable account is the manageable account. It is consultable in an orderly fashion to find the whatness and the nameable parts of the enterprise. The task, the enterprise, as a describable one is findable in such accounts. They also furnish the aboutness of the task, the step conditions leading to a finished project. The use of sledgehammer is not findable in this orderly account and yet it is imaginable if one were asked to search for a Why such a hammer was used because a worker could locate the very reason for its use. That it is bad practice does not erase this direct findability, but then it is a workman's findable.

There is a sense in which both parties – OSHA and tire servicing personnel – know better than each other what goes into safe workplace conditions. OSHA, with its top-down logic, provides for an overriding safety mechanism of generalized (even though they may seem quite specific in their detail) 'safeguards' which provide for conditions which are theoretically, that is deductively logically, sufficient to meet accident events as activities or conditions which get out of hand. There is a sense in which OSHA brings 'order' to the workplace environment by setting out the logical conditions whereby accidents of known kinds, i.e., within their experience as knowable events, are 'prevented' in first a logical sense and secondly, in a physical sense. Hence, the unembarrassed preventability analyses of accident data. Standards are drawn up to encompass areas of the workplace environment as a way of meeting specifically known accident types. They are deductive in this sense in that they are specifically designed to meet a collection of features posed as the 'problem.'

OSHA accepts and believes that the mechanics of safe conditions are already known, at least with old line mechanical operations of manufacturing as opposed to, say, levels of exposure to toxic chemicals, and that the Occupational Safety and Health Act of 1970 merely put teeth into the standards. This means that OSHA's mission of enforcement of safe workplace standards, being incomplete, allows for the playing off of a deductively logical sufficiency of a standard's provisions for solving the 'problem,' while in fact one can only see the problem *mitigated* in accident statistics. This mere mitigation is supposed to be the result of a lack of full compliance with the standards in the thousands of workplaces forming American industry. It is thought *only* to be that.

The workplace personnel in turn 'know better' than any standards provisions what safe work conditions consist of as in fact they know their job as a reasonable account whose particulars are made up of trained-in pieces of work procedure and remarkable features of the parts they work with. The trained-in pieces of procedure for truck tire personnel are the items mentioned by the manufacturers of the wheels in their servicing manuals. These manuals speak of the wheel as an object with a proper, reasonable assembly, with parts and tools to be used. It is a how-to with some technical specification as to the *product* parts, i.e., types of wheels, serial numbers, but whose assembly description is so straightforward as to provide for the only reasonable talk about the parts that is necessary to get the job done. Thus talk about the wheels by tire personnel uses those items furnished in service manuals. These items form the relevant mentionables about the object worked on and how (i.e., the what-ness of how it is worked on). A search for what could be wrong with multipiece rims finds these mentionables problematically posed for their omission, i.e., it is imagined that it is these things which, when omitted, given that they form the official remarkables of the object, are potential trouble spots if they are omitted. These items are not talked about specifically by tire personnel as the *cause* of *specific* accidents, but are believed in as reasonable candidate items for the cause of accidents.

This is not to say that there is not observed treachery in the object itself, in sprung rings and mismatched parts which in fact must be nevertheless assembled and made to work. This is also not to say that the pieces of procedure offered by the manufacturer in its manual are not correct or are incomplete as an account of what needs to get done to in fact accomplish the task. They are not pristine accounts with no 'hints' about possible trouble spots. It is, however, these trouble spots which are seen as attached to their *step* in the assembly operation by tire personnel, hence it is step talk which is the focus of attention in accounts of what goes into safe tire and wheel assembly. What is not, of course, available in the shop manuals of manufacturers is the lore of particular wheels. This is passed on by word of mouth and gained by experience in servicing particular wheel types. Yet at the same time, it is step difficulty that makes a particular wheel type remarkable in this way. The continuous side ring which has to be slipped over the wheel base, rathher than a split ring which is prised open somewhat to snap into the gutter of the base, is remarkable because there is continued concern as to whether it is truly 'centered' on the rim base but only as a seating step condition (we will use 'condition' here to refer to an interim state accomplishment in task completion). The center split wheel, split into two halves of a wheel, each with a rim edge, is problematic because the two halves need to be aligned properly for their interference fit. This is also a seating step remarkable because once the tire is mounted over such an assembly one can no longer 'see' the interlock. It is the necessary accomplishment of the work as consisting of a series of required step conditions which furnishes remarkable items in the account of multipiece rim assembly. It is the step that is the referential item, but we shall see later that the step of making something happen, of reaching the interim goal condition, is not the same 'step' as the natural account's step.

The wall charts used for instructing truck tire servicing, furnished by both NHTSA and the Rubber Manufacturers Association (RMA), were made up by wheel manufacturers. They consist of a series of steps with accompanying photographs which display the proper sequence of events and more importantly, they show the application of tire tools on the wheels and point up the design features of wheel types. They also furnish warnings and a list of do's and don't's. The wall chart presents an abbreviated view of the rim assembly process in that it displays a small selection of the steps involved if steps are considered to be pieces of directed action which have a completeness to them within a rather small span of activity. Checking is such a 'step.' Prising up the edge of a lock ring is such a step while prising it off all around the circumference of the rim is another step. A step is in fact as wide an encompassing reference as one wishes to make it. 'Remove the lock ring,' 'demount the tire' are both step instructions in the sense of what happens next, but they each encompass a number of smaller considerations, such as forcing up an edge of the lock ring up out of the rim gutter with the forked end of a tire tool and then working a tool under the lifted ring around the rim to free it entirely from the gutter without bending it, or having to 'chop' the bead of the tire away from the rim with an adze-like tool on both sides of the rim and removing the inner tube and tube liner. The wall chart is an abbreviation but in fact not this kind of abbreviation where steps are made to merely reflect gross stages of goal conditions.

The adequacy of the wallchart instructions and warnings was never questioned in the comments submitted to OSHA in its proposed rule-making. That it is irremediably an abbreviation of tire servicing is not seen as problematic by either those who designed it or those who use it as a guide. Indeed, as a set of instructions posed as a natural account of what must be done in order to accomplish a tire change on differing types of rims it is straightforward and informative. The warning items are highlighted although the major warning which serves as the danger signal that a hazard exists in servicing the wheels is phrased somewhat as a disclaimer in 'failure to comply' items. The wall chart is an adequate how-to but is it in fact an adequate proposal of the hazard involved in servicing the multipiece rim? There are some identifiable reasons why it isn't.

OSHA takes the philosophy of positive instruction. That is, it, as a matter of policy, proposes that only the right way, the correct way, the safe way of doing a thing be shown. Its reasons for choosing this method of instruction is the belief that showing a workman how to do something a wrong way will give him ideas about shortcuts. Since there exists a great effort toward simplification in work effort, this is a warranted assumption for shortcutting prevalent in the best of trained personnel. What this positive view only approach does, however, is to remove the consequentiality of particular actions from consideration. In their place, films 'demonstrating' the force of a rim separation propose to elicit respect for the danger involved yet it is a danger unspecified as to the configuration which triggers the separation. In fact there is nowhere evident an analysis of just what the mechanism of separation is, no compilation of engineering reports pointing to just this failure in components, design or service. OSHA standard provisions provide for a containment policy, that is, it is a policy of restraint of the separations it assumes will take place. Its preventive quality is one of preventing injury when the rims separate. It is a fact of the multipiece rim that the assembly can in fact 'look good,' that there be no visible fault in its configuration or the parts used and yet an explosive separation will occur. It is this indeterminancy which is respected and which invites remedy or ignoral by service personnel. Old hands ignore it as 'it hasn't happened to me yet, it won't now.' To novices it is an invitation to endless concern until the rim is out of their work area, after that it doesn't matter.

That the consequentiality of specific actions has been removed, or more correctly, not made present in the instructions, means that *all* contingency considerations are irrelevant to the instructions. The only consequentiality presented in the instructions is that at the end you will have a mounted wheel assembly. Even the do's and don'ts do not point to their consequences and are left as mere admonitions. The wallchart reflects the activity of effecting a tire servicing as an occasioned adequate account which can be posted for personnel to read. The OSHA statute requires familiarity with both it and the contents of the standard itself. That knowledge, a knowledge of an adequate natural account and a top-down logic designed to contain the separation occurrence, is what comprises the formal solution to the problem of multipiece rim servicing.

Local structures

There is a certain class of activity and its attendant objects which is referenced neither in the OSHA standard specifications nor in the manufacturers' service manuals. The activity could be referred to as *ad hoc* but that would miss their systematic character and the predictability of their presence. They are personalized and they are contingent on things being at hand. They are safeguarding activities undertaken by tire service people and they arise in and through reasoning about the task as a task with consequences for the safety of the workman. These safeguarding activities are formed of situated logics. We will speak here only of safeguarding behavior by service personnel and not of the logic of shortcutting or substituting although they exist as well.

By situated logic we mean that structure of particulars and inferences which operationally link them together as a framework for attaining some goal. Decision-making is structured into this framework once it has been established as the only *possible* subsequent inferences that can be made given the structure's schema. The structure arises as a theory of goal attainment, not in general, but quite particularly this goal, in this setting with these conditions. The schema forms a 'logic' in that the structure of the schema can be and is consulted in future for reasonable and effective moves. It is also formulated purposefully to solve some goal problem so that it is a specific solution algorthm for solving it as a *reasoned* mechanism. That it is therefore reasonable, i.e., reasons can be made for its existing, inferences and the collection of items it uses, why *these* pieces of information or parts of a phenomenon and not others. They are assembled for goal attainment and no other reason. They may incorporate a discernible *reference* to some formal criteria, like deductive validity of an argument, but in fact they do not operate in this manner. They are not 'invalid' for this reason because their only true criterion is the accomplishment of the goal in mind, the one for which they arose and were developed for. They are logical in the sense that not just any structure will do. They are carefully reasoned schemas whose validity lies in the goal's attainment and not in any formal logical criteria. That they do not meet these formal validity criteria is of no practical interest to those who use them, for the arguments they pose are worldly arguments of practical decision-making. This indifference to the claims of formal logic as a way of finding fault with them is a worldly indifference, that the world's work is not up to that, i.e., what formal deductive logic could possibly say about the world's ways. Situated logics are above all else practical accomplishments.

We will speak here of two pieces of the situated logic of truck tire servicing and will not elaborate the entire logic of multipiece rim assembly. These two segments were observed over a period of two days' observation at three truck tire service facilities, two manufacturer's service shops, and one truck fleet garage. The two pieces of logic are of a different character. One is a version of personal safeguarding and the other is what we shall refer to as an example of 'embodied logic.'

The piece of personal safeguarding logic centers, like the OSHA standard's concerns, on containment of a separation. Since separations are seen as unpredictable by tire servicing personnel, personal safeguarding arises as a way of meeting this unpredictability.

OSHA requires a safety cage but since a majority of the work of a shop may be done out in the field, containment must be effected in other ways. The methods used are substitutions, that is, reasoned replacements of an *ad hoc* but systematic nature which are posed to serve as well as a safety cage, given the aboutness of the safety cage as a stopper of flying parts and a container of those parts. These methods are, in fact, even used in the shop.

Substitution Variation One is the use of a manufactured, slightly U-shaped bar referred to in the ubiquitous term, a 'suicide bar.' The bar is slipped through the holes of the rim base disc so that the ends cover the lock ring on either side of the ring. This is kept in place while the tire is aired. Variation Two is a substitute for this and consists of sticking a tire tool through the holes of the rim so that one of its ends is wedged under the base disc and the other extends out over the edge of the tire, covering as it does the lock ring. Variation Three focuses more on the containment aspect of a safeguarding device and utilizes a chain wrapped through the base disc holes and in effect around the wheel so that it is 'tied up.' These are *ad hoc* solutions to a reasoned problem of containing or deflecting rim parts upon separation. They are systematic in the sense that once such a solution is found, it is used repeatedly and, of course, offers itself to imitation. The structure of the reasoning is straightforward. Anything that can be placed between the rim parts and the worker and contain them during a separation is the goal. The mechanics of the substitutions use simple analogies to the major perceived functions necessary to contain or deflect rim parts.

These devices are not mentioned in the OSHA standard nor were any comments on such safety devices submitted to OSHA in its rule-making question on proper restraints. This is a piece of practice which is added onto the procedural steps spoken of earlier. It is a personalized step, an old hand's trick. That it 'works' attests to the infrequency of rim separations rather than the effectiveness of bars and chains as restraining devices. When they don't work they in fact add to the problem. The bar or tools and pieces of the chain become missiles propelled along with the rim parts. (The chain is used in part as a backup for a shortcut, airing up a tire on a vehicle.) The OSHA specification requires a device which will withstand one and a half times the explosive force of a separation. Subjective estimates about what will contain such a force, the strength of bars or chains, is based not on pounds of force, but on perceived relative strength. In this way too it is a reasoned approach to safeguarding, but the physics of the problem overwhelms it when a separation takes place. It could be argued that personal safeguarding of this kind consists only of a psychological reassurance device by workmen. But this presupposes the knowledge of the engineer of the inability of these measures to meet the forces of a separation and poses psychological mechanisms as tricks of the mind in what is really a rationally determined world. Situated logics do not consist of faulty reasoning, rationalizations, or self-delusion except in privileged analyses using a contrasting situated logic.

The second piece of logic is an example of an embodied logic. An embodied logic consists of the reflexive interaction of task logic and object design. This means that a mutual determination of what is to be done and how exists between the task as a goal and the object as one with which the goal is to be accomplished. One might say the object is that *within* which the task is to be accomplished if by that it is understood that the object poses the possibilities for that accomplishment in its design features and that the task is the reaching of a goal condition of some kind and not simply activities constituting an operation. We are then talking about goal-directed decision-making in the utilization of a physical object which is the instrument for bringing about that goal. When we speak of the design features of the object we are not referring to its intended effective performance of some operation alone. It is not merely the designed-in purposeful function for which the object was built but we refer to the object's design features as the sum of what it invites the user to make of it, to do with it, to manipulate within it, intervene into and tease out of it. In this way, an object *invites* actions taken with it and on it when the goal is to get to some end condition *through* that object. Embodied logics consist of the particular situated logic of object use. They are a subset of situated logics in that they arise in and about object use as a localized product of interaction with one particular object, be it a tool, a machine, or an instrument panel. Situated logics, in a more general sense, focus on the logic structures of broader enterprises which may include objects or pieces of embodied logics as their subset.

It should be kept in mind that we are centering on goal achievement in both situated and embodied logics. These logics arise only for the purpose of accomplishing some task. They are specific to that task yet may reflect the enormity of the context within which it resides. That 'enormity,' of course, is represented in the situated logic as threads of structure representing the consequentiality and effects perceived as affecting the operation of attaining the goal at hand. Thus, a system may have many goals residing within its overall framework but situated logics form a specific relational structure determining particular goals in the sense that to locate a situated logic you must first locate the specific goal being worked on and then examine the logic surrounding it which is determined by the overall system parameters. The logics are localized to the extent that they are directed to specific task accomplishments and are determined by the particulars of the system in a unique way for that task. There exists a set of these situated logics within any system, a set of uniquely structured schemas to deal with specific goals at hand existing within the system. Analytically, these schemas are findable only by locating the goal at hand as the focal point and examining the structure of its effective logic. The structures form logics in the sense that the schema consists of locally perceived particulars and operations which form consistent patterns of inferences based on the needs presented by the goal at hand.

Embodied logics are situated logics existing around and centering on some object's use. They reflect some elements of the larger system within which they reside but are so concentrated as to appear to exist solely in and as the object's use. The embodied logic of multipiece rim servicing is relatively simple as compared to more elaborate objects, for example, machine use. Yet it is extensive enough that we will only examine a piece of it, albeit a most important piece. The goal around which the piece of embodied logic we will consider is the 'seating' of the ring. More specifically, it is perceived as the seating of the lock ring. The construction of the lock rings, and here we speak only of those wheels where a ring slipped into the rim gutter forms the basis for a mechanical interlocking of parts, is such that they either snap into the gutter formed by the rim (either of a side ring or on the wheel base itself), or slip over the rim edge and form a loose fit under the rim lip. The 'seating' of the ring thus consists of setting it in proper configuration for the airing up process to take place whereby the interlock is held fast by air pressure exerted on the tire bead under the interlocking rim parts.

Concern for seating the ring is not over when the snap-on is completed and the airing step ready to take place. It is not the case that these are two independent steps, seating and airing, for the goal of securely seating the lock ring is one which encompasses the airing process because the goal is to seat the ring *without a separation taking place*. The embodied logic of the rim assembly here consists of the continued interaction with the rim during the airing up of the tire. This is not checking work in the sense of looking or inspecting alone. The rim assembly, because of its design features (and here we speak only of these rims with outer locking or side rings) invites a continued concern in the form of physical contact with the rim while it is airing. The airing up takes three minutes or longer, during which time contact is maintained with the ring parts in a concern that they are properly centered or properly alligned for interlocking to occur. It is visual contact to be sure, but the compelling invitation of the object's design is for *physical* contact with the ring itself and this takes the form of using a hammer on the ring while the tire is being aired.

This is an old hand's concern. It is, literally, keeping 'in touch' with the ring while it is being set by the air pressure building under it. It, the setting, is the goal of the servicing operation in that it is the most consequential part of the operation for those who know a separation can occur. Novices will abandon the area to an extension air chuck, the recommended procedure, where a safety cage is not available, in keeping with OSHA's determination that standing outside the trajectory of the rim parts is the best solution to avoiding injury. Yet novices face that awful moment when they have to return to the rim to remove the air chuck. It is the mystery of whether the ring has set properly that awaits them. It is proposed that for this reason – the existence of that mystery – a way of keeping in contact with the rim parts is built up and forms part of the old hand's practice. The use of a safety cage is often shunned because the worker 'can't see' the ring well enough in the cage. Poking at the ring seating evolves into the old hand's studied tapping of the ring assembly at intervals during the early stage of the airing process. The assurance of a proper seating lies in this contact and the parts themselves 'invite' this contact by being a set of interlocking edges and relatively loosely fitting parts at the beginning of the airing up step.

The RMA wallchart makes reference to use of a hammer only in this way: 'NEVER [red caps] hit tire or rim with hammer [black small case letters].' This is listed among the do's and don'ts. The OSHA proposed standard specified that 'under no circumstances shall any attempt be made to adjust the seating of the side ring and lock ring(s) by hammering, striking, or forcing the components while the tire is inflated, so as to avoid any violent separation.' (44: 24256 FR.) The final standard on this point read: 'no attempt shall be made to correct the seating of side and lock rings by hammering, striking or forcing the components while the tire is pressurized.' (1910.177 (f) 8.) At first sight this appears to cover only the extreme case, hammering on a fully inflated wheel to ensure the rings are snug under the rim gutter. But when it is remembered that safety cage use is required by the final standard after 3 psi, since 10 psi was considered too dangerous a level without a restraining device by those commenting on the standard proposal, then it is realized that it is not merely the extreme case that is being referenced here.

Since a truck tire takes from 90 to 120 lb per square inch of air pressure, we are talking about a dangerous separation condition after only 8 to 11 per cent (the 10 psi level) of the total air pressure has been administered. Ten psi takes only a few seconds to add to a deflated tire so the mechanical danger level is reached in those first few seconds of airing, yet the overriding concern of the workman *throughout* the airing process is the seating of the ring and he 'keeps in touch' with that seating process by contact with the ring(s) using a long handled tool, with either a hammer or a tool with a head which can serve as a hammer. The design features invite the knocking down of the lock ring to keep it under the rim gutter and a hammer device is chosen to accomplish this. That this activity continues over the course of the airing implies that this piece of embodied logic, the very thing that should *not* be going on, is, nevertheless, the very thing that is so compelling. And compelling in a 'logical' sense, given the understanding of how situated logics work.

Policy and local practice

What can be seen to exist here is competing versions of what safety is, the top-down logic of safety standards in the work place versus the *in situ* logics of safe work performance. Formal safety logic, that of the official account posing safety measures as deductively effective, and deductively findable for that very reason, is based on natural accounts of accidents which use only whatness and aboutness items in referencing the task the accident happens within. These are ways of talking about the task and not about the content of practice. Practice can be seen to be a playing off of these whatness and aboutness items in the formation of a situated logic for getting the task done, not in talk about it, but in its physical realization. It is the situated logics of practice, of personal safeguarding and compelling pieces of embodied logics which are in effect safe practice for the worker. What is ignored in official safety, the regulation of safety, is this local practice. It can be argued that this is what 'performance standards' are all about. They form a lid on local practice in that whatever goes on as local practice, is acceptable so long as accidents don't occur. Accident containing devices, like the safety cage, positive-action-only training and 'warnings' form the 'lid.' They specifically ignore local practice as a function of this bottom line concern.

It is argued here that formal safety, safety accounts, top-down logic, and containment concepts consisting of physical barriers of warnings between the worker and the accident are incapable of *finding* an accident. They are remedial measures based on an accident analysis which fails to see the productive character of accidents. And by productive character we refer to the situated logics in places which attend and inform the doing of the work task. Formal accident theory treats accident, that is injury, events as failures in a normally functioning enterprise. The actions leading to the injury are 'errors' and 'faults' expressed in terms of unsafe practice. It is argued here that accidents are findable in the situated logics which form actual task practice and this is the very thing formal accident theory does not, indeed as it is now structured, cannot, touch.

It can be argued that formal safety, as an overriding device, does not *have* to touch actual task practice, that only a point of control has to· be instigated, physical or warning limits against what local practice can produce. In this way a safety cage and clearing the trajectory path of the rim parts is posed as a limiting device on whatever local practice might produce by way of incorrect ring seating, mismatched parts and other localized 'errors.' Warnings take up the slack where physical devices cannot completely contain the potential accident event. Hence, a warning not to lean against the safety cage since the impact of a separation can be transferred through the cage device to anything in contact with it. It is assumed that to do otherwise than offer controls as a limiting maneuver, is to engage in an endless listing and finding of things not to do, that the list would have to comprise the whole of small bits of bad practice, 'dumb' moves, and that last ditch explanatory item, reckless disregard for safety precautions. Physical restraining devices are, in fact, one way of translating warnings into effective reality by substituting a physical restraint for the action warned against. It is proposed here that it is not an endless list of activities that has to be recounted, warned against or protected from, but rather the nature of the situated logics in use which structure local practice, both good and bad, and that it is these structures which must be elucidated in order to first *find* the accidents and then prevent them.

Safety regulation is the regulation of accidents and not of safety as such. This appears to be a somewhat fussy mincing of words here but what is meant is that, despite the formal account's claims that it is safety work (that is, the routinization of a work task so as to be mishap-free, by whatever means) that it is up to, safety regulation is an attempt at accident containment which is not the same thing as accident prevention in its truest sense. The evaluation of this work resides solely in accident statistics for this reason. Regulation knows its effect only in counting mishaps or their converse, 'safety records.' But this is not the only way regulation knows its effect, it also knows it through the *imagined* effectiveness it supposes, based on the logic of its formal deductive encompassing account of what constitutes the lid on accident events. That the lid is deductively sufficient, based on reasonings about accident description natural accounts, means that there exists a reasonable excuse (not meant in any pejorative sense here) for the accidents that do occur *vis-à-vis* the regulations in effect: that is, that there is not full compliance with the regulatory provisions, indeed, there *cannot* be full compliance given that these accidents are taking place. This is so because regulatory provisions are designed to be overriding control devices. That accidents occur nevertheless can only mean that these control devices are not in force in the field. It is this logic which allows an unabashed reading of accident accounts for the accident's 'preventability', with the training category taking up the slack where the lack of physical restraining devices can't be invoked as the cause.

Regulation is, of course, not as straightforward an affair as merely discovering what to do to control some situation. That those events still occur is often taken to mean that regulation isn't working. Many reasons are offered for this, most of them centering on the compromise nature of the regulatory process: standards weakened by private interest lobbying when they are set out, selective enforcement practices, the need to drag matters through years of civil suits in the courts. Regulation is compromise, to be sure, but we would offer an *additional* element to what determines its effectiveness if that effectiveness is measured only in terms of numbers of accidents with injuries. As an example, we will take the issue of restraining devices for the multipiece rim. The safety cage is accepted as the premier restraining device. The specifications, however, were intentially left open so as not to limit innovation in future devices. Thus, the one and a half times the force of the explosive power of a separation was taken as a performance standard in that any device must meet that as a requirement rather than any close design features. There were a few 'inquiry' comments made to OSHA about other restraining devices but these were posed as information gathering by interested parties as to what might be banned from use and not statements from these parties as to what *should* be banned from use.

The restraints we know that are used in the field as substitutes for a safety cage do not necessarily meet the one and a half times the force criterion. A heavy enough chain might contain 20 tons of explosive force but that is not the point here. The point is that no one, as part of the regulatory process of submitting comments in preparation for standards promulgation, condemned *ad hoc* restraining devices, nor were there *any* comments received on the adequacy of the wall chart serving as both instruction and warnings for rim assembly. It is simply the case that there was no motivation to do so. Manufacturers would not condemn the use of *ad hoc* restraints because to do so is to recognize their use in the field and this could conceivably constitute 'foreseeable misuse' of the wheel product, a theory in strict products liability under which they could be sued by injured workers using such devices. Moreover, unless they specifically warned against the use of such devices, they can be sued for 'failure to warn' under the same products liability law. In addition the manufacturers would not comment on a wall chart they helped put together as being inadequate in any way.

Would employers, some of whom are manufacturers of wheels and tires running service shops or truck fleet companies under worker's compensation, complain about *ad hoc* restraining devices? Would employees? Would attorneys representing either the defense or the plaintiff's side of civil personal injury law suits, thus weakening their respective theories of what constitutes adequate protection?

In fact, none of the parties to the regulatory situation would make such comment. To call this an unintended consequence of the regulatory process is to leave it as a weak designation for an area thus seen as some kind of error. Such unintended features of regulation are in fact structurally determined aspects of the regulatory process. The question of what to do to prevent accidents now appears to be irremediably swamped by a process which has a life of its own . It is a small wonder that the simple question of what is to be done becomes a little issue in comparison to the competing forces of regulatory control: lobbying by special interest groups, compromise standards, selective enforcement and questions of real concern which, not inadvertently, but systematically fall through the slats. Nor will this change for regulation is not that kind of finely tuned instrument for solving safety problems. It is not regulation's specifications that reside in the workshop as delimiters of getting the job done safely, it is the structures of local practice, the situated logics of effective and safe as well as unsafe procedure which are left untouched by a formal safety theory whose effectiveness is measured only in accident/injury counts. It is these structures which must be elucidated in order to *find* accidents, to unravel their systematic production and thereby to intervene in the processes which bring them about as not mysterious failures but the ordinary occurrences that they are.

Appendix 1: examples of accident summarizations*

*These summaries were used by OSHA as multipiece rim accident data.

Date of Incident	Source	IIHS Log No.	Involved Person's Name and Address	Location of Incident	Component Manufacturer, Size, Design and Vehicle Type (if known)	Nature of Incident; Extent of Injuries (if known)
10/28/72	NHTSA Defect Investigation 215	69	Herman E. Savoy Easton, Maryland	C. & D. Bandag Co. Main Street Preston, Maryland	(Rim) Goodyear 22" KW; (ring) Goodyear 20' KW; unknown truck type	Received fatal head injuries when the locking ring separated from a Goodyear KW rim as he was inflating the tire and wheel assembly.
9/8/72	Goodyear claim correspondence	39	Samuel Giles, Sr.	Unknown	(Rim) unknown; (ring) unknown; Trailmobile trailer	Fatally injured when an unidentified design of multipiece rim separated while he was attempting to mount the assembly on the right rear axle of a Trailmobile trailer. Mr Giles was a tire service store employee.
9/5/72	NHTSA Defect Investigation 150	141	Virgil L. Kersten Orlando, Florida	Texaco service station 1–4 and Lee Road, Orlando, Florida	(Rim) unknown; (ring) unknown; unknown truck type	Seriously injured when an unidentified design of multipiece rim separated explosively.

Date of Incident	Source	IIHS Log No.	Involved Person's Name and Address	Location of Incident	Component Manufacturer, Size, Design and Vehicle Type (if known)	Nature of Incident; Extent of Injuries (if known)
8/22/72	Goodyear claim correspondence	04	James Anderson Killian, Blythewood, South Carolina	Able residence Rabon Road near Highway 555 Blythewood, South Carolina	(Rim) Goodyear 7.00-20KWX; (ring) unknown; unknown truck type	Received a fractured skull and lost his left eye when the locking ring from a Goodyear KWX multipiece rim separated explosively as he tapped on the inflated assembly to properly seat it on the axle of a truck.
00/00/76	Letter to IIHS	237	James W. Burks Texas	L. Lewis Transportation Co.	(Rim): Kelsey-Hayes 20x6 RH5° (Ring): Firestone 20x6 RH5° 1966 Ford 600 truck	The victim was struck in the face and legs by the side ring of an RH5° rim. His face was crushed causing him to suffocate to death. The tire and rim had been assembled and aired three days before the incident.
00/00/76	Kentucky Workmen's Compensation Board	248	Witheld by Kentucky Workmen's Compensation Board	Service Station	(Rim): unknown; (Ring): unknown; unknown truck type	Received injuries to mouth and teeth when struck by a locking ring of a multipiece rim which exploded when injured party struck the partially inflated assembly with a hammer to seat the ring.

Date of Incident	Source	IIHS Log No.	Involved Person's Name and Address	Location of Incident	Component Manufacturer, Size, Design and Vehicle Type (if known)	Nature of Incident; Extent of Injuries (if known)
00/00/76	Kentucky Workmen's Compensation Board	246	Withheld by Kentucky Workmen's Compensation Board	Service Station	(Rim): unknown; (Ring): unknown; unknown truck type	Received severe facial lacerations when struck by a locking ring from an unidentified multipiece rim. The victim had inflated the tire in a safety cage and then rolled it to the truck. It exploded as he was mounting the assembly on the vehicle.
3/22/69	Goodyear claim report	64	Eugene Pierce Salt Lake City, Utah	Interstate Motor Lines Salt Lake City, Utah	(Rim): Goodyear 7.50–20KW; (Ring): Goodyear 6.50-20KW; unknown truck type	Received fatal head injuries when the locking ring from a Goodyear KW multipiece rim disengaged as he inflated the tire following assembly. Mr Pierce, who was an experienced tire mechanic, inflated the tire 15 ft from an inflation safety cage.
3/21/69	NHTSA Defect Investigation 150	171	Robert W. Scholl Newark, California	Nelson Tire Co. San Leandro, California	(Rim): Firestone 20 × 7.6 RH5°. (Ring): Firestone 20 × 6.5 RH5°; 1969 International Harvester truck	Received unspecified injuries when an RH5° rim separated when he was adding air to underinflated tires on new trucks.

Date of Incident	Source	IIHS Log No.	Involved Person's Name and Address	Location of Incident	Component Manufacturer, Size, Design and Vehicle Type (if known)	Nature of Incident; Extent of Injuries (if known)
3/21/69	Goodyear claim report	36	Laurel Hamblin Illinois	Unknown	(Rim): Goodyear 7.50-20KW; (Ring): Goodyear; trailer	Received compound fractures of the right tibia and fibula resulting in amputation when the locking ring from a Goodyear KW multipiece rim separated as he was inflating the tire on a trailer owned by his employer, D & Z Trucking.
00/9/69	NHTSA Defect Investigation 150	144	Austin L. King Tulsa, Oklahoma	Unknown	(Rim): Kelsey-Haynes RH5°; (Ring): RH5°; unknown truck type	Injured when the locking ring from an RH5° multipiece rim mounted on his truck separated explosively.
00/24/69	NHTSA Defect Investigation 150	160	Franklin C. Wettles Hardeeville, South Carolina	Service station Bill Green's Service Station Hardeeville, South Carolina	(Rim): Kelsey-Hayes 20 × 6.5 RH5°; (Ring): Firestone 20 × 6.5 RH5°; 1955 Chevrolet 1.5 ton flatbed	Received a fractured skull, forehead lacerations, and a crushed arm when the RH5° multipiece rim he had assembled separated as he was inflating the tire.
00/1/69	Goodyear claim report	29	Joseph Edward Evans	Shell Truck Stop Belvedere, South Carolina	(Rim): Goodyear KW; (Ring): Goodyear KW; trailer	Received fatal head and neck injuries when the locking ring from a Goodyear KW multipiece rim disengaged when Mr Evans struck the assembly with a hammer to seat the ring after he had inflated the tire to 90 psi.

Date of Incident	Source	IIHS Log No.	Involved Person's Name and Address	Location of Incident	Component Manufacturer, Size, Design and Vehicle Type (if known)	Nature of Incident; Extent of Injuries (if known)
6/19/69	NHTSA Defect investigation 150	150	Leonard McNabb Riverbank, California	Unknown	(Rim): Budd 90170; (Ring): Budd; unknown truck type	A tire serviceman was killed when the locking ring from a multipiece rim separated, crushing his face and skull, as he was inflating the tire he had mounted.
00/13/77	New York Workmen's Compensation Board	319	Withheld by State of New York	Unknown	(Rim): unknown; (Ring): unknown; unknown truck type	Sustained injuries to his hand when a multipiece rim exploded while tire was being inflated in safety cage.
00/3/77	Puerto Rico State Insurance Fund	341	Name withheld by Puerto Rico Juana Diaz, PR	Service Station Juana Diaz, PR	(Rim): unknown; (Ring): unknown; unknown truck type	Received permanent injury to right arm when struck by an exploding multipiece rim which separated upon inflation of the tire.
00/22/77	Puerto Rico State Insurance Fund	342	Name withheld by Puerto Rico (Age 20) Ponce, PR	Service Station	(Rim): unknown; (Ring): unknown; unknown truck type	Received facial injuries when a multipiece rim mounted on a truck exploded as air was being added to tire.
00/1/77	OSHA Region V	330	Gene Skidmore	Mobile Repair Shop Republic Steel Corp. Warren, Ohio	(Rim): unknown; (Ring): unknown Slab carrier vehicle	Fatally injured when a multipiece rim exploded as he was removing a wheel from a slab carrier vehicle.

Date of Incident	Source	IIHS Log No.	Involved Person's Name and Address	Location of Incident	Component Manufacturer, Size, Design and Vehicle Type (if known)	Nature of Incident; Extent of Injuries (if known)
12/30/76	Puerto Rico State Insurance Fund	336	Name withheld by Puerto Rico (Age 60) Arecibo, PR	Automobile Parts Store Arecibo, PR	(Rim): unknown; (Ring): unknown; unknown truck type	Sustained injuries to left forearm when a multipiece rim exploded as the tire and rim assembly was being mounted on a truck.
12/21/76	Washington State Department of Labor and Industries	297	Withheld by State of Washington	Metaline Falls, Washington	(Rim): unknown; (Ring): unknown; unknown truck type	Suffered shock, severe back contusions and three fractured ribs when a multipiece rim exploded 15 minutes after the tire had been inflated.

		Multipiece Truck Rims		Summary of Reports of Explosive Separations Causing Accidents Since January 1 1972	
Victim's Name/ Location	Accident List No.	Rim Type	Time of Accident	Injuries	Factors Involved in the Accident
Robinson, J.	1	K Type	Apr. 1973	Fracture of arm	Victim had twenty years' experience as a tire repairman
Rodrigues, R.	2b	RH 5°	Sept. 1975	Skull fracture, brain damage, left with permanent limp	Separation occurred while checking air pressure at service station. Victim was fourteen-year-old boy
Romero	2b	RH 5°	After 1973		Separation occurred while adding air to low tire on school bus
Savoy	Article in *Baltimore Sun*	KW	Oct. 1972	Death	Separation occurred during inflation
S???	Summary in IR 150	RH 5°	Sept. 1972	None	Separation occurred on moving vehicle causing it to go out of control
Shelbyville, Ky.	14		Mar. 1976	Bruised thigh	Separation occurred after safety cage was used
Smiley	1	Budd BW	Mar. 1974	Death	During vehicle mounting, fatigue crack found in metal
Smith, B.	2d		Oct. 1977	Fractures of leg and jaw	Separation occurred while checking air pressures
Smith, Cleo	1	LWD	Mar. 1973	Blindness in one eye, part of skull missing	Separation occurred during mounting on vehicle, mismatched parts
Somerset, Ky.	14		July 1976	Severe facial lacerations	Separation occurred after safety cage was used
Tisdale	1	L&D	Mar. 1972	Skull fracture and facial lacerations	Victim's car was hit by wheel thrown off by truck
Walker, R.	2c	5° Com.	1974		
Walker, A.	2b	RH 5°	Approx. 1973		
Wayne, Pa.	2a		1976		

3 Kung Fu: toward a praxiological hermeneutic of the martial arts

George D. Girton

The systematic field-work for this paper was conducted over a three-month period at the Wah Que Studio of Kung Fu. Wah Que means 'for everyone' in Chinese, Ark Wong is fond of saying, and he has been teaching Kung Fu to everyone there since about 1964, when he was one of the first teachers to open his doors to students who were not Chinese. Although he is sensitive about filming, he is generous with his apparently limitless knowledge of Kung Fu, and holds a short session of his class at the end which is devoted to teaching responses to different attacks. In the two years I have been there, he has never done the same thing twice in these sessions. What I don't believe I have emphasized in the body of this paper, however, is that it is possible to learn how to fight without actually fighting, and to do this by means of acting the various formal single-person exercises. How this happens I am not fully sure, but as Ark Wong says, 'When you are experienced, your body knows how to move.'

But without a synchronous sound-visual record, the almost unbelievably detailed way in which instructed action works will have to be largely taken as a matter of faith. Indeed, the summary observations in this hermeneutic will have to be taken as illustrative of theoretical points, rather than as findings. In some cases it is not explicitly suggested that observations about Kung Fu as instructed action can be read as insights into instructed action more generally. For this I apologize to Harold Garfinkel, whose lectures on instructions as a part of the enterprise they are required to undertake have deeply informed this inquiry into practical action and whose insights have virtually dictated that the inquiry take the form of a praxiological hermeneutic.

In other cases it is not explicitly suggested that observations about instructed action in Kung Fu can be read as insights into

Kung Fu more generally. But the issue of 'Kung Fu more generally' will be encountered later on.

Opening remarks

It is only partially due to the growing availability of informed popular views of Kung Fu in manuals, movies, and on television that we have decided on the present treatment. Kung Fu is an interesting subject in its own right, well worthy of ethnographic treatment independent of the entertainment trends of the times. But several popular martial arts movies have appeared on the US movie market (although the 'fighting movies' have been making the circuit of the Chinese movie theatres of the world for quite some time). An episode of 'Kung Fu' recently replaced 'All in the Family' as the top Nielsen-rated show on television. Ohara Publications, Martial Arts Supplies Co. and other martial arts firms are capitalizing on this, selling the accoutrements of the arts, as well as a series of manuals,[1] detailing some of the many styles of Kung Fu.

But these sources cannot be taken seriously in their entirety as documenting the art of Kung Fu, limited as they are by the restrictions of their media. Indeed, there is much to object to in them.

The fighting movies, never steeped in moral reflection, depict simple peasants carrying out wars of bloody vengeance against the most mundanely evil villains history has been able to construct: gamblers, smugglers, corrupters of the pure, and once the fighting gets going, murderers of friends. Villain and hero alike turn the quiet world into one of confrontation, turning the confrontation into controlled and skillful violence at times seemingly for the sheer pleasure of it all. In these modern morality plays the weapons of the modern world are abandoned in favor of all manner of chains, swords, knives, clubs, and natural weapons such as hands. Whether you boo the villain or cheer the hero, the conflicts are esoteric, explicit, and clever enough to make any Sam Peckinpah movie look like the innocent play of a six-year-old. To those who abhor violence, the fighting movies are the latest perversion. The fighting movies make me nervous.

Television's weekly series 'Kung Fu' suffers similarly from the necessity to adhere to a narrative format. The plot alternates between the protagonist's training in the legendary Shaolin monastery in Northern China and his encounters with the logic of the American Western Frontier – a sort of 'chow mein western,' if you like. For the general viewing audience, perhaps the best lesson that can be drawn is that at the limiting point in the war of all against all, when one's lack of competence in a culture rivals that of an aphasic, profound physical skill and spiritual training are needed to survive. Indeed, it is tempting to inspect this television series in order to illuminate an article by Alfred Schutz entitled 'The Stranger,' but that would distract us from the praxiological reading we hope to develop. One might think that it would be possible, indeed advisable, to largely ignore the training methods depicted as largely fictional, the 'Kung-Fu philosophy' as script-writers' inventions. And why should we criticize as not being fact what is, after all, intended as fiction? But the fact of the matter is that practitioners of Kung Fu can and do treat fragments of these films as what Harold Garfinkel refers to as production accounts.[2] We promise to develop this later. First we must turn to the more serious how-to-do-its of Kung Fu – the pictorial manuals.

The manuals, with profuse illustration but sparse commentary, provide the closest approximation to didactic discourse on Kung Fu. How I would like to say that they can be divided into two categories – those which can be used by anyone and those which can be used only by practitioners! For this would allow me to make a strong argument that Kung Fu is at the very least an occult discipline, if not an occult science. Indeed, some manuals seem intended to confuse readers with their inaccuracies and omissions, with their failure to spell out most detailedly, without leaving any doubt, extremely intricate series of hand, body, and leg movements. And they insist on using the most enigmatic and paradoxical language, for example, 'All movement should be executed smoothly and with continuity. They should not be rigid, but firm and soft'[3] is a typical example of one of these discursively intractable production sentences.[4] They are not intractable because they are bad grammatically, though they often are bad grammatically. Further, they are not intractable because their makers never went to school and so don't know how to make a manual. But they *are* intractable to 'discursive' interrogations in that to read them in that way is to miss fundamentally the essence of what is contained in them and implied by them. They cannot be read as a report, but they can be read praxeologically, as a how-to-do-it, by anyone, not just by practitioners.

This of course introduces the question: Is what one can learn from one of these manuals really Kung Fu? The answer is neither yes nor no, for it seems that there are features of Kung Fu that one can learn only from a master of the art, and in fact this insight itself is a recurrent theme *in* the manuals, an aspect which does not seem to be in the interests of Good Advertising. But the question as to whether it is 'really' Kung Fu cannot be directed to manuals alone. In fact that question, along with another, 'What really happened?' is one of the major themes of the praxiological hermeneutic, both in actual interactional scenes where the teaching of Kung Fu is being carried out, and in actual scenes where manuals alone are used. There are here extant two issues which are analytically distinct, but which appear together in the question of the Kung Fu manuals. The first issue is that of instructed action as the use of manuals, which can be read praxiologically by anyone. The second is the issue of whether or not the result of that reading is Real Kung Fu. This second issue cannot be resolved generally. The answer would have to depend upon whether a practitioner did the reading and how he did it. It is true that practitioners learn things from manuals that others could not learn. In any case, when manuals are given a praxiological reading, they can be seen to exhibit a sense and unity which they do not have when read discursively.

On the other hand, we shall have to discount other large parts of the manuals as being of not direct praxiological, but great discursive value, especially those portions which deal with histories and indigenous theories of the arts. For along with the pictures, sequences of pictures, selected instructions, and points of interest to potential and actual practitioner alike, there filters in a variety of those theories which have been developed by long-time practitioners or 'masters' of the art. The existence of these theories places us in a difficult position relative to our wishes to give these manuals as sensible a reading as possible. Is it the case that we can follow the instructions, but we cannot transform discursive presentations into instructions? Would that an account could be given, but it may be that we shall have to eschew a treatment of histories of the art, of formularized theories about them, of their appreciated versions. Further, practitioners often give (non-praxiological) symbolic meanings to the formal systems of movement in the art. We shall have to reject any comprehensive treatment of this as well, only noting for the present that it seems plausible that the histories, the theories, the appreciated versions, the philosophical systems, all appear in the manuals not by virtue of the fact that their writers figured that those parts of the manuals could be turned to immediate practical use, but that they were a part of knowing how to talk for those who took the art seriously, and that if you wanted to study the art you might also come to talk like that to those who would have questions of theory, of appreciation, of philosophy, of history. That is, those parts of the manuals are things that authors figured 'should go' in manuals by virtue of the fact that those maxims and stories they taught in their classes found their way into writing. Maxims and stories in the context of an actual Kung Fu class do seem to have the character that they are indeed indexical and cannot be properly understood except by refusing to treat them solely as discourse, and subordinating all that looks like discourse in them to a practical reading of them for the advice and instruction they contain.

Now the question of how important are the varied formularized ways of talking to the learning of the art is extremely interesting. The question of what part that talk plays in the doing of the teaching is also very interesting. Indeed they could provide access to just what it is that makes the martial arts arts, and not merely systems of fighting. If we are to respect and take seriously the claims of masters of the art, then at some point these systems must be come to terms with. For the present, however, it is sufficient to take note of these interesting aspects, and use the talk which is done by masters and teachers only in the manner of anthropological quotes used to illustrate points which we wish to make, rather than inspecting it thematically for its self-organizing character. At this point an aside is necessary.

It would seem that in any area, not just in Kung Fu, where a body of knowledge is accessible in formularized form, either as a series of specified and repeatable body movements or as a litany or series of stories in any oral tradition, or even as a body of scientific knowledge available in the form of journal articles, etc., a distinction of some kind must be made. There is a difference between that body of knowledge, as a coherent unity, and the art which it is directed toward developing, improving, or merely sustaining. In scientific research this is reflected in Michael Polanyi's observation that although the findings of science had spread far and wide, and its maxims were legion in the junior high schools of the world, it seemed that authentic productive scientific research had remained limited to roughly the geographical area in which the scientific revolution took place. If true, this is of course remarkable. Its implications for the study of Kung Fu (for something like the same distinction abides here) are relatively extensive.

First, there is a difference between the art and the systematized formalizations of the ways of learning it. There is another difference between the art and the organizational settings in which it is learned and taught, but this is a different difference. We do not mean to equate 'systematized formalization' with 'organizational setting.' But the existence of a difference between the systematized formalizations or 'training programs' for the art and the art itself means that we shall have to abandon the notion that we can undertake, with the motivations appropriate to these enterprises, studies of historical development, cartographic representation of the geographical spread, or even a bibliographic investigation of the writings about what seem at first glance to be merely a set of body movements. In a way this is a great shame, for it is in the martial arts particularly that this kind of study could draw on an already formulated vocabulary of movements of the kind which Ray Birdwhistell for example has had to spend a great deal of time formulating, and with limited success at that. Consider the advantages of operating with 'kinemes' which have already been specifically formulated for self-defense application, and which are performed with an eye to attain constant and explicit awareness of those movements! It would doubtless be a tremendous contribution to the study of non-consciously organized, informal body movement, orientation and skill to see how such things work with formal systems of body movement. So it would be possible to interview and film not only the older practitioners of the art, but also the newer ones, questioning them as to their memories of innovations and borrowings, etc. But these would not form an adequate description of the competence involved in the learning and mastery of a martial art any more than linguistic geographies can provide more than an occasional glimpse into the way the learning and mastery of language on the occasions of the interactions of which it forms a part. Indeed, without a ponderous insight into the workings of imitative movement and its transmission, an insight which might not be available to everyone, that is, without the generation of a separate art, that of the access to the historical spread and distribution, it would seem necessary to describe in more than merely a formal manner how even a single actual movement was done, and what that meant in terms of mastery of the art.

Second, this means that perhaps the art is something different from the concatenation of specifiable movements. Perhaps it lies also in terms of abilities, qualities, and similar invisibilities. Consider the following quote from a practitioner's account:

> I found out today that I had been doing certain movements wrong, for at least a long time; say a year for some, several months for others. One of them was that I was holding my thumb wrong on my hand, not that it wasn't tight against my hand, but that I was holding it tight against my hand in the wrong place. Now this was something that I was used to from Uechi-ryu karate, where various portions of my hands always caused me trouble in controlling them, and I have just now been able to pay attention to it again. I was told that the way I was punching, with my thumb held in such and such a way

was not powerful, and that I should have to change in order to do it correctly. Now that in itself is not surprising. What was surprising was that as soon as I integrated this new piece of information into my kata, they in turn became more integrated and felt more powerful and flowing. So the amazement is the large difference the way you hold your thumb can make in what you do.[5]

In any case, properly speaking it is not the formalized system of talk and movement itself which constitutes the mastery of the master. Indeed, the movements which manuals of the art aim to provide adequate instruction for, and to which considerable time is devoted in the teaching of a novice at a Kung Fu school, *themselves* have the properties of production sentences. That is, they are deeply indexical, they are not treatable in a collectable fashion except as by the use of a swarm, they are enactments, and so on. This being the case, although it would be productive to investigate their historical spread by interviewing aged practitioners, taking films and poring over old manuals, doing the work of historical reconstruction as well as the synchronic constructive analysis which would be necessary to view the particulars of the swarm as an objective, rather than a lived unity replete with all the organizational work that goes into making it one, it would seem that a necessary prior task would be the description of how that second level of production sentence worked. That is, it would seem that a better description of practitioners' competence could be developed, especially in so far as it was initiates' competence, knowledge, and orientations. There is reason to believe that such a treatment would have to go more deeply into the structure of events than history, geography, or naivety could take us.

But our aside has taken us far afield, as at first we intended no more than an admonition of extreme care in the choosing of an order of fact from which to construct an adequate account. This turns out as well to be a problem for practitioners who are engaged in learning the art, in the form of locating an authoritative version.

In spite of the defects of manuals, movies, and television, practitioners who know how to look turn to them for depictions of fragments of training and fighting which represent discrete and nameable styles and schools of Kung Fu, and read these fragments as production sentences. The fragments are, in this sense, 'alchemical formulae' although it turns out that they yield to nonpractitioners as well. That is, the sequences of photographs in the manuals, the sequences of film in the films and television programs, may be viewed in (at least) two ways. One has to do with them as seeable as appreciations or descriptions of a scene.

Or evaluated under the auspices of some aesthetic. As neutral descriptions, if there be such a thing. The other is to see the sequences as do-able, as part of some step-wisely organized or organizable sequence or actions which, if followed, if really followed, would give the desired result. Now for an observation. Practitioners of Kung Fu as a matter of routine return from the fighting movies with a few new techniques in their repertoire. Or they can be seen to be performing motions which could have only been derived from a known manual of the art. Or they imitate something from the television show. Indeed one devotee was so taken by TV's depiction of the ritual shaving of the heads of initiates into the Shaolin monastery that he shaved his own head. He is still sometimes called Caine after the protagonist in that series, although his hair has long since grown back.

At any rate, the question of whether it is all 'really Kung Fu' is independent of whether real Kung Fu can be learned from the movies. An acceptable account of some movements which 'appear' at the Kung Fu studio is that they come 'from the movies,' although this is in some sense viewing fragments from other parts of the world and attributing the sensible unity of the situation to them. The question of what is really Kung Fu is of course a question which, in the details in which it is worked out, is a standing preoccupation of the initiate. Since one is an initiate for a long time, the problems of initiates are not trivial. But further, it might turn out that a detailed investigation into the acquisition of mastery could, by virtue of finding the details of bodily transformation and the concomitant 'horizontal' modes of being in the world, locate such questions within the sphere of the sciences rather than in philosophy: on the basis of actual, pointable-to, and embodied particulars.

So let us now turn to considerations of the reflexive character of instructions, and the unity which confronts the initiate.

Introduction to the ethnography

> I will explain what the term Kung Fu means. 'Kung' means the 'work.' 'Fu' means somebody. 'Kung Fu' means the skilled man. Since the martial arts are very popular in China, the majority of the people take it for granted that 'Kung Fu' means the 'working man' has reached the apex in the art of self-defense. (Ark Y. Wong, *The Secret of Kung Fu*)

In providing for the elements of an ethnography of a Kung Fu studio, the elements of which are used by members (and one corner of which would be tapped into by strangers) it would be appropriate, in the interests of more complete description, to provide some description of the more complete natural language competence displayed by students, the teachers, and whosoever was engaged in producing the social order of the studio as a routine matter. This would be the first component of a 'dispassionate' ethnography – for it is surely the case that not everyone who comes to the Wah Que Studio is a practitioner. Since Mr Wong, the teacher and proprietor, runs his herb office/martial arts store there, and since he is a bastion of Chinatown's aged people and has a lot of friends, there is a steady stream of visitors, potential and actual customers, injured people coming to see him in his capacity as the local 'Chinese doctor' and various other people who come for reasons unrelated to a general curiosity about the art, although there are spectators too.

I imagine that it would be possible to provide a 'flow chart;' a categorization device for whosoever entered the door and climbed the stairs, and then to find the ways in which they and whoever was in the school were concertedly producing their respective positions in that chart. And, indeed, entering faces are monitored to find if they are new faces, interesting and storyable in various ways. Indeed, one of the ways in which they are of immense interest is the way in which the information gained from their monitoring is used in the anticipating and carrying out of the course of actions which will occur during the ensuing class. By 'immense' is not meant that such questions constitute the 'essence of the art' but instead that in addition to whatever 'added skills' (where added skills is meant to evoke something like a kinesiologist's conception of skill) people come to the school for the purpose of acquiring, they also have the task of getting through the class as best they can. That is, they have the vulgar skills of the mastery of embodied natural language (to use a gloss) necessary to bring off the co-production of the class as an orderly event. You might not believe it to see it, but it's orderly.

Now this last observation is not news in the area of ethnomethodological researches. It is mentionable here mostly in contrast to a current ethological notion which is being adopted into behavioral studies, with Erving Goffman as one of its proponents. This prevalent view involves seeing an individual as surrounded by an Umwelt, or dwelling in a 'surround' which he is monitoring for its potentially dangerous aspects. Although there are other theoretical reasons for criticizing this view, here there is a stronger criticism. One of the notions of this prevalent ethological view is that parties in settings can monitor best what happens at entrances to enclosures, rooms being the kind of things they are. The claim being made *here* is that parties monitor openings, doors, and *from* doors but not for possible dangers. Or, rather, the possible dangers are both considerably more neutral and more dangerous than heretofore set forth, at least by ethological theorists. More neutral in that the danger would not consist of a horde of attackers, armed to the teeth, bent on vengeance, bursting through the door (although this did happen in a San Francisco Kung Fu Studio, with disastrous results). More dangerous in so far as the disruption of the social fabric itself is a danger greater than mundane dangers – but this really isn't in the same league, for who could imagine such an event, if it could even be called that, while it is easy enough to imagine a horde of attackers or a peaceful guest. At any rate, parties to the setting of the Ah Que Studio *do* 'monitor' or 'attend' occurrences for the not necessarily disruptive impact they will have, or mutually will be made and seen to have, on the course of the class. Not the least of which is the arrival of the teacher, or 'sifu' as he is called.

B: (*pointing to door*)
A: (*turns, looks at door*) Oh, Sifu's here.
B: Now there'll be law and order.

In our terms, there was order all along, even before the door was pointed to. For although there is a veritable melee of pre-class warmup, stretching, exercising, chasing, and playful sparring going on, and aside from the fact this is itself orderly in that it does sequentially there rather than later, during the class, B is already standing in a horse stance facing the front of the studio, which means thaat the door is within his field of vision. But this is not making B out to be in error, for it is surely the case that in substantive terms the teacher plays a large part in organizing the class.

But now the problem of ethnography arises in a puzzling manner. In our quest for how members might 'come to see with members' eyes,' we begin to see the learning of the art as 'grounded' in what for Alfred Schutz was the paramount reality: the commonsense world of everyday life. That is, even while initiates and masters alike are orienting to what we might name a 'finite sub-universe of meaning,' that of *acting*, they orient to it as the reason for being there, as an accretion onto the everyday world, as an addition to it. In terms of a more ethnographic motivation, we face the problem we will face later with regard to movement: that without fully describing the commonsense world, we wish to describe acting as a related phenomenon.

The ambivalent status of an ethnographic enterprise

By raising the notion of ethnography as ambivalent, we do not mean to introduce a discussion of the varying degrees of certitude which an ethnographer, a detailer and analyzer of 'the life' may have about his observations and their 'validity.' We mean instead that there are at least these two aspects to an ethnography which is conducted under social scientific auspices: the first is that in some way based on a 'detailed observation' of everyday life, that it utilizes commonsense notions through and through in carrying out these observations. Better still, the world which it seeks to bring to the professional audience is a world seen in common, heard in common, felt in common and in these ways a world which is sensible-in-common. That is what is meant by 'commonsense' – that a world as seen, heard, felt, and known in common is assumed and relied upon by ethnographers. There are further issues having to do with the sensibility of the organizational world from a members' and again, from an ethnographers' 'standpoint.' But these may be subsumed under this larger topic, that of the world as made up of discrete, accountable, observable, and reportable fragments, and the prevailing use of this notion of the accountable world by lay and professional ethnographers alike to make sense of individual situations, to negotiate social scenes in which they must participate rather than being mere witnesses, to be mere witnesses, to become members. All this is one 'valence,' if you will.

The second has to do with a preoccupation of rigorous describers who, while concerned with knowledge about situations as accountable matters, find themselves motivated to provide insight into what situations could after all be about, about how accountability worked, in detail of some kind. By this is not meant that 'good' ethnographers should and do become more 'aware' of their own practices, although this is certainly recommended. Instead we mean that ethnographic studies, even when conducted from the advantageous members' perspective nonetheless unavoidably speak in a detached way which does not fully retain the motives, the views and beliefs, the schemes of relevances, the practical maxims, the knowledge, and the artistry which obtain in the field that the ethnography holds as a topic. Conversely, in so far as the ethnography is in congruence with its topic in these respects, does it not assume doctrinal aspects? We must reserve a thematic treatment of ethnography in general for a later work. Let us just say for the moment that there is a deeper sense of ethnography, in which perhaps the notion could be saved. If we abandon the curiously geometric metaphors of 'perspective' and 'standpoint' and adopt instead a notion of 'pathness' or being on a path, ethnography as depending upon a 'manualized' reading and presentation of the facts of life would then assume the character of 'writings from the path.' The following remarks have the character of summary observations about Kung Fu as instructed action. Instructed action more generally, and Kung Fu in particular, is like a finger pointing at the moon. Concentrate on the finger, and you will miss all the heavenly glory.

Acting

It isn't only because acting is instrumental to an understanding of the organizational arrangements of the setting of Wah Que studio that an extended treatment of it is called for. It is also because it is instrumental to the learning of several of the arts of Kung Fu that it merits treatment. Indeed, an investigation into acting *sans* organizational setting would be deep and interesting, and would probably lead us far further into the essence of the art than we can go in a more properly ethnographic treatment. In any case, acting is found massively *in* organizational settings and is amenable to description. Further, before one learns the arts of Kung Fu through acting, the learning of acting itself constitutes a first order of instructed activities.[6] In so far as the end result, or any partial end result, is derived from the inspection of and operation on production sentences, acting is derived from an inspection of and operation on production sentences.[7] An expansion of the sense of 'in so far' in the preceding sentence is appropriate but only in the context of a more detailed description of the way(s) people learn acting. They do learn it by doing it of course, but the reflexive character of the settings in which instructing/learning takes place[8] prohibits our speaking of this learning as the mere passing along of information, or bits of information. Less closely watched and described, that might seem to be the case. Conversely, a more detailed description could be expected to find how instructing/learning as a gloss of the ways practitioners were finding-acting-for-themselves was an extremely crude way of speaking.

At first glance, even at first protracted inspection by an interested potential student, the acting of any of the forms appears as an incongruous and intractable series of dancelike movements. An occasional movement in the puzzling dance is evidently a punch, or a block, or some self-defense technique. Kicks are particularly obvious. But for the most part the naive observer is hard put to figure out just how the person who is acting is moving his hands and feet, let alone what it all means. There is, prior to watching for the purpose of figuring exactly what the actor is doing (watching for what he is doing being prior to watching for the purpose of making it retellable, or, in this case, redoable) such a thing as competent critical observership. What a ponderous name! But as a task it is ponderous in its own way, at least to the doer of it. It entails watching someone who is acting, especially (for the convenience of our example) someone who is acting something for which the observer does not know the specific moves, watching it not *for* the specific movements in any way, but watching for qualities of movement. Are there any lapses of concentration or continuity in the flow of movements one into the next? Are they being performed with sheer physical strength, or does the strength more subtly flow from within? Are they always visible, or is the acting being done too fast to see everything? Does the person doing the acting have 'control'? If competent critical observership were an interview, these are some of the questions the observer might be asking. Of course it is not really an interview. It is only watching and is perhaps more delicate than the asking of questions. Perhaps, also, more difficult.

What the watcher actually does is to watch just the movements, not the pennants on the walls, or, more to the point, not the color of the actor's clothes nor the expression on his face. He must concentrate very hard, though it is not necessary to frown, bug out his eyes, or otherwise appear to be concentrating in order to concentrate. Indeed, sometimes by looking 'softly' (though always just the movements) he can see better, and see more. One who has competently critically observed is then in a position to comment on the 'performance' he has just seen, engage in conversation about it, and adjudge the effectiveness of the acting in the terms in which he has watched it. In the social situations in which this occurs, there is usually plenty of room for controversy, gossip, and revision of opinion. But this kind of watching does not seem to be essential to at least the first stages of learning acting except in a tangential, perhaps gently inspirational way. Watching others, the beginner can find them to be excellent in a way which he wishes to duplicate, for example, 'I would like to be able to move with the same kind of definiteness and accuracy as he.' Or (and this does not have to do exclusively with the watching), finding himself in the presence of the talk resulting from competent critical observership, the beginner can feel comfortable in his enterprise and perhaps learn from their talk. But in this last he must be more careful. There are other kinds of observership, where the observer is watching specifically to learn, or, knowing the movement, specifically to be critical of and to the person who is doing them, as a matter of teaching them and correcting or changing either gross errors or slight nuances of manner. The first of these will concern us later, though the latter is important too.

The primary reason that acting looks like dance is that it is a single person activity which is pre-programmed. Fighting sets and freestyle sparring are usually pretty clearly evident as just that – fighting. Acting's 'essence,' or more mundanely, purpose, is not always immediately evident from its appearance, and its particular and minute applications even less so. It is, however, *not* dance, and teachers of Kung Fu are usually careful to emphasize this. Properly carried out, however, it doesn't really look like an expressive dance. A grandmaster acting the dragon is a terrible sight, carving world out of air with vanishing hands.

Acting is the contemporary version of a very ancient and legendary collection of self-defense techniques. They were supposedly taught by an Indian priest named Da Mo, or Bodhidharma in the Shaolin, or Sillum monastery in Northern China, where Da Mo traveled around AD 500. This collection of movements was later expanded and enriched by Kwok Yuen around AD 1600, with the help of a few famous fighters of the time. Even this much is not known by most beginners, a knowledge of the history of the art not being necessary to learn how to move one's body in determined patterns, or to fight. But the movement patterns of acting are not the very first movement patterns taught, nor is freestyle fighting taught or encouraged among beginners, if at all. The first pattern taught is '*walking*,' or '*walking the horse*,' in which the rank beginner is taught first how to stand in a '*horse*' stance and then how to move that first stance across the floor. He is taught how to punch, some elementary blocks and then, perhaps somewhere near the end of the first lesson, begins to learn how to *act*.

Retrospectively, from the standpoint of a practitioner who has learned how to act it is possible to describe acting as consisting of a collection, or ordered series of *sets*. A set in Kung Fu and some other Chinese systems of the martial arts is a term roughly equivalent to *kata* or *form* in Okinawan and Japanese systems and *hyung* in Korean systems. They are initially encountered as a series of evident and discrete self-defense techniques. Care is generally taken to see to it that beginners are correctly instructed in the fundamentals, or basics, and that they have the proper stance at the same time that they are doing the corresponding hand movements in the sequence. If a simple 'mechanism' would suffice to account for how the sets were learned, it would probably be imitation. In detail, however, this simple imitation does not turn out to be so simple, and it is not all there is to the learning of the sets, or the learning of Kung Fu. What is involved is to watch someone else doing a movement, and then to produce that movement so that although any other could see that it was in fact the same movement, from the standpoint of the person doing it, it would not look the same.

An argument could be made that the beginner in seeing part of his body is seeing it as an object from a slightly different perspective than he would the body of another doing the same movement. Then, instead of making the more difficult and total transformation from 'the movement as done by his body' to 'the movement as done by my body and experienced from within rather than merely watched,' he would be able to work on that part and the movements it makes, looking at them until he no longer needed to look at them any more in order to do them. Indeed, characteristic errors which beginners make in learning certain movements seem to suggest that, at least in some instances, something like a failure to make this transformation seems to be operating. For example, one particular circular arm movement is often incorrectly performed counterclockwise instead of clockwise. And there are some jumps in which the whole body turns 180 degrees that are particularly difficult to learn. On the whole, however, it seems appropriate to say that although 'outer' movements of the limbs would be amenable to treatment in terms of an informational model, subject only to the obstacle of the changing perspective of an object (thereby treating one's own body under the auspices of an idealization of 'object,' that is to say, treating it only as a physical object, visible from all sides, perspectival, and thereby identical with the appearance to others of the 'target' or teacher's movements). It would be difficult to deal with movements of one's own body which were, strictly speaking, out of line of one's own sight. This would include both major elements of posture, like the leaning or straightness of the body, and minor ones, like hip and shoulder placement and motion. Failing a more complete outline of a phenomenology of the body, it does not fall within the intentions of this investigation to develop this point further. Our primary concern is instructed action.

Thus far we have been writing about imitation as if a single imitation would suffice for the learning of a movement. What really happens is not a single imitation but, in a successful interpretation, a series of them. Someone who knows the set shows the movement to a beginner, the beginner copies it. Then he does the sequence by himself, if he can, and is told if he did it correctly, and maybe some mistakes that he made. Usually he will be shown again, if he asks. These are the major imitations, but the minor imitations are just beginning. They entail watching an authoritative version of the movements again and again, inspecting it whenever a question occurs as to the correctness of one's own version. Then the change is made so that the beginner's practices are in accord with the authoritative version. But that is only part of the story. It is a desirable activity, even for sets a practitioner has long known, to watch a master performing them, watching even for portions of the practitioner's own acting that he was relatively sure about, in order to uncover hidden errors in the way he was doing the sets, and to find how he might be doing them differently. This results in a continual articulation of the practitioner's own version so that eventually he will at no point in the set be unaware of the way he is doing some movement. In addition to being aware of the movement, he will be doing it correctly, or differently if what he is performing is an adaptation or innovation based on his own personal style, or even the best he can do considering the limits of his physical abilities. How simple this seems! Consult the authoritative version again and again until finally you have it right. In fact, there is more. The beginner cannot always see that he is making an error, and indeed cannot know to look to some or all of what he is doing in order to locate errors in his own performance. There are films and other people to help with this. A more troubling difficulty is finding the authoritative version to imitate, especially since a practitioner may see a truly wonderful version only once or twice.

Most of the sets are named after animals, and historically are said to have been derived from the observation of animals in combat. The names of the sets taught at the Wah Que studio are the Small Cross, Butterfly, Combination, Blackbird, Palm, Snake, Tiger, Dragon, Crane, and Leopard. The list is potentially endless but these are the only sets which the class acts regularly. However, to treat them only as a list of titles subsuming a discrete and unchangeable collection of movements is to hide far more than we would reveal.

On the matter of Styles of Kung Fu

We would like to reverse the use of style with a lower-case 's' to indicate that we are talking about the manner in which an individual does a set, and have Style, with a capital 'S' mean something like 'name brand' of Kung Fu. This latter usage is more common.

Although it is a well known and recognized notion that there exists a multiplicity of distinct Styles of Kung Fu, as is the case in many of the other martial arts, we cannot find the unity of the art by providing a rigid definition of what would be legitimately included or excluded from the corpus of Styles of Kung Fu. If members did not rather casually treat it as a corpus with, of course, the usual reservations, unless we talked about the problems of defining what was the corpus we would not have warrant to talk about it as a corpus. Indeed, to think of it only as a corpus is to miss essentially its most interesting character: it is always viewed by members from the standpoint of their own or someone else's competence.

I am continually learning of the existence of Styles I had not heard of before and which are mentioned nowhere in the available literature. So as well as the five family Styles and the Style of the five animals, there is a ten animals Style, Praying Mantis Style, Wing Chun Style, White Crane Style, and so on, each one of which has what could be called a 'substantive thematic core.' More Styles could be named, along with a few sentences characterizing the substantive thematic core of each. This listing, however, would be trivial in that it would not definitely, in a definite manner, definitionally decide what should or should not be included in the corpus of Styles as a legitimate version of the art. Just as crucial, it would not define or specify just what it was that united them all under the same rubric.

A cursory examination of available writings raises apparent reasons for dismissing this problem as a false one. According to Kong and Ho:[9]

> The term Kung-Fu is a colloquialism of Southern China which has come to mean any of the martial arts. Literally, it can be applied to anyone who is talented and proficient in a particular field.

Or, as Ark Wong explains:

> 'Kung' means the work. 'Fu' means somebody. 'Kung Fu' means the skilled man.[10]

It seems, does it not, that our worries about the unity of the art are empty worries. Without some notion of unity, then what kind of a question is our other worry, about whether a given Style shall belong to the corpus? If it is a martial art, it belongs. The search for an objective unity, at least to find in some definiteness and detail what that unity consists of, imposes artificial constraints on the way in which we are to conduct our interrogations. Kong, Ho, and Wong seem to imply, at least to these passages, that concerns of unity of corpus and membership of style in corpus are not really members' questions. This would indeed be the case if we could take these two quotations as indicative of the state of the art (or arts). But a problem arises here. In a search to find all the possible talk about this matter, one finds sooner or later that the same problems arise with the talk as did with the Styles themselves. On some issues the collection of quotations will be contradictory, on others in accord, or skewed, or perhaps clearly not even talking about the phenomena in the same way. The same property which we had sought to eliminate in the investigation of the Styles we find cropping up again in the talk about the Styles. Namely, is there a unity to the corpus of talk, and what talk does or does not belong to that corpus? This is especially crucial when it is realized that most of the talk is being done by the practitioners of the Styles. Is the problem then an academic one, having to do with documentation? Couldn't these difficulties be surmounted by actually visiting the environs of known or reported Styles and then limit one's inferences about what the essence of the art must be to what could be seen, not depending upon what could be heard or read? Not really, for although the visible must form an important and perhaps necessary component of ethnographic description, we must not give ourselves over to a tyranny of the visible. There is more to Kung Fu than can be seen. Bringing ourselves into the presence of those Styles which we have heard of as offering contrast or similarity with known Styles or even an unheard of or unusual curiosity will not help. For to then deduce or infer from what the Styles had in common, with qualifications and footnotes for individual variations, would only be to substitute for quotations other fragments of the world, fragments, nonetheless, whose coherence would be no less problematic by their having been witnesses. Fragments, furthermore, whose place within the rest of the Style from which they were drawn as exemplars would remain unelucidated, as the rest of the Style remained hidden from view.

But it is largely on the basis of a notion of rigor in description that we are disallowing ourselves from conducting a loose and far-ranging survey of the styles of Kung Fu and more or less closely similar martial arts. For it is surely the case that for members, addressing these same questions of the collection of Styles as a coherent collection, it is precisely the character of the experience, in the situations in which they can actually be witnessed, learned, and learned from, as a lived experience in the course of a retrospective-prospective praxiological (rather than merely critical or vicarious) career, that makes the collection available as a boundless collection. Each Style can be and is inspected to find the coherence of the art in so far as such an inspection is possible, and in so far as such a coherence can be found, it is found in this way. In the conversations that go on around the edges of Kung

Fu class news is traded of new schools opening up, replete with stories of their advantages and shortcomings, and discussions of whether or not it would be worth anyone's time to go to them to learn.

The crux of the matter of Styles is, that to members the collection, or to use Garfinkel's term, the swarm, of Styles is horizonally available in the following way: as those Styles known and witnessed which one could come to learn, as those Styles known and not yet witnessed which one could come, to know, witness, and learn, as those Styles neither known nor witnessed but whose existence somewhere one would have no reason to doubt, etc. In short, available as an open, horizonally boundless collection, upon and boundless in the way that one's life is open and boundless. But these remarks have been directed to elucidating the character of the 'corpus,' or better, swarm, of Styles. There is also the matter of the swarm of movements. For the Styles only confront an investigation which goes beyond the boundaries of the setting in which Kung Fu is taught. It remains to be seen that some of the same questions arise, and in greater detail, when movements are addressed. In connection with this, it is necessary to discuss the 'five animals' as well as the five 'family' Styles which are taught at the Wah Que studio of Kung Fu.

The five animals

'You have to know the five animals. Even if it is hot, no matter, you act the five animals.' (Ark Y. Wong)

The Snake, Tiger, Dragon, Crane, and Leopard are collectively known as the 'five animals' in Kung Fu or Shaolin Temple boxing, as it has also been called. They are sometimes incorrectly thought of as the basis for the expression 'the five-formed fist' of Kung Fu. Five-Styles, or the five-formed fist, is instead based on the family names of the originators of ways of doing certain basic techniques: Li – blocking; Hung – punching; Choy – horse stance; Mawk – kicking; Fut – cutting or chopping with the edge of the hand. Choy Li Fut Kung Fu, for example, emphasizes the horse stance, Li type blocking, and cutting with the edge of the hand. Of course in most schools each of these five 'family' Styles is utilized to some extent – it is a matter of emphasis. Ark Wong claims to be the only one in the world teaching all five. Although it is hard to know how seriously this claim should be taken, in any case I know of no other person who is teaching all five animals to whosoever would come to learn them. The five animals are sequences of eighty-two (the Tiger) to 108 (the Snake) self-defense related movements. The five animals are not the only animal sets. We mentioned the Butterfly and the Blackbird, which are taught at the Wah Que Studio, but there are numberous others, such as the Monkey, White Crane (a different crane), Deer, Bear, Horse (different from horse stance), Elephant, and so on. These sets are different from Styles, although any one of them could conceivably form the thematic core of a Style. I think there is even a donkey set of animal acting, but I have not seen it. The five animals, however, are somewhat different, and have connected with them certain maxims. That is, by acting the animal movements, a student is practicing or improving in some area of self-defense skills. On the wall of the Wah Que Studio is a sign in both Chinese and English which reads in English:

Dragon acting – known for ferociousness and lightness. Stalks and attacks with swift counter movements.

Tiger acting – strengthens bones and develops agility in striking and jumping.

Snake acting – is continuous acting. This develops internal power and speed. Both long and short hand styles are used.

Leopard acting – develops destructive striking power.

Crane acting – develops alertness, balance, and coordination.

Beside the description of each kind of acting is a picture of the teacher standing in a posture which, it turns out, is typical of, or characterizes, that 'animal.' Next to the sentence describing Crane acting, for example, Ark Wong is pictured standing on one leg with his arms outstretched, as if to imitate a crane aboout to fly. But from this little sign a potential member[11] or other person who did not already know would not be able to infer what for the person engaged in an actual learning career is vital knowledge: that acting was more than the standing in a determined ritual pose which seems to be part of either Chinese or turn-of-the-century ritual photography. If he did know about acting, he would not be able to infer from the sign that those animals were taught in their full and rich form. In fact, even from watching the class it would be difficult to tell if the sign were correct in all that it promised to the hopeful. The Snake is acted at almost every class, but the others much less frequently, with a wait of as much as two months between occasions on which the Leopard is acted. This largely has to do with the fact that if nobody knows an animal, it cannot be acted, and if one, or maybe two people know it, that it will be acted is an unlikely possibility. They may be doing it on their own, rather than as a class activity, but to an observer who is counting on the announcement of an activity to find its name, and this is something that does happen, what they might be doing is totally mystifying. There have been occurrences of the following nature: Ark Wong says, 'Come to act the tiger.' Then, it turns out that there aren't enough people who know it there at the time and he says, 'Later on,' which is a way of canceling the present activity. 'Later on,' it turns out, can mean later that day or a few days later, but what it really means is 'not now' with respect to the activity which was about to begin.

Movements and movement in Kung Fu

Thus far we have discussed the notion of Style, and some Styles, making the point that they exhibit to members who are 'on the path' the properties of a swarm of Styles rather than a collection of Styles. But much of our discussion of Style, as well as some forthcoming remarks about movements, has relied on an implicit notion of what neutral movement, commonsense movement, might be like. We wish to deepen and make more precise this critical notion, and here there is little risk of pedantry or misguided precision. Instead, the only risk is not enough precision. For it is not just important to members what a movement is. It is crucial. Ideally, we might be able to characterize 'movement' in general as it naturally occurred, and then provide how movement or movements in Kung Fu were similar to or contrasted with the naturally occurring version. Unfortunately, this would take us over into a rather large independent domain of social scientists, not to mention those dancers academically inclined; the domain of the study of natural bodily movement. There is no reason to expect ahead of time that we would be able to 'characterize' naturally occurring movement sufficiently well in order to point out the contrasts. Suffice it to say for the present that whereas in everyday life there is a variegated mix of spontaneous and planned, controlled and uncontrolled movements, running the gamut from precise to awkward,[12] in and beyond the sets of Kung Fu, each movement is controlled, precise, and made with the full knowledge of the practitioner that exactly that movement is being made.

But the heart of our remarks on movement and movements have to do with the set not merely occurring temporally, but as being performed as a course of action-over time, without pause. Stretching the language a bit, it could be said that sets have their 'own' time, one which has no breaks in it, and which, if it is parsed, is not significantly parsable by watch, but by movement-in-the-set. But that is an aside.

Fortunately there is additional warrant for proceeding in our description of Kung Fu movement and movements without a further elucidation of natural movement, cultural movement, etc. This warrant lies in the fact that initiates do not encounter the movements of Kung Fu in thematically elucidated contrast, they merely learn to do them as another region of the world, so to speak. The movements do not stand in contrast in the way that a reasoned argument distinguishes, makes distinctions. Instead they confront initiates, beginners, practitioners as a practical task: to move like that and *just* like that, where 'that' is some authoritative version.

The first notion of movement is related to the sets as the product of first order production sentences – the imitation of the authoritative version provided by a teacher. This first notion also surfaces elsewhere, where regulation or control of more than one person doing the set at the same time is required, such as in a room that is really too small for everyone to be acting without bumping into one another. This first notion of movement relies upon the [movement's] congruence with a portion of an ordered count, upon the obviousness of the movement, and upon its separability from other adjacent movements. Upon as well, the comparability of movements one with another, and with body-glosses, or visual examples of not-movements-in-Kung Fu, as possible errors. For example when Ark Wong says, 'Follow dees, don't put too close, don' metch too fah dey kick *you*,' he is exemplifying the proper hand position at the completion of a movement in one of the sets by relying upon that separable notion of movement, exemplifying the desired hand positions with his own hand, putting it too close to his leg on 'close,' too far on 'fah.' 'Dey kick *you*' is the consequence of improper hand position. The movements under the aegis of this first notion are not just comparable, but are clearly reproducible. They are recognizable by reference to them as 'kernels' rather than 'fringes' of meaning, as literal and explicit rather than metaphorical and vague. They are, however, not accessible by virtue of being the motion of arms as objects through a Cartesian three-space, but instead are the movements of one's own arms, legs, etc. in relation to the rest of one's body. They are dance-notational rather than analytic geometrical and perhaps more important, they only assume their character as movements as movements-in-an-enterprise. Not a general enterprise, but the specific enterprise of learning the set of which they are a part. This conveniently introduces *the second notion of movement*.

Inasmuch as the movements occur in an ordered sequence,

whereby one movement follows another time and again, it is soon seen that, in terms of discrete movements, movements which are otherwise similar are different by virtue of occurring after movements whose final positions are different. But the essence of the second notion of movement rests upon the continuous uninterrupted performance of what was originally and painstakingly learned as a sequence of movements, and upon the fact that when the set of movements is performed in this way, the question of final position disappears. Or, rather, appears in subtler form. Namely, that in this embodied calculus the 'final' position may be placed *anywhere* in the course of a set and what came before it may then be inspected for its possible value and applicability as a self-defense movement. That it is a movement in Kung Fu, there is no doubt. As unthematized, however, its possible application or applications remain hidden.[13]

It is not only because the phrase 'meditation through movement' is sometimes associated with Kung Fu that Heidegger's distinction between calculative and meditative thinking comes to mind in connection with these two notions of movement. For movement is as important to Kung Fu as thinking is to philosophy, and the differences between these two kinds of thinking are very much the same as the differences between the two notions of movement discussed here. Calculative thinking, which races from one prospect to the next, which never stops and collects itself, which is part and parcel of technology, would correspond to our first notion of movement, in which the meaning and application of each discrete and separable movement is known. The technology in Kung Fu is the technology of the sets as a discrete and finite collection of movements. Critical in the understanding of this first notion of movement as part of a technology is the notion of technical efficacy and application, the notion of the collection of movements as a known and knowable collection of self-defense *techniques*.

Our second notion of movement corresponds with Heidegger's 'meditative' thinking. Inasmuch as 'the meaning pervading technology hides itself,'[14] and meditative thinking entails having the comportment which 'enables us to keep open to the meaning hidden in technology, *openness to the mystery*,'[15] our second notion of movement entails, as a necessary part of doing it properly, that it is meditative movement in this sense: that it is exploratory not in the sense that it lays the plans for exploration, but in the sense that it demands that the practitioner engage himself with 'what at first sight does not go together at all,'[16] namely, the interstices between the discrete movements. Notice, however, that thus far we have said little about whether meditative movement can take place outside of the technology of the sets, nor, indeed have we mentioned whether the movements of Kung Fu can take place outside the sets. Or, to discard the somewhat puzzling topological metaphor in favor of a more human one, not on the path of the sets. This raises again on a more specific level, and because of that specificity in a more vital and necessary way for the practitioner engaged in learning the art, questions which we encountered with regard to the matter of Styles of Kung Fu. The answer is much the same but it has greater situational practical import. The movements are to be treated as a swarm, rather than a collection of movements.

The movements of Kung Fu as constituting a swarm

Above we referred to the movements of 'animal' acting as a collection of movements.[17] This has been handy enough, but they instead display the properties of a swarm. This summary observation is one which leads us to conclusions of descriptive richness and depth. Although fighting with concomitant theoretical talk has been known to exist in China for roughly four millennia, the exercises as a set of movements are said to have originated with a set of eighteen movements taught by Da Mo, or Bodhidharma. This exercise was known variously as the I Chin Ching (not to be confused with the I Ching), the eighteen Arhan Hands, and some untitled versions. CC Hu, who found ten versions in a search through historical documents, notes that it is not traceable to documents of the time at which it was purportedly taught, and that the earliest references to it occur about 1,000 years later, when accounts of it appeared in popular historical novels. In any case, it was later expanded to 108 movements, then Kwok Yuen's expansion occurred, to 172, and so on. But then something catastrophic in terms of its import for Kung Fu as a system of bodily movement, unified in the way a natural language is a unified system. This was accounted for as the fall of Shaolin monastery. O Hu, in attempting to verify its existence, surmised this reason for its fall. Although it had been apolitical for over a millennium, the involvement of monks highly trained in Wu-Su, or military skills, in political espionage, battles between local warlords, and other such mundane matters aroused the ire of the powers that were. Kung Fu in the presence of political reality became politically vulnerable. The secret monastery was located and destroyed, although it is said that many of the monks escaped, and were able to defend themselves against five to ten people. Small wonder that they escaped. The mythic meaning of this parable to practitioners aside, the modern lesson which can be drawn is that disciplines, sects, groupings once energized by political motivations will not be able to survive for more than several centuries. The ninja in Japan are perhaps the classic and best-researched case of this. Ninjitsu today is really only practiced by a very small number of individuals who do so in the interests of 'keeping the art alive,' a state in the evolution of an art when it may be safely assumed that it has long since passed away. It must be said that an equally plausible alternative account is that the Shaolin monastery vanished along with hundreds of other more conventional monasteries in the book and monastery burning that were so frequent in China's history.

However, the historical accounts tell little of how unity can be found by practitioners today. In terms of the way a single movement is done, that movement properly done can be read to find the coherence, consistency, and overall unity not just of that movement, but of the entire art. John Gilbey[18] relates the story of a man from Indiana who had, by poring over obscure Tibetan texts, and in the following of their instructions reading into them their specific import as instructions for an art of self-defense, come to know, practice, and eventually master only one technique. This technique became for him a method of self-defense which was effective and rewarding enough to be safely be called a system, although it could not be called Kung Fu, nor had he trained directly under a master.

The existence of so many stories of the expansion of the collection, its refined spread, its irreparable losses, are the ways in which members provide for that collection as a bounded set of elements, knowing full well that that collection is unbounded for them. The elements are the individual movements, the counts, the techniques. They vary in length from a single short hand motion to a much more lengthy combination of kicks, sweeps, blocks, and what to practitioners are rather subtle esoterica, but what to someone who does not know looks more like a repetition of the movements which came before, or is not visible at all.

With regard to membership in the collection[19] there are movements which do not belong to Kung Fu, both in the grander terms of their belonging to another Style of boxing or bodily movement, and also in terms of situated movements which one might do in an actual class, but which would be either wrong or not to the point. They would be situated in a class in the following way: practitioners would not have occasion to ask unmotivatedly whether or not a movement was 'in' Kung Fu, and would happen to be in the physical setting of a Kung Fu classroom. Instead, they would be asking if it were in Kung Fu and would they thereby have occasion to learn it, master, or hope to learn it and master it. It would be situated further in that there would be such a thing as doing a movement incorrectly, or doing something which not only wasn't a movement in the art, but which could even be harmful. Occasionally Ark Wong admonishes the class not to learn Pa-Kua (a soft, or 'internal' system of Chinese boxing) unless they are much more experienced, otherwise it could kill them. But consider the following account of a milder case:

> I remember when a friend and I were having an impromptu contest to see which one of us could stand in a horse stance the longest. This was the second contest in a row, two others having just finished their contest when one of them stood up out of his horse stance, his legs quivering with exhaustion. We had been standing there just about ten minutes, when from behind, Sifu called everyone to come and act the Snake. They started lining up, but we remained, keeping on with the contest, an unusual move for both of us, who act the Snake every time. Then Sifu called to us, 'Don't stand in the Horse, come to act.' We both turned around and got in line for the Snake. He repeated, 'Don't stand in the Horse, that's no use, don't waste your time. You can stand like that all day, no good. You know why?' Embarrassed, I shook my head. 'You have to stand like *this*,' he said, and as he spoke, he lowered himself so that his thighs were almost parallel to the ground, but not quite.

To talk about collections of movements as strict mathematical entities, with boundaries and boundary conditions like mathematical sets, or even the universes within which the sets fall, is to do some injustice to the exigencies of the occasions on which the movements occur, great injustice to potentiality, and greater injustice to embodied action and the practitioners' being-with the unfolding of self-defense techniques in their presence. To try to describe the movements as a collection with mathematical properties would be to derive this description only at the expense of the integrity of the situation. In so far as the collection of movements was rooted in the situation, as seems to be the case, the description would be a mal-description. That is, talk about the collection, or various collections of movements in Kung Fu is metaphoric at best, and successfully metaphoric perhaps on only those occasions when the metaphors can be read for their instructing character.

Now it is surely the case that instructing metaphors are employed, but not with reference to this calculative kind of movement. A case might be made that the instruction 'Turn your body' could be metaphorical. It is unavoidably a gloss inasmuch as it cannot be understood from the production sentence 'Turn your body' alone which way the body is to be turned, how far, where the movement begins and ends, whether the head remains at the same level, does it matter which way one is facing, how fast the movement is to be done, and so on. Compare, for example, the reading of this production sentence alone to accomplish the instruction, in which the practitioner must be rather finely attuned to the bodies of his fellow students around him in order to see more or less closely how they were turning their bodies, with the case in which the teacher actually manipulates the student's body so as to show him the beginning and ending positions, teacher turning practitioner's body further if it needed to be turned. Only *that* would constitute a more literal passing along of 'instructional information.' But to say that 'Turn your body' and other sentences of that ilk are metaphorical would not allow us to reserve the use of that term for another situation where metaphor does seem to be employed: in the matter of Style, and in the application of some of the maxims about doing the second kind of movement, meditative movement.

Style with and in meditative movement

By small 's' style, we mean the way in which acting is done, as matter of openness – something like what Heidegger called openness to the mystery, but an openness with concomitant, relatively well-known practical resources. As a matter of the application of metaphor, a practitioner might act the Dragon, for example, slowly; quickly; strongly, as fast as possible; with more or less attention to form; trying to think of the application of some, any, or all of the movement; trying not to think of anything in particular; lazily so as not to forget it; just lazily; trying to begin each movement rapidly and without hesitation; etc. all the dragon-possible styles. Ark Wong, being the teacher, is always exhorting students to 'act right.' In finding what 'right' consisted of, they might go through many of the above styles on subsequent actings of the dragon, or they might do some of them in spite of his exhortations, i.e. acting lazily. In any case, they are examples of actual styles of actual acting of the dragon. They have the character of prescriptive metaphors whose only serious meaning inheres in their prescriptiveness. In taking them as emblematic and descriptive of the various forms the practitioner must take them as prescriptive in order to find how they would be descriptive. When the practitioner reads on the wall that dragon acting is known for ferociousness and lightness, he can only find the serious sense of how this might be so by acting the dragon ferociously and lightly. In using the maxims to direct his acting of the dragon, the practitioner would be treating the dragon as a production sentence of the second order. The first order production sentence was the set of instructions by which the dragon-as-calculative-movement was originally learned. The crux of the first order production sentence was somebody else's acting of the dragon. The practitioner's own acting of the dragon is the heart of the second order production sentence. It must be understood that these remarks recommend the reading of collections as collections of instructions, in the case of Style, style, and movements, and further recommend that members read these collections in this way. In that way the movements themselves become available as instructions; discretely available in movement as calculative, but unveiling themselves as qualities in movement as meditative.

That we have concentrated in this hermeneutic on calculative movement and the accountable aspects of the art is a matter which requires no apology. Some readers will be disappointed that less was said about the other facet of movement, which we called meditative. This aporia is unavoidable inasmuch as all efforts to be didactic about the nature of 'essence' of meditative movement leave its significance as a matter of practitioners' concern with being on the path, veiled.

Those who know the Tao
do not need to speak of it.
Those who are ever ready
to speak of it, do not know it.[20]

Appendix

The following are manuals which I purchased at the Wah Que Studio, as soon as I found that they were furnished at the same price as everywhere else.

Da Liu, *T'ai Chi Ch'uan and I Ching*, Harper & Row. A moderately followable illustrated manual of what is sometimes referred to as one of the 'soft' martial arts. Tai Chi Ch'uan means, roughly translated, 'grand ultimate fist'. Its sixty-four positions are associated with the sixty-four hexagrams of the I Ching in one of the more philosophically articulate of martial art doctrines.

Fon, Leo, *Sil Lum Kung-Fu*, Ohara, written by a Christian

Minister turned martial arts author, this contains a partially usable presentation of Lin Wan Kune ('the continuous and returning fist') which is the first formal exercise in Sil Lum (Shaolin in Mandarin dialect) style Kung Fu. Some of the applications depicted are implausible.

Fong, Leo, *Choy Lay Fut Kung-Fu*, Ohara Publications. Contains the first formal exercise from Choy Lay Fut Kung-Fu. I am not confident of its correctness. Choy Lay Fut is sometimes colloquially known as 'long hand' because of its wide-sweeping 'haymaker' punches and emphasis on attack, rather than defense.

Kong and Ho, *Hung Gar Kung-Fu*, Ohara Publications. Contains a fairly long two-person prearranged sparring exercise and one of the best English treatments of Kung Fu's elusive philosophical concepts. The treatment is, of course, praxiological. A fairly good introduction to the art.

Lee, J. Yimm, *Wing Chun Kung-Fu*. This style was founded by a woman. Although the manual begins with a diatribe against formal exercises and that way of training, recommending that 'what you learn today you can use today,' it contains and places strong emphasis on Sil Lim Tao, which is just such an exercise. Because of its two-person exercises, similar to 'push hands' of Tai Chi Ch'uan, Wing Chun is sometimes colloquially known as 'sticky hands', although Wing Chun itself means 'beautiful springtime' in literal translation.

Lee, Ying-Arng, *The Secret Arts of Chinese Leg Manouvres in Pictures*. When I bought this book Ark Wong said, 'Oh, kicking.' It also contains a partially alchemical history of the arts which is of only partial reliability, although nonetheless extremely interesting.

Lee, Ying-Arng, *Iron Palm in 100 Days*, McLisa Enterprises. Contains more historical details not found elsewhere, as well as one good, simple breathing exercise 'to increase your power.' Contains some interesting and intelligible theory, although the English is difficult at times.

Wong, Ark Yuey, *The Grand-View of Kung-Fu*. A puzzling book with xeroxed photographs. Possibly intended as for appreciation only, although it contains one good breathing exercise and a section on the horse stance.

Wong, Ark Yuey, *The Secret of Kung Fu*. Three hundreed pages of pictures from the life of a master. One formal exercise, scarcely usable in the form presented here, and three good breathing exercises. Makes the inside of the school available as a mneumonic to one who has been there.

Wong, T. YY. and Lee, K. H., *Chinese Karate Kung-Fu*. Contains a version of the Sil Lum form depicted in Leo Fong's book by that title. It is less clear on the hand movements but more clear on the foot movements. Has a section on 'Iron Hand Training', with the characteristic disclaimer: 'Although the ability to break bricks bare-handed is not essential in the "internal and external" system, special chapters are included in this manual to satisfy those who like to specialize in this stunt.'

Other sources include:

Black Belt Magazine is for the most part of little praxiological use, although it can serve as a helpful introduction to the heterogeneous martial arts.

New Martial Hero. A Chinese language martial arts magazine to which you can turn to find what kind of a thing sequences of pictures are without the accompanying commentary. Surprisingly, I have occasionally found it to be of some use in providing photographs of phenomena that I had heard about. Pictures can be extremely suggestive in depicting new and original training methods.

This is just a beginning of a collection of these manuals – a more extended treatment would locate more. I know of more that are not currently available without writing away for them.

Notes

1 For an annotated bibliography, please see the Appendix to this chapter.
2 A production account is the product of operations on production sentences. So what we are saying is that practitioners view fragments of these films as having been learned, learned as Real Kung Fu, and as providing an example of it. They also, however, treat the fragments as production sentences.
3 Kong and Ho, *Hung Gar Kung Fu*.
4 A production sentence is that part of a set of instructions which derives its serious sense as part of the enterprise which it is used to conduct, i.e. an instructed enterprise.

5 Fieldnotes, 1971.

6 Even practitioners of the Wing Chun Style of Kung Fu, after decrying the acting of forms, then go on to teach a basic form which, they say, is extremely important for mastery of the system and should be practiced every day before everything else.

7 Linguists, and others acquainted with linguistic modes of investigation, may be puzzled, indeed alarmed at the 'imprecise' use of 'sentence' here to denote an object in the world which syntactically need not have sentential construction. We can only answer that our usage is drawn from an inspection of manuals, where the instructions do occur primarily in sentences. Interactionally, however, it is by no means the case that instructions take sentential or, for that matter, clausal or phrasal form. In this investigation, for example, soundless fragments of situations are extremely important parts of production sentences. To criticize the use of 'sentence' is not to criticize the fundamental point.

8 Rather than the reflexive character of settings in general.

9 Hung Gar Kung Fu, p. 9.

10 *The Secret of Kung Fu.*

11 There is, at the door, a line on the floor proclaiming in white painted lettering 'members only' in English and Chinese. But this is different from our usage of the term.

12 Though it must be understood that all of these may be found to have ordered properties.

13 In the Uechi system, formerly called *pang gay noon*, this became a thematic, almost doctrinal point of the system: that not only were the applications hidden, but even movements were hidden in a special way. That is, the movements which were explicitly present in the more advanced sets seisan and san-se-ru were present in the basic set, sanchin, in subtle and unarticulated form. Further, that it was the unending task of the practitioner to find, in sanchin, how the meaning of what he had been doing was hidden from him. Indeed, George Mattson goes so far as to claim that unless the inapparent techniques are discovered by the practitioner, rather than being pointed out by someone who already knows, they will be useless to him.

14 Heidegger, *Discourse on Thinking*, p. 55.

15 *Ibid.*, p. 55.

16 *Ibid.*

17 About 450 movements in the five animals, depending on how you count.

18 Secret fighting arts of the world.

19 Here the notion of membership which has been implicit in our investigations all along, i.e. competency in natural movement if not natural language, is particularly exquisite. For the query to the practitioner almost always goes something like 'do you know' some style or another, or, from other practitioners less advanced, do you know some set. Whether a practitioner knows a Style or set is not itself exclusive criteria of including it or excluding it, so the

exquisiteness is not mathematically neat, but lies instead in the
notion that individual movements are to be mastered.

20 *Kung Fu Meditations and Chinese Proverbial Wisdom Meditation*,
Far Out Press.

4 Features of signs encountered in designing a notational system for transcribing lectures

Christopher Pack

In contrast to the conventional theories of signs, which provide for the features of signs in light of the correspondence between the sign and its referent, this paper proposes a theory of signs as provided by the work of designing a notational system. In the first half of the paper, I outline the theories of the sign-relation held by C. W. Morris, C. J. Ducasse, John Wild, and Alfred Schutz. I show that a correspondence theory of meaning underlies each of these theories. In the second half of the paper, I demonstrate that the sign vehicle, as well as the designer, are missing from such an account of the sign-relation. These features stand as essential elements of the work of designing which consists of the constitution of the correspondence between the sign and its referent. Finally, I show that construction of correspondence is situated work. Once the correspondence has been constituted, the sign offers no trace of this work, thereby providing for the findings of the conventional theories of correspondence.

In his article 'An Introduction to the Phenomenology of Signs' John Wild states that 'all knowledge . . . would seem to involve the interpretation of signs and symbols.'[1] For Charles Morris, 'human civilization is dependent upon signs and systems of signs and the human mind is inseparable from the functioning of signs – if indeed mentality is not to be identified with such functioning.'[2]

The aims of this paper are to present the reader with first, a brief introduction to the present state of sign theory, with particular emphasis on the 'sign relation' and second, to present some preliminary findings of my own encounter with signs which might suggest the foundations of a new theory of signs accessed through the work of designing a notational system.

The theory of signs is a theory of intersubjectivity

A traditional concern of sociological theorizing is the relationship between the 'I' or 'ego' and the presence in the world of the 'Other'. That is, how can 'I' come to know and move through the world with the 'Other'? How is it that 'I' can come to know what the 'Other' means while at the same time he comes to know 'my' meaning? How is it that while 'engaged' with the 'Other', 'I' can find 'myself' in relation to 'him'?

For George Herbert Mead this problem is answered by a theory of signs based on his notion of the 'significant symbol or gesture.' As Natanson states on behalf of Mead: 'The basic mechanism whereby the social process goes on is gesture. The social act is effected by means of gestures.'[3]

> The significant symbol is then the gesture, the sign, the word, which is addressed to the self when it is addressed to another individual, and is addressed to another in form to all other individuals, when it is addressed to the self.[4]

Thus, the significant gesture displays two essential features. First, 'the individual making the significant gesture places himself in the position of the individual to whom his gesture is addressed.'[5] Secondly, 'from the point of view of the other, the individual then regards the content of his own gesture.'[6] As Mead further states:

> The fundamental importance of gesture lies in the development of the consciousness of meaning in reflective consciousness. As long as one individual responds simply to the gesture of another by the appropriate response, there is no necessary consciousness of meaning. The situation is still on a level of that of two growling dogs walking around each other, with tense limbs, bristly hair, and uncovered teeth. It is not until an image arises of the response, which the gesture of one form will bring out in another, that a consciousness of meaning can attach to his own gesture. The meaning can appear only in imaging the consequence of the gesture.[7]

Thus, according to Mead, meaning is found in a correspondence between the gesture or symbol displayed by 'self' offered to the 'Other,' which in turn constitutes the 'self.' Meaning or 'significance' is found in the possible interchangeability of the 'self' and the 'Other.' This interchangeability is grounded in the correspondence between the sign or gesture and what it 'means' as it is available to both the 'I' and the 'Other.' In light of this correspondence between the gesture and its meaning, 'an individual is able to respond to his own language as the other responds to it, to mean by a word or symbol what the other means by it.'[8]

For Alfred Schutz this relation of correspondence between the sign and its referent may be specified in relation to Husserl's notion of 'appresentational pairing.' In his use of appresentational pairing Schutz is addressing:

> that particular form of pairing or coupling, which Husserl calls 'appresentation' or 'analogical apperception.' The most primitive case of a coupling or pairing association is characterized by the fact that two or more data are intuitively given in the unity of consciousness, which, by this very reason, constitutes two distinct phenomena as a unity, regardless of whether or not they are attended to.[9]

Thus, in consideration of an object in the 'outer world' – for example, a red cube – 'this perception involves an apperception by analogy of an unseen backside, an apperception which, to be sure, is a more or less empty anticipation of what we might perceive if we turned the object around or if we walked around the object.'[10] Thus:

> we may say that the frontside, which is apperceived in immediacy or given to us in presentation appresents the unseen backside in an analogical way, which, however, does not mean by way of an *inference* by analogy. The appresenting term, that which is present in immediate apperception, is coupled or paired with the appresented term.[11]

Yet, according to Schutz, the appresentational pairing need not be restricted to objects in the outer world, where the appresenting and appresented member are co-present in the immediacy of perception.

> In his study *Erfahrung und Urteil*, Husserl has shown that a passive synthesis of pairing is also possible between an actual perception and recollection, between a perception and a recollection, between a perception and a fantasm, (fictum), and thus between actual and potential experiences, between apprehension of facts and possibilities. The result of a present element of a previously constituted pair 'wakens' or 'calls forth' the appresented element, it being immaterial whether one or the other is a perception, a recollection, a fantasm, or a fictum. All this happens, in principle, in pure passivity without any active inference of the mind.[12]

In the notion of appresentation Schutz provides for a theory of correspondence between a sign or the appresenting member and its referent or appresented member. Through this correspondence, knowledge of the 'Other' is made possible to the 'I' and vice versa.

> the Other is from the outset given to me as both a material object with its position in space and a subject with its psychological life. His body, like all other material objects, is given to my original perception or, as Husserl says, in ordinary presence. His psychological life, however, is not given to me in originary presence but only in copresence; it is not presented, but appresented. By the mere continuous visual perception of the Other's body and its movements, a system of appresentations, of well ordered indications of his psychological life and his experiences is constituted . . .[13]

Thus, although the formulation of 'correspondence' differs for Schutz and Mead (in light of Mead's 'social behaviorism' and Schutz's notion of 'appresentational pairing'), both provide for the possibility of knowledge of the 'Other' through a correspondence between the use of a sign and its referent as available to both the 'self' and the 'Other.' This correspondence between the use of a sign and its referent as available to both the 'self' and the 'Other.' This correspondence provides grounds for intersubjectivity in that once the 'I' and the 'Other' encounter that correspondence the sign may have the same meaning to *whosoever* might encounter it, *wherever* they might encounter it. Thus, as Schutz states: 'Through the use of signs the communicative system permits me to become aware, to a certain extent, of another's cogitations and, under particular conditions even to bring the flux of my inner time in perfect simultaneity with his.'[14]

Four versions of the correspondence theory of meaning

For the varieties of this theory of correspondence we might turn to four theorists: Charles W. Morris, C. J. Ducasse, John Wild, and Alfred Schutz. I wish to offer a brief summary of each theorist's formulation of the sign-relation, or the correspondence between a sign and its meaning. In addressing each formulation I wish to avoid discussion of their distinctions between natural and arbitrary signs, marks, indications, signals, and symbols. Although these distinctions speak to the features of signs and the sign-relation, I wish to focus solely on the characteristics of the correspondence between a sign and its meaning. In my use of 'sign' I wish to refer to the most general features of the above collection.

Charles W. Morris

Morris, by way of a behaviorism similar to Mead's, provides the reader with his theory of signs with the aid of two examples. In the first example, a dog has been trained to go to a certain place to receive food when a buzzer has been sounded. In this case, according to Morris, the buzzer is a sign to the dog that food is to be found in a pre-arranged place in a way similar to the fact that dark clouds are a sign of rain. In the second example, a man (A) is traveling in his car to a town. He is flagged down on the road by a man (B) who informs man (A) that the road ahead is blocked by a landslide. Man (A) then turns on to a side road so as to by-pass the obstruction and reach his destination. In this second case, the utterances of (B) as heard by (A) (as well as by (B³)) are found by Morris to constitute a sign of the presence of the obstacle on the road ahead for both (A) and (B).[15] He finds, by way of his effort to specify the sign-relation, four elements common to both of these occasions of sign use.

(a) The fact that both the dog and the person addressed behave in a way which satisfies a need-hunger in one case, arrival at a certain town in the other.

(b) In each case the organisms have various ways of attaining their goals.

(c) The buzzer is not responded to as food nor the spoken word as an obstacle; the dog may wait a while before going for food and the man may continue to drive for a time down the blocked road before turning off to another road.

(d) Yet in some sense both the buzzer and the words control or direct the course of behavior toward a goal in a way similar to (though not identical with) the control which would be exercised by the food or the obstacle if these were present as stimuli. . . . The buzzer and the words are in some sense 'substitutes' in the control of behavior for the control over behavior which would be exercised by what they signify if this was itself observed.[16]

In light of these four features of the encounter of the dog with the buzzer and the man with the warning, it may be said that the buzzer and warning are present to the organisms in a sign-relation. For Morris:

If anything, (A), is a preparatory-stimulus which in the absence of stimulus objects initiating response-sequences of a certain behavior family *causes* a disposition in some organism to respond under certain conditions by response-sequences of this behavior-family, then (A) is a sign.[17]

In other words, (A) stands as a sign in virtue of the fact that as a 'preparatory-stimulus' it 'influences a response to something other than itself rather than causing a response to itself.'[18] In the case of the dog, the sign is the buzzer; for the man, it is the warning of the obstacle ahead. In the absence of either the food or the landslide, the organisms respond to the sign *as if* these stimuli were present. Thus, the meaning of the sign is provided by a sign-relation in which the presence of the sign (buzzer or warning) corresponds to the presence of the referent (the food or the landslide).

Morris then goes on to specify the essential elements of this correspondence. These elements are (a) the *'sign'* as manifested by a 'sign vehicle' ('a particular physical event such as a given sound or mark or movement which is a sign'[19]); (b) an *'interpreter'* or 'any organism for which something is a sign . . .';[20] (c) the *'interpretant'* or 'the disposition to respond because of the sign . . .';[21] (d) the *'denotatum'* which is 'anything which would permit the completion of the response-sequence to which the interpreter is disposed because of the sign . . .;[22] and (e) the *'significatum'* or those conditions which are such that whatever fulfills them is a denotatum.[23] Two aspects of the correspondence between the sign and the 'response-sequence' which it elicits are 'signification' and 'denotation.' Thus,

> in the example of the dog, the buzzer is the *sign*; the dog is the *interpreter*; the disposition to seek food at a certain place, when caused by the buzzer, is the *interpretant*; food in the place sought which permits the completion of the response-sequences to which the dog is disposed is a *denotatum* and is *denoted* by the buzzer; the condition of being an edible object (perhaps of a certain sort) in a given place is the *significatum* of the buzzer and is what the buzzer *signifies*.[24]

In the case of the driver on his way to town, the utterances of (B) are signs which are spoken to (A) the *interpreter*, which gives rise to the *interpretant* or 'his disposition to respond by avoiding a landslide at that place in the road . . .'[25] In addition (B's) warning *denotes* 'the landslide at that place' or the *denotatum*, while at the same time signifying 'the conditions of being a landslide at that place' which is the *significatum*.[26]

C. J. Ducasse
For Ducasse, in contrast to Morris, the sign-relation is provided for as a 'mental event . . . rather than as a relation between

97

certain physical events and certain other [physical events].'[27] The sign-relation, according to Ducasse, 'is the kind of mental event consisting of this, that consciousness of something causes us to become conscious of something else.'[28] In specification of his use of the notion of causation in providing for the correspondence between the sign and its referent Ducasse states:

> When . . . I speak of consciousness of something *causing* consciousness of something else I use the word 'cause' in the sense which I believe it always has in experimental situations, namely, to mean such change as is introduced in an otherwise unchanging state of things – the 'effect' then being the further change in that state of things immediately following the change introduced.[29]

Thus, in the case of Ducasse, the sign-relation inhabits the consciousness of the interpreter. Furthermore, the structure of the correspondence between the sign and its referent or 'meaning' is provided as that of 'causality.'

In this version of signs, the essential elements of 'signifying' is provided in terms of a tetradic relation. That is: (a) the '*interpreter*', 'namely, the set of mental habits possessed by the person concerned [which] constitute the kind of mind he has';[30] (b) '*the context of interpretation*, namely, the kinds of things of which at a given time he is conscious, whether clearly or unclearly';[31] (c) '*the interpretandum*' or '. . . a kind of change supervening in the context of interpretation and thus functioning as cause';[32] and finally (d) the '*interpretans*' or 'another kind of change immediately following it and thus functioning as effect.'[33] All four of these conditions must be present for the sign to offer its meaning. As Ducasse states:

> Although we do say, for instance, that a mark consisting of a little cross is a symbol of addition, the fact is of course that at times when that mark is not present to a mind, it does not symbolize addition or anything else. Moreover, even when it is present to a mind, it does not symbolize addition unless that mind has been trained in a certain manner; for obviously such a mark does not symbolize addition to the mind of a Hottentot or other wholly illiterate person. And further, even when the mind to which that mark is present is one trained as our minds have been, the mark does not symbolize addition unless the mental context in the mind at the time is of a certain kind, viz., mathematical; in a religious context, for instance, that mark obviously symbolizes for us something very different from addition.[34]

John Wild
As we have seen, to Morris the sign-relation is essentially a triadic structure composed of the interpreter, sign, and significatum. (The denotatum is only required for the fulfilment of the interpreter's 'goal' – 'while a sign must signify, it may or may not denote.'[35]) Similarly, for Ducasse, the sign-relation requires (a) an interpreter's consciousness (which provides for his 'mind' in Ducasse's sense, as well as the 'context of interpretation'); (b) the presence of a sign or 'interpretandum', and (c) the referent or 'interpretans.' In contrast, Wild offers a dyadic theory of the sign-relation. That is, the sign is *really* connected with that which it signifies irrespective of the presence of an 'interpreter.' The correspondence between the sign and its referent is a *'real'* relation rather than a 'causal' one as provided by Morris and Ducasse.

As Wild states:

> Both Morris and Ducasse take the position that instead of being connected by a real, extramental relation apprehended by the interpreter, the sign is connected with the signatum only with some efficient, causal effect which the former exerts on the interpreter. This is responsible for the psychological subjectivism which characterized both theories.[36]

Thus, according to Wild, smoke is a real sign of fire whether or not an interpreter is present.[37] To the interpreter 'the sign-relation is an object of knowledge, not an efficient cause of knowledge.'[38] The sign-relation stands 'as something discovered not made.'[39] For Wild, 'a sign is anything capable of manifesting something other than itself as an object of the knowing faculty.'[40] Yet Wild is quick to point out that the notion of 'manifesting' is not to be confused with either Morris's or Ducasse's notion of 'signifying'. As he states:

> Light manifests color. The microscope manifests the cellular structure on the slide. But neither the one nor the other *signifies* the object manifested. Knowing is a kind of manifesting and signifying is a kind of knowing. All signifying is knowing, but all knowing is not signifying. Thus nonexistent entities, like mermaids and centars, may be known or represented, but not signified.[41]

According to Wild there are three essential conditions which must be met by (A) for it to stand as a sign of (B).

(1) (A) must be more knowable than (B), as the footprint of the animal is more knowable than the animal.
(2) (A) must be dissimilar to (B), as smoke to fire.

(3) (A) must be related to (B) as the symptoms to the
disease.[42]

The interpreter comes to 'find' the sign through the 'noetic act'
whereby he enters into the real relation between the sign and the
signatum. In light of the presence of the interpreter, Wild provides
for the correspondence between the sign and its 'meaning' as
follows:

> Knowing the sign causes knowledge of the signatum as
> knowing the foundation of any relation causes knowledge of
> its term. Thus in knowing the relation of similarity which (A)
> has to (B), we cannot say that (A) efficiently causes the mind
> to bring (B) into existence without denying the extramental
> reality of the relation. (A) is a moving *specifier* in a formal
> sense, leading the mind to a terminating specification in (B).
> . . . The sign only *begins to specify* the object, and leads the
> mind formally or noetically to the signatum which completes
> the specification.[43]

Alfred Schutz

As mentioned, to Schutz the sign-relation or the correspondence
between the sign and what it signifies is provided by way of
Husserl's notion of 'appresentational pairing' which

> is characterized by the fact that two or more data are intuitively
> given in the unity of consciousness, which by this very reason,
> constitutes two distinct phenomena as a unity regardless of
> whether or not they are attended to.[44]

Yet, as the interpreter encounters the appresentational reference,
several orders of the relation between the sign and the referent
are offered. Schutz provides for these orders as follows:

(1) the *apperceptual* scheme whereby 'the order of objects to
which the immediately appreceived object belongs if
experience as a self, disregarding any appresentational
references . . .'
(2) the *appresentational* scheme which is the 'order of objects
to which the immediately appreceived object belongs if
taken not as a self but as a member of an appresentational
pair, thus referring to something other than itself.'
(3) the *referential* scheme which stands as 'the order of objects
to which the appresented member of the pair belongs
which is apperceived in a merely analogical manner.'
(4) the *contextual or interpretational* scheme which is 'the
order to which the particular appresentational reference

itself belongs, that is, the particular type of pairing or context by which the appresenting member is connected with the appresented one, or, more generally, the relationship which prevails between the appresentational and the referential scheme.'[45]

In an encounter with a sign-relation we may take any one of these schemes or orders as a 'home base' which comes to constitute our interpretation of the basic order of the appresentational relation.

Schutz then goes on to describe the relation between these orders by way of Bergson's theory of order. According to Schutz, Bergson's theory, when applied to the orders of the appresentational relation, provide that

> we may interpret the appresentational relation by taking either the apperceptual, appresentational, referential, or contextual scheme as a system of reference. In doing so the selected system of reference becomes the prototype of order. Seen from it, all the other schemes have seemingly the character of arbitariness and mere contingency.[46]

Furthermore, the scheme of order which we 'select' is not one to which we are committed throughout our encounter with the sign-relation, but we may and do continuously shift the 'prototype' scheme 'in the natural attitude of daily life.'[47]

Having thus provided for the various orders and their relationship to one another, Schutz then goes on to provide three principles which govern any changes in the appresentational reference or sign-relation. These principles might be thought of as speaking to the essential features of the correspondence between the presence of a sign and what it 'wakens' or 'calls forth' as its referent.

(1) *The Principles of the Relative Irrelevance of the Vehicle* provides that: where (A) appresents (X), (X) may enter into a new appresentational pairing with (B); where (B) will appresent the same appresented object (X) as in the original pairing between (A) and (X). Some consequences of this principle are:

(a) the meaning of an appresentational relation is *independent* of the character of the sign vehicle which appresents it. For example: 'the meaning of a scientific paper is independent of whether it is printed in this or that typographical style, written in typescript or longhand, or read out loud to an audience . . .'[48]

(b) Similarly, 'the possibility of substituting one vehicle for another is one prerequisite – but only one – for translating the same appresentational content – at least to

a certain extent – from one sign system to another one
. . .'[49]

(c) Two new possibilities are provided:[50]

    (i) both (A) and (B) appresent object (X). In this case both (A) and (B) are 'synonyms.'

    (ii) or it may be the case that (A) becomes detached from its appresentational reference to (X) and thereby no longer offers itself as a sign of (X).

(2) *The Principle of Variability of the Appresentational Meaning.* In this case as in (i) above, both (A) and (B) stand as signs of (X), yet 'the appresentational meaning changes with the substitution of (A) by (B) although the appresented object (X) remains the same.'[51] For example, 'the Commander in Chief of the Allied Armies of D Day, 1944 . . . and the thirty-fourth President of the United States are [both] names denoting Dwight D. Eisenhower, but each appresentational reference is a different one.'[52]

(3) *The Principle of Figurative Transference.* This principle involves a change which is the opposite of that found in relation to the 'relative irrelevance of the vehicle.' That is, (A) which appresents (X) enters into a new relation with object (Y) and possibly even object (Z). The possible consequences of this change are:

(a) that sign (A) may then appresent two or more objects – (X), (Y), and (Z) – thereby providing for the 'equivocal use of the appresenting term,' (A). According to Schutz, this feature 'makes the construction of higher levels of appresentational relation possible.'[53]

(b) *or* the appresentational relation between (A) and (X) is forgotten while the relation between (A) and (Y) stands. This possibility thereby provides for a 'shift in meaning.'[54]

In summary, in each of these theorists' versions of the sign-relation, a correspondence is set up between the sign as encountered by the interpreter and its referent or meaning. This correspondence provides for the presence of the sign as 'directed to' its meaning. Thus, the dog in Morris's example responds to the buzzer 'as if' the food were present. The encounter with the buzzer 'means,' or corresponds to, or is directed to the presence of the food. This correspondence then is the foundation of inter-subjectivity for it provides the possibility that given the presence of the correspondence between the sign and its meaning 'I' may respond to the sign of the 'Other' '*as if*' it was 'I' who was directing the sign to the 'Other', and vice versa. Thus, in this sense, the relation of correspondence permits the possibility that a sign has the same meaning to whosoever might come to it on any occasion. In other words, this correspondence permits the interchangeability of the 'I' with the 'Other' and thereby establishes intersubjectivity.

The situated constitution of correspondence: designers' work

The features of the sign vehicle as transparent

As Morris states:

in semiosis something takes account of something else mediately, i.e., by means of a third something. Semiosis is accordingly a mediated-taking-account-of. The mediators are *sign vehicles*; the taking-account-of are interpretants; the agents of the process are interpreters; what is taken account of are designata.[55] (emphasis added)

In the correspondence theory of meaning, the meaning of a given sign is not to be found in the sign *but in the correspondence* with its referent, in the sign-relation. Thus, for Morris, 'the buzzer is not responded to as food nor the spoken words as the obstacle.'[56] Furthermore, in Ducasse's formulation of the sign-relation, 'consciousness of *something* causes us to become conscious of something else.'[57] John Wild states that 'the essential function of a sign is to lead the mind (not behavioristically but noetically) to something *other than* itself. . . . (A) must be dissimilar to (B) as smoke to fire.'[58]

In Schutz's formulation:

the object, fact or event called sign or symbol refers to something other than itself. Smoke is a physical thing given to our sensory perception. It can be seen and smelled and chemically analyzed. But if we take smoke not as a mere physical object but as an indication of fire, then we take it as manifesting something other than itself.[59]

Thus, in that the sign directs the interpreter to 'something other than itself,' (X), its features are provided for only in terms of its function of 'manifesting' the meaning of the sign. The interpreter is directed by the sign to the referent, which thereby provides for the sign to be found by an interpreter not as an object in the world, but in terms of its meaning. Thus, the correspondence theory of meaning provides, in Schutz's terms, for the 'relative irrelevance of the vehicle.' That is, (A) may function as a sign of

(X) just as well as (B) may function as a sign of (X). The meaning of (X) is not to be found in the character of either (A) or (B) but only in terms of the sign-relation or correspondence between (A) and (X), (B) and (X), or (A) and (B) and (X). Thus, in that the character of either (A) or (B) is rendered irrelevant to the interpreter, their features stand as transparent in the light of the sign-relation.

The designer as a missing person

In the provision for meaning as corresponding to the referent, each theorist provides an essentially triadic formulation consisting of the interpreter-sign-referent. Thus, in the formulation of inter-subjectivity provided by the theory of the correspondence, 'my' meaning is available to the 'Other', in that the correspondence between the sign and referent is in hand. Yet this theory of correspondence disattends to the work of the 'I' in providing for or coming *to* the sign offered to the 'Other.' Thus, in Morris's example of (B) warning (A) of the landslide ahead, (B) plays no part in the character or formulation of the features of the sign--relation. The theory of signs as a theory of intersubjectivity provides only for both the 'I' and the 'Other' as entering into the triadic structure of meaning as the interpreter-sign-referent. Thus, the conventional theories of correspondence provide for the work of 'I' in 'designing' the sign for presentation to the 'Other' as being essentially invisible. The designer then, in these formulations of sign theory, is provided as a 'missing person' in the structure of meaning.

Features for the designer's work – an ethnography of the work of designing a notation for lectures

In contrast to these features of the correspondence theory of meaning, what I wish to propose might be glossed at present as a tetradic theory of signs consisting of the designer's work-sign-interpreter-referent. That is, I wish to offer the work of the designer in constituting the correspondence between the sign and its referent. In my encounter with the work of constituting this correspondence, both the designer and the features of the sign vehicles disclosed in the source of the work, are found as essential features of signifying. Furthermore, one feature of the constitution of correspondence is that once constituted, this correspondence provides for both the designer and the features of the sign vehicle as missing. Thus, rather than 'fault' the theories of correspondence as offered by Morris, Ducasse, Wild, and Schutz, I take these theorists at present as elegant spokesmen for the features of the sign-relation in the movement *from* the sign to the referent by the interpreter. Yet my claim is that such an account provides for the work of design as a 'hidden topic.'[60]

I wish to offer as evidence for the presence of designer's work some preliminary findings by way of an 'ethnography' of an encounter between myself and the design of a notational system for lectures. The 'setting' arose during some summer work for Harold Garfinkel. A transcript of class lectures was prepared by a typist with the use of a tape recording of the lecture. I was to add missing words, correct punctuation, and check that the typed transcript was an accurate record of the lecture on the tape. Unfortunately, the resulting transcript proved to be unreadable, or at least readable only through great effort. (See Appendix, Exhibit I.)

Given this problem, my job was to devise a method to 'render'[61] the lecture as 'present' to the reader. I found that work to be impossible without altering the text in some way – mostly through the use of some signs, or a notational system. Thus my 'charge' was to present to the reader by way of a transcript the substance of the lecture.

Three notational systems were used. (See Appendix, Exhibits II–IV.) In the first transcript (II), I provided for what I was calling 'phrases' as a criterion for gathering utterances together in sentence-like structures. A second type of transcript (III), was generated by the use of standard 'Jefferson Conventions' as used in conversational analysis. And, lastly, a third transcript (IV), was organized around an attempt to 'display' silence as found on the tape to the reader. This was accomplished by 'pairing' the silence, or lack of talk, with space, or lack of writing.

The charge

Being a worldly task, the charge of providing for the talk in these transcripts was formed up under the following practical constraints:

(1) The 'rendering' would re-present to the reader the substance of the lecture.

(2) The rendering would not involve much time on my part since the task could easily become overly expensive for the returns obtained. On the other hand, the rendering had to offer the lecture as readable since I was being paid to provide something. (Thus efficacy became a thematic issue.)

(3) The representation of the lecture would be packaged in

such a way as to offer the material in an efficacious manner to the reader. That is, the substance would be gleanable from the record through a first reading or 'informed' glance;[62] and, at least, the material would stand as readable.

(4) The rendering would offer to the reader the same accessibility to the material as held by the audience or hearers of the lecture. Thus, this requirement directs the transcript to the situated features of the lecture which serve to offer the identity of the material *as* lecture. This identity provides for the possible existence of cutoffs, restarts, repairs, silence. It provides for the 'charge' of the representation of *lecture*, rather than a literary exposition. Its representation as lecture provides the material with a certain tentative air – a certain latitude with respect to the substance of the talk and its organization.

(5) The rendering stands as public record. That is, it stands as a re-presentation of the lecture, independent of both the original lecture and the tape of the lecture. In other words, the substantive material in the lecture would be offered to who-so-ever might find their way to the reading.

Angst
Given the 'charge', the first feature of designing I encountered may be collected under the term 'angst'. That is: where do I begin? The aim is the development of a notational system which can reproduce in readable form the talk of Harold Garfinkel and John O'Neill as it is available from a tape. Yet one just can't 'plunge into the work.' Here is the tape – what does one do with it? Here is three hours of talk that I am charged to reproduce in writing – how am I to do it?

In my presence to the tape, a hearing offers: talk (both distanced and close), agreement to start, breaths, silences (both long and short), all varieties of 'non-dictionary' utterances, 'repairs,' the shuffling of papers, people walking, cars passing, unexplained knocks, and various other 'background noises.' What would a system designed to capture all the above look like? How do I get such a system out of a typewriter and onto paper?

Furthermore, in the designer's presence to the paper such features as the following appear: the paper stands as an object; there are two sides to the paper; one can only write on one side at a time; the writing is provided as a contrast between the presence of the work and the 'blankness' of the page, and any combination of this contrast is available; these marks on the page are encountered in two-dimensional space; texture is available, i.e. the paper can be smooth or rough; and the paper is flexible, i.e. it can be folded and bent to take multi-dimensional shapes. In light of their imagined character, both these lists stand as combinable and expandable in an encounter with them in use.

These features stand as possibilities in light of the 'charge' to represent on paper the talk as spoken. These possibilities stand as manipulate-able. They present a 'world of possibilities' to the designer, a world that offers itself to aid in making the lecture-talk demonstratable to whoever comes to it. That swarm of possibilities is the foundation of what I've called the 'angst'. They represent the ways of representation independent of the 'charge'. That is, they are uncommitted possibilities in the face of a commitment to establish the record *as* the talk. The 'charge' or the 'project-at-hand' is to provide for the record *as* talk 'in situ' through and *despite* the features of the record.

Favored features

Angst is offered as a descriptive term for this encounter between the 'world of possibilities' and the 'charge.' Out of this angst, as directed by the project-at-hand, emerges what might be called the 'favored features.' That is, out of the sheer presence of the tape and paper to the hearer, both begin to suggest their own solutions to the following question: How do I get the features of talk out of a typewriter?

The tape offers words, pauses, and talk by Harold Garfinkel and John O'Neill. These features offer the 'highlights' to the designer. They suggest what are, or might be, notable features of the talk. They offer to the designer certain possible and contingent structures. Furthermore, in conjunction with the suggestions as offered by the tape, there are the favored ways of the paper. For example, the paper offers the unfolding character of a given string of words as displayed by the movement of the eyes starting from the left and progressing to the right, reaching an end, and returning to the left once again. There is the presence to a reader of a columnar series of such progressions which come to form images on the paper, page after page. There are things like the sharp, discrete, and delineated character of the left-hand margin. There is the use of indentation or spacing to mark off segments of a something from a something else.

In both these cases these suggestions are offered to the designer as generated by the characteristic appearance of the talk on the tape and the look of the paper. This characteristic appearance offers the favored features of the tape and paper to the designer. They stand as possible resources to the designer whose task is to provide for the talk on paper *as* the talk on the tape. They stand as weighted possibilities – 'weighted' in that they offer a strong but subtle case for their use, 'weighted' in their familiarity as a resource in fulfillment of the designer's requirement for efficacy. In this sense, 'favored' speaks to their seductive character.

Yet, these features stand as suggestions rather than as answers to 'angst'. They are suggestions presented out of the world of possibilities *in light of* the 'charge.' They stand as *'possibilities;'* they are in the air, and the air is swarming with them. Yet, these suggestions are faulted in that they do not provide the answers to the 'angst' of the designer, but they do provide a place to begin.

Questions
Once under way, the encounter between the 'charge' and the ways of the sign vehicle generates questions. These questions and their answers come to illuminate the features of the work of design as well as the ways of the paper and typewriter. Furthermore, these questions are encountered as problems found only in the course of the work of providing for the correspondence between the notation and what it represents.

In order to illuminate the features of this questioning, thereby providing for the features of the work of design as it encounters the ways of the paper and typewriter, I now wish to turn to two problems which arose in the course of that work. These questions involve the issue of how to provide on paper the presence of silence and interruptions on the tape.

Some features of notating silence and interruptions
This question was found in relation to the presence of gaps on the tape, gaps which constituted pauses in the ongoing talk. The question arose: How do I provide for the silence as see-able? In part, this question was answered by the design of the third version of the transcript (IV), which was directed toward this goal. I encountered silence in the course of transcribing the beginning of the talk between Garfinkel and O'Neill which was noted as follows:

```
HG:     alright
JO:     mmhum
HG      okay?
JO:     churely
(33 second pause)
```

The problem of providing for the presence of silence was found at that point at which the 33-second pause was encountered. One particularly striking feature of the talk was the length and feeling found in listening to that first long silence. The presence of this silence stands as notable in light of the hope that if the talk is captured on paper as spoken, the sense of the talk as spoken will also be found. In other words, in light of the 'charge' to provide for the talk as spoken 'in situ,' this silence stands as a presence which might provide the sense of what was said between Garfinkel and O'Neill.

One feature of this presence of the silence was that it is found as 'nothing happening.' That is, given that the tape provides for what happens in the conversation only in terms of an audio record, the lack of talk is found as an absence. A contrasting version might be provided in terms of a video record where the lack of talk might be provided in terms of the speaker's eating, walking, looking through some papers, shrugging their shoulders. In light of this feature of the tape recorder, the silence is found on the tape as a 'gap' or an absence of notable talk.

A further feature of the silence as found on the tape is that it displays a beginning and an end. When this boundedness is transposed in terms of paper's way, it gets translated into a linear space. Furthermore, in light of its presence on the tape as a 'gap,' the silence then stands as linear space bounded by talk.

Therefore, in light of these features of the silence on the tape, at the point of the 33-second pause, the question arises: How do you make the silence seeable? That is, in light of the ways of the typewriter-paper (which will become visible in the work of providing for the silence notation), how do you notate silence in such a way to provide for its sense *as* silence to a reader?

An idea I developed for displaying the silence, suggested as favored in light of the paper's way and by the features of the silence on the tape, was to provide for silence through the use of the space on the typewriter keyboard. That is, each blank space on the page would be provided for as corresponding to a silence found in the talk between John O'Neill and Harold Garfinkel.

In order to provide for the presence of silence by the use of a space, provision must be made for the presence of the reader. Thus, in providing for the space as signifying silence, that space must be found *as in* the talk to whosoever might read the transcription, and must be found *as* silence on each occasion the reader encounters the space. The presence of the space *as* silence is provided by a rule of correspondence or a rule-of-use.

In the construction of the rule-of-use, each space which is present *as* silence to the reader must come to stand as a length of time set up to correspond to a timing of the silence on the tape. A constraint I encountered in the constitution of this rule of correspondence was that the timing of each gap must be standardized. That is, given the features of space – that each space is offered one at a time – the presence of each space must correspond to a given length of time. Furthermore, since each space is offered to the reader as corresponding to a length of 'clock time,' this correspondence must be provided by the designer as a consistent structure.

When this time correspondence was provided, I encountered the feature of silence as offered by the tape, and the features of the ways of paper, in the constitution of the rule-of-use. For example, one rule-of-use that might be tried would be where one space is equivalent to one second. Yet, in this use, the problem arises as to how to represent a silence found on the tape which is less than a second, in light of the ways of the space (i.e., the space stands on the paper as an indivisible object). Another rule of use which might be tried is where one space equals one half of a second. Yet the same problem arises regarding the silences which are less than half a second. How are these silences to be provided for by the presence of the space, in that the space is set up to correspond to the precise length of the silence on tape? These two tries, therefore, have excluded the representation of two classes of silences – all those silences less than a second and all those silences lasting less than a half second.

Furthermore, in the provision that the space corresponds precisely to the silence on the tape, the time segment to which the presence of the space corresponds must be provided as an additive entity. That is, the time segments must be combinable such that any length of silence might be captured through multiple spaces. For example, in relation to the first try where one space equals one second, the question arises not only as to how I can provide for silences less than one second, but also how a silence of one and half seconds can be captured by the notational system.

In light of these problems, the rule-of-use which was utilized in the case of transcript (IV), was one space equals one-tenth of a second. In this way I avoided the problem of providing for a silence which is less than the timing associated with the space. Also, the problem of providing for the spaces as additive entities was eliminated. However, in relation to this use, I encountered different issues which were presented by the ways of the paper.

The first of these issues was encountered when I tried to represent the first silence of the page which lasted thirty-three seconds. That is, in light of the rule-of-use, the first silence required 330 spaces. While I was counting out the spaces of this silence, I encountered the end of the line. At this point the question arose as to how I would provide for the difference between the space as silence and the space as a 'non-relevant' space found in the margin of the paper. This problem occurred only in relation to the end of a line of silence spaces as these spaces encountered the right-hand margin. In contrast, this problem of differentiating between the silence spaces and the non-relevant spaces of the margin, was not encountered with respect to the left-hand margin. That is, since writing on a typewriter starts precisely at the left-hand margin, the character of the left-hand margin unfolds as a defined edge. Thus, in relation to differentiating the beginning of a silence space, the precise presence of the left-hand margin provides a resource for the distinction between the silence spaces and non-relevant spaces of the margin. Yet this delineating character of the left-hand margin disappears in relation to noting a three-minute silence which would call for using 1,800 spaces, thereby creating a blank page.

On the other hand, the right-hand margin does not seem to display the same precision. That is, the words on the page stop at the closest possible point to what has been established as the margin. This fact seems to offer the right-hand margin as a shaggy presence. Thus, in that the rule-of-use provides for the space as precisely corresponding to one-tenth of a second, this shaggy presence becomes a problem to the transcriber 'charged' with the precise representation of silence. Thus, in coming to the end of the first line of silence, the question arose: How do I turn the system off?

In addition, since the rule-of-use has established the relevance of the presence of a space on the page in a strong way, the presence of a space found *anywhere* on the page is implicated as a notation of silence. Thus, given the use of this notation procedure, the spaces betweeen words are found as silences lasting one-tenth of a second. Furthermore, the second silence on the tape is found between two utterances, thus the notation for silence must differentiate the inter-word non-relevant spaces from inter-word silences. Hence, the question arises again as how to differentiate the non-relevant space from the relevant silence space.

In this case, the inter-word spaces, as displayed on paper, are bounded by writing. Therefore, not only should the end of the silence be notated, but also its beginning. Thus once again I was involved in the work of constructing a notation to provide for the beginning and the end of a silence space. Yet, in the search for this sign, I was constrained in two ways. First, this notation should be found on the keys of the typewriter. Although signs might be written in the most efficacious way of creating the signs is by utilizing the typewriter's keys. Second, the notation should not be implicated in any previous use. That is, the notation must signify to the reader the same referent each time he encounters it in the transcript. In other words, the notation must be provided for as a consistent structure.

In transcript (IV), the problem of the presence of the margin and the problem of inter-word spaces and silences, are solved by using a '/' to signify the presence of silence. Thus, a rule of correspondence is constructed which states whenever one encounters the presence of a '/ /', a silence is found within. That is, the presence of these signs bound the silence. For example:

JO: churely /   /
        / . . . (to be continued for 286 more spaces)   /

Yet, in the provision for the silence space through the use '/ /', I encountered another problem. That is, in using the '/' to provide for the beginning and the end of the silence or the creation of the silence space, I found that this sign had been used previously to capture the presence of an upward intonation pattern. For example:

1 HG: alright
2 JO: mmhu
3 HG: okay/
4 JO: churely/   /
          / . . . (to be continued for 286 more spaces)   /

Thus, although the silence was encountered early in the transcript in line 4, the use of the '/' representing upward intonation was provided in line 3.

The question that is generated with respect to this earlier use of the '/' is found in relation to line 4. That is, is JO's 'churely' spoken with an upward intonation or does the presence of the '/ ' provide for a silence starting at the point of its appearance? Thus I encountered what might be called the designer's problem of consistency, whereby in the constitution of the rule of correspondence, the designer is required to provide for the signs as consistant structures. The use of '/' then, provides for both the presence of an utterance which displays an upward intonation, *as well as* the beginning of a silence space. Again, I had to search for a notation to replace either one these uses. Once more, the typewriter is consulted for a key which has not been used elsewhere. In this case, the solution might be found in the 'favored' use of the '?' to provide for the presence of an upward intonation.

A further instance of the work of constituting the rule of correspondence is found in relation to one problem I encountered in providing for the length of an interruption. That is, in the design of transcript (II), I had provided for the co-presence of the overlapped and overlapping phrases by way of a rule-of-use wherein the beginning of the overlap would be offered by aligning each utterance in relation to each other. For example:

```
JO:      . . . -the talk of occasioned maps it gets under way
HG:                          Yeah well I was going . . .
```

Thus, in this case, the interruption begins where John O'Neill's 'it' is overlapped by HG's 'Yeah.' While disregarding the problems which arose in providing this scheme, a problem arose in relation to how I might provide for the *end* of the interruption. In other words, how do I provide for the presence of interruptions on the transcript when it was found that the written overlapped and overlapping utterances display the length of interruption differently then the same overlap encountered in the tape?

In contrast to the length of the utterances as spoken, the ways of writing offer the length of the utterances in light of writing linear organization. For example:

```
JO:      it gets under way
HG:      yeah well
```

In this case, while both utterances as spoken are the same length, the writing provides for JO's utterance as lasting longer than HG's. Thus, with respect to this feature of writing, the question developed as to how I would provide for these utterances as being co-present in interruption.

The solution to this question was the use of underlining to represent the length of the overlapped and overlapping utterances. Thus, this example would be notated as follows:

```
JO:      . . . -the talk of occasioned maps it gets under way
HG:                          Yeah well I was going . . .
```

Yet in the course of transcription I found that I had earlier used underlining to note the presence of a stressed utterance. Thus the designer's problem of providing for the sign as a consistent presence occurred once more. Since the underlining now stands as a sign of the length of the overlap and also as a sign of a stress utterance, the sign offers itself as an ambiguous presence to the reader. Thus, given these two uses of the underlining, how would I notate the presence of an utterance which is both stressed *and* found in overlap. Hence, the work of the rule-of-use is not only to make the occasion of use sensible, but also by way of that sensibility, to provide for the identity of the sign as a feature of talk found 'in situ.' Thus, in light of this problem, I was again in search of notation available from the keyboard which would not be implicated in a previous use.

Conclusion

My interest in the problems which emerged in these two examples is not directed to their solutions as practical problems. Instead, I am interested in the work of designing as this work encounters these problems in the constitution of the rule-of-use. In this sense, the questions or problems which emerge as a result of the encounter of the 'charge' with the ways of the paper-typewriter, illuminate the work of designing a sign.

One element of the designer's work is the features of the sign vehicle, i.e., the ways of the paper-typewriter. In other words, the notational system is constructed in light of the presence of the ways of paper-typewriter to the designer's work. For example, in constituting a rule-of-use to provide for the space as silence, the encounter with the presence of the right-hand margin and the inter-word spaces as features of the sign vehicle, required a notation for differentiating silence space from the non-relevant spaces. In contrast to the theories of signs offered by Morris, Ducasse, Wild, and Schutz, which provide for the sign vehicle as transparent, the work of designing offers the ways of the sign-vehicle, as encountered in the course of that work, as an essential feature of the sign-relation.

A further feature of the work of designing with respect to the ways of paper-typewriter was that these 'ways' were disclosed only in relation to the course of work of providing for the presence of the sign. For example, the right-hand margin was found as a feature of the notational system only in relation to the use of a space as sign of silence. Furthermore, both the notation and the presence of the right-hand margin were found *right there* in the transcript as it unfolded. That is, I was sitting at the typewriter, counting out the number of spaces needed to notate the first silence. The typewriter stopped at the right-hand margin. It was at *just that point* that the problem of providing for the end of silence was encountered. Thus, in that the work of designing is disclosed on the occasion of the constitution of the rule-of-use, the work of designing encounters the ways of paper and type-writer; that work is encountered as situated work.

Furthermore, in addition to the situated presence of the work of designing, the 'charge' stands as a third element of that work. That is, the 'charge' provides that the notation on the page must provide for the presence of what it notes (e.g. the silence or interruption) to whosoever might come to it on any occasion of use. Thus with respect to this feature of designing, a rule-of-use is constituted whereby a correspondence is provided between the presence of the sign on the page and its referent. It is in light of the work of constituting this correspondence that the problem of providing for the sign as a consistent structure is encountered. Once the work of design constitutes this correspondence, the sign stands in the place of the referent. Hence, when the '/' appears on the page the 'sense' of that presence is provided by the rule-of-use *as* the bounding of a silence space. Thus, like the four theories presented in the first half of this paper, the 'sense' of the sign, as provided by the rule-of-use, directs the reader *from* the sign to the referent. That is, the rule-of-use provides for the presence of the '/' *as* the bounding of silence. Thus, to a reader, the '/' has nothing more to say; the sign stands as unquestioned – its presence on the page is only provided for by the rule-of-use. In light of this work of designing, the features of that work as disclosed only in the course of annotating, disappears once the rule-of-use has been constituted. Hence this feature of the work of constituting the correspondence between the sign and its referent provides for the sign's own invisibility and thereby, provides for the findings of the conventional theories of signs.

Appendix

Exhibit (1)

DISCOVERED TOPICS
Logical Properties of Occasioned Maps
HG to John O'Neill 2/10/73
Dept of Sociology, UCLA

HG: I don't want to be talking about discovered topics; I want to be talking first of all about the logical properties of occasioned maps. The discovered topic consists of the logical properties of occasioned maps; finding then that what kind of thing the logical properties of occasioned maps would be is finding what they are, would then find that – finding that this will be signs of as an occasioned map – as a discovered topic would thereby would be directed to pulling together the logical properties of occasioned maps and other discovered topics as the – thing I'm looking to lay out

John: (It's how the   ?) for some simplest question for which the talk gets in the way of occasioned – the talk of occasioned maps.

The Missing What

HG: Yes, well, I was going to speak about – Let me tell you about some things that provide motives for interest in occasioned

115

maps, so that reading occasioned maps, we're coming onto something that – it's not that I happened to be in the street one day and asked somebody, 'How do I get to your house?' and they drew me a map and I could see from what they drew. That's why I was going to be interested in it. The ( )

Exhibit (II): The Phrase Transcript

Rules-of-use:

Phrases are organized into clusters.

/ /	=	editorial comments
( )	=	utterance is untranscribable
———	=	simultaneous talk
-	=	cutoff utterance
(0.0)	=	time of silence in seconds
/	=	upward intonation

HG: ummm/tape is turned off and on/
JO: mmhum
HG: okay?
JO: churely
    (33.0)
HG: I don't want to be talking about discovered topics
    I want to be talking first of all about (3.0)
    my whwhat I'm – I want to be talking about the
      logical properties of occasioned maps (1.0)
      (JO:) mmhuh
    the discovered topic consists of the logical
      properties of occasioned maps (JO:) mmhuh
    right?
JO: okay
HG: finding then what kind of – what kind of thing the
      logical properties of occasioned maps would be
      you would then find (1.0) uhhumm (3.0)
    In let's say finding what they are would then find
      ummm that it's a – it's a that it (6.0)
    finding that this is – that this can be – that this will
      be spoken of as a occasioned – as a discovered
      topic would thereby ahh (3.0)
    would be directed to be-to-to pulling together the
      logical properties of occasioned maps and other
      discovered topics as the ah (1.0) as the ah as the
      achievement-as the thing we are looking to lay
      out

JO: mmhuh
HG: /throat clearing/ummmmmm (75.0)
JO: (the-it is by ark) for some uh simplest occasion for
which for which uh uhmm the talk ge-gets on
the way occasioned – of occasioned – the talk of
occasioned maps – *it gets under way*

HG: *yeah well I was*
going to speak
about
let me tell you about some things that – that
provide motives for interest in occasioned maps
(*before* we even)

JO: *ummmhuh*
  HG: so that coming on occasioned maps we're coming
on to something that
it doesn't – it's not that we happened – that I
happened to be on the street one day and asked
somebody *how* do I get

JO: *no*
to your *house* and they drew me a map and I could
see from

JO: *right*
HG: what they drew _____
JO: *quite*

Exhibit (III): The Jefferson Conventions

Rules-of-use

Capitals signify a relative increase in volume.

(( ))	=	editorial comments
( )	=	utterance is untranscribable
(0.0)	=	time of silence in seconds
//	=	interruption starts here
*	=	interruption ends here
_____	=	stressed utterance
/	=	upward intonation
	=	downward intonation
.	=	cutoff phrase
-		
.hh	=	in-breath
=	=	this utterance is closely followed by the next

HG: alright
JO: mmhum
HG: Okay
JO: churely
(33.0)
HG: .hh .hh .hh ummm ((tape off))((tape on))
(24.0)
HG: .hh ((laughter far in background)) .hh I don't want
        to be talking about discovered topics I want to be
        talking first of all about (3.0) My whwhat I'm – I
        want to be talking about the logical properties of
        occasioned maps (1.0)
JO: (mmhuh)
HG: the discovered topic consists of the logical
        properties of occasioned maps
JO: mmhuh
HG: right/
JO: okay
HG: Finding then what kind of – what kind of thing the
        logical properties of occasioned maps would be
        would then find (1.0) uhhmm (3.0) in let's say
        finding what they are would then find ummmm
        that it's a – it's a des – that it (6.0) Finding that
        this is – that this can be – that this will be spoken
        of as a occasioned – as a discovered topic would
        thereby ahh (e3.0) would be directed to be – to –
        to pulling together the logical properties of
        occasioned maps and other discovered topics as
        ahmmm as the ahh – as the – the big – as the
        achievement – as the thing that we're looking to
        lay out. alright/
JO: mmmhuh
HG: .hh ((clearing throat)) ummmmm
(75.0)
JO: (the – it is how the ark) for some uh simplest
        occasion for which uh uhmm the talk ge-gets on
        the way of occasioned – of occasioned – the talk of
        occasioned maps//it gets under way
HG: Yeah well* I was going to speak about – let me tell
        you about some things – that – that – provide
        provide motives for interest in occasioned maps (//
        before* we even) – so that coming on occasioned
        maps we're coming on to something that – it doesn't
        – it's not that we happened – that I happened to
        be on the street one day and asked//somebody//

how*do I get to your hou//se* and they drew me
a map and I could see from what they drew

JO: ummm
JO: No
JO: right
JO: quite=

Exhibit (IV): The Silence Transcript

Rules-of-use

(( ))	=	transcriber's comments
/ /	=	silence is found within where one blank space = .1 second
( )	=	utterance is untranscribable
*	=	in-breath
-	=	cutoff phrase
___	=	simultaneous talk
?	=	upward intonation

HG: alright
JO: mmhum
HG: okay?
JO: churely/(33.0)   /
                                                         /
                                                         /
                                                         /
                                                         /
                                                         /
                                               /
HG: ***ummm ((tape turned off))((tape on))/(24.0)   /

                                           /** I don't
want to be talking about discovered topics I want
to be talking first of all about/(3.0)   /
My whwhat I'm – I want to be talking about the
logical properties of occasioned maps/
(1.0)   /(JO:)(mmhuh)(HG:) the discovered
topic consists of the logical properties of
occasioned maps

JO: mmhuh
HG: right?
JO: okay

HG: finding then what kind of – what kind of thing the logical properties of occasioned maps would be would the find /(1.0)   /uhhum/
(3.0)   /in lets say finding what they are would then find ummm that it's a – it's a des – that it/(6.0)   /
                        /finding that this is – that this can be – that this will be spoken of as a occasioned – as a discovered topic would thereby ahh/
(3.0)   /would be directed to be pulling together the logical properties of occasioned maps and other discovered topics as ahmmm as the ahh – as the – the big – as the achievement – as the thing that we're looking to lay out alright?

JO: mmmhu h

HG: *((clearing throat)) ummmmmm/(29.0)   /
                                                            /
                                                            /
                                                            /
                                                            /
                                                            /
                                                            /
                                                            /
                                                            /
                                                            /
                                                            /
                                                            /
                                                            /

JO: (the – it is how the ark) for some uh simplest occasion for which uh uhmm the talk ge-gets on the way of occasioned – of occasioned – the talk of occasioned maps it gets under way
(HG:) yeah well I was going to speak about – let me tell you about some things – that – that – provide motives for interest in occasioned maps (before we
(JO:) ummm even) – so that coming on occasioned maps we're coming on to something that – it doesn't – it's not that we happened – that I happened to be on the street one day and asked somebody how do
(JO:) no I get to your house and they drew me a map and I could see
(JO:) right
from what they drew

JO: right

Notes

1 John Wild, 'An Introduction to the Phenomenology of Signs,' Philosophy and Phenomenological Research, vol. VIII, no. 2, 1947, p. 217.
2 Charles W. Morris, 'Foundations of the Theory of Signs,' International Encyclopedia of Unified Science, University of Chicago Press, 1938, p. 1.
3 Maurice Natanson, *The Social Dynamics of George H. Mead*, Public Affairs Press, Washington D.C., 1956, p. 8.
4 George H. Mead, 'A Behavioristic Account of the Significant Symbol,' in *Selected Writings: George Herbert Mead*, Bobs-Merrill, 1964, p. 246.
5 Natanson, p. 8.
6 *Ibid*.
7 George H. Mead, 'What Social Objects Must Psychology Presuppose?,' in *Selected Writings: George Herbert Mead*, Bobs-Merrill, 1964, p. 246.
8 Natanson, p. 13.
9 Alfred Schutz, *Collected Papers I: The Problem of Social Reality*, ed. Maurice Natanson, the Hague, 1071, p. 295.
10 *Ibid*.
11 *Ibid*.
12 *Ibid*., p. 297.
13 *Ibid*., p. 314.
14 *Ibid*., p. 326.
15 Charles W. Morris, *Signs, Language and Behavior*, George Braziller Inc., New York, 1955, p. 6.
16 *Ibid*.
17 *Ibid*., p. 10.
18 *Ibid*., p. 8.
19 *Ibid*., p. 20.
20 *Ibid*., p. 17.
21 *Ibid*.
22 *Ibid*.
23 *Ibid*.
24 *Ibid*., p. 18.
25 *Ibid*.
26 *Ibid*.
27 C. J. Ducasse, 'Symbols, Signs, and Signals,' Journal of Symbolic Logic, vol. IV, no. 3, 1939, p. 42.
28 *Ibid*.
29 *Ibid*.
30 *Ibid*.
31 *Ibid*.
32 *Ibid*., p. 43.
33 *Ibid*.
34 *Ibid*., p. 41.
35 Morris, 1955, p. 18.

36 Wild, p. 223.
37 *Ibid.*, p. 230.
38 *Ibid.*
39 *Ibid.*
40 *Ibid.*, p. 229.
41 *Ibid.*
42 *Ibid.*
43 *Ibid.*, p. 230.
44 Schutz, p. 295.
45 *Ibid.*, p. 299.
46 *Ibid.*, p. 301.
47 *Ibid.*, p. 300.
48 *Ibid.*, p. 303.
49 *Ibid.*
50 *Ibid.*
51 *Ibid.*, p. 304.
52 *Ibid.*, p. 304.
53 *Ibid.*, p. 305.
54 *Ibid.*
55 Morris, 1938, p. 4.
56 Morris, 1955, p. 6.
57 Ducasse, p. 229.
58 John Wild, p. 229.
59 Alfred Schutz, p. 294.
60 This term is borrowed from Harold Garfinkel. For the purposes of this paper 'hidden topic' may be thought of as a naturally organized phenomenon whose features are essentially missing in the account of their structure.
61 This term is again borrowed from Harold Garfinkel. In my use in this paper it might be thought of as reproducing or bringing to light the features of the talk between Harold Garfinkel and O'Neill.
62 'Informed' here means informed by the topic or organization of the talk on the tape, as pre-given to a reader's encounter with the transcript.

5 Introduction to a hermeneutics of the occult: alchemy

Trent Eglin

This essay is intended as an introduction to an on‑going study in the hermeneutics of occult philosophy and science. It is restricted, first, to predominantly methodological issues, and second, to the study of alchemy as one among many occult sciences via which considerations of method, as regards the entire corpus of those sciences, might best be illustrated.

The study itself seeks, on the basis of its own preliminary findings, to approach the occult sciences in a unique fashion. It is an approach which relies overwhelmingly on at least earlier work of Harold Garfinkel, and may be regarded as an attempted application of methods developed by him. As such, the approach may be termed ethnomethodological.

The specific practices of ethnomethodology require and are deserving of studies in their own right, and to attempt a proper explication of these would inevitably take us far afield of the direct concerns of the present effort. Moreover, the present effort is, itself, designed merely, and by way of a beginning, to place us in the presence of a phenomenon which would justify the application of those practices.

Heretofore, the Occult Sciences – the origins of which are irreparably obscure and the present extent of the activities of which is practically unassessable – have come within the province of students of history, sociology, philosophy, religion, philology, the classics, and – with both moderate and deceptive success – of psychology. That these representatives of the analytic sciences have obscured the salient and, indeed, remarkable features of the occult sciences becomes clear on the occasion of a careful reading of their own research 'confessions;' while each of these disciplines have claimed much for their findings with regard to the occult sciences, for our purposes, the outstanding results of their labors have been, on every hand, what they have felt constrained to omit, to gloss, and to dismiss as unassimilable within the frame of their legitimate researches.

The occult sciences present a problem for scientific analysis precisely because recognizably sanctionable methods of observation – be they lay or scientific – of reportage, of description, of organizing evidence and formulating accounts – i.e., of saying-in-so-many-words exactly and only in the ways one can be *seen* and can *make oneself seen* to be saying-in-so-many-words – rely upon the reflexive or embodied character of natural language formulation for their cogency and their sense. The reflexivity of natural language formulation *as an inexorable and essentially uninteresting* presence on every occasion of rendering an account gives rise to appeariential evidence of paradox, contradiction, absurdity, inconsistency, and the rest of the list of incompetences reported with respect to the occult sciences, often as research findings.

It is, at the same time and in strong contrast, a reflexivity which, *in practice*, is prominantly and characteristically 'taken into account' – i.e., is *essentially interesting* – in occult, as opposed to analytic, science, and not only demarcates the occult sciences' chief divergence from the analytic sciences, but guarantees their victories one and all.

The admittedly least sophisticated and yet perhaps most telling indictment against analytic forrays into the realm of the occult is simply researchers' persistent unwillingness and – with reference to the sanctioned and sanctionable legitimacy of their researches – inability to take the practitioners of the occult sciences seriously; to attend to these practitioners' claims and representations as anything other than epiphenomena, if not instances of fraud and chicanery; to resist the ever-present temptation toward reduction. All studies of the occult or arcane sciences which fail to take into account the claims of its practitioners can in no way assess those practitioners' methods or victories, and are consequently capable of bringing into view little more of ultimate interest than the invidiousness of their own investigations.

Our studies would thus take most seriously the universal insistence of the occult scientists that no matter the guise, no matter the variety of allegorical accoutrement, no matter the seeming diversity stretching across time and cultures, we are, when attending to the legitimate documents of the occult sciences, in the presence of a unitary body of thought in no wise deficient in empirical referent, in consistency, cogency, reproducibility, and specifically, in no wise lacking in sheer efficacy; that is, that we are in the presence of a true and radical science.

Although we shall see further on what is to be gained by this methodological posture, one potential benefit comes immediately to mind, viz., the occult scientist remains no longer the mute *object* of our researches, but is transformed instead into their inexhaustible *resource*, indeed, their guarantor. We are, as well, subsequently in a position to free ourselves of the inevitable historicization with which studies of the occult are generally burdened, i.e., free to confront the data unencumbered by the restrictive sense of the historically and epistemologically situated character of occult science as insisted upon and reaffirmed in previous research. This would involve, in brief, the suspension of the relevance of and reliance upon dubious chronologies, arguments pitting theories of diffusion against theories of simultaneous discovery, and, ultimately, of any causal reduction which invariably undercuts or trivializes practitioners' claims.

> The esoteric doctrine is the common property of mankind, and it has always been thus. In all the various great religions and philosophies of the world, the student will find fundamental principles in each, which, when placed side by side and critically examined, are easily discovered to be identic. Every one of such fundamental principles of religion or philosophy or doctrine is in every great world religion or world philosophy, hence the aggregate of these . . . contains the entirety of the esoteric doctrine, but usually expressed in exoteric form. (G. de Purucker, *Occult Glossary*

The *prescriptive suspension* of the relevance of historical and cultural diversity as concerns occult science in general, requires, inevitably, a distinction between *exoteric* or popular versions of occult teachings wherein historical and cultural diversity is in full and rich evidence, and an *esoteric* or exclusive version wherein the sense of the universal profession of unity of method and content is to be sought. And, indeed, the distinction between the exoteric and the esoteric is explicit, virtually universal, and where referred to, its overarching importance is insisted upon. It is this insistence which renders our hermaneutical enterprise a conceivable one.

For most academic inquiries into the occult, the exoteric, i.e., myth, legend, religious history and, indeed, all lay-oriented representations and understandings of cosmogenesis, anthropogenesis, the nature of man and the visible order as well as of the gods and the invisible order, is inevitably seen as and understood to be a collection of accounts, standing, for all practical purposes, for the things and events for which the accounts are seen as names and (some kind of) descriptions. So, for example, religious histories are commonly taken as (in some sense) descriptive accounts – however attenuated displaying, minimally, the features of similar and all too familiar activities of, simply, producing an account, as Garfinkel says, for-all-practical-purposes. From the point of view of this methodological presupposition, such histories reveal their patent defects as 'factual accounts' when juxtaposed with the order of facticity which we, as contemporaries of science and partakers of its methodological ideals, may be said to know so much better. This, it need be added, remains the case even though such accounts would not be regarded as in any sense deficient as *mythic* accounts which are treated *sui generis*. When such accounts are treated as mythic, the emphasis of resultant studies is inevitably reductionistic and the student is invariably in the dubious position of, from the start and perforce, knowing more of related events – psychic or physical – than those who formulated them 'for the telling.' We will confront this problem again later on. In any case, approaches to the documents of the occult sciences, and to the documents of religions, treat them as formulations unfortunately (whatever else they may be) deficient in observation, in logic, in sense, in completeness, in cogency, etc.; i.e., as the products of methodologically untrained minds, products for which the victories of science and analysis stand as correctives.

The intentionality and 'meaning' underlying the documents in question are thus taken to be initially opaque, and given as 'the problem;' an opacity and a problem for which the analytic reductions, be they psychological, sociological, anthropological, historical or whatever, may be brought to bear as method and as remedy. Where occult formulations, on the exoteric side, overlap with areas of observation organized by modern scientific disciplines, the deficiency of the former is frequently merely noted and the features of the apparent discrepancy are rarely thematicized, themselves, as objects of investigation. Thus, for the modern astronomer, astrology is simply primitive – not to say 'poor' – astronomy; for the modern chemist, Alchemy is simply primitive – not to say 'poor' – chemistry, to cite two more obvious examples. It is indeed the order of these misrepresentations that is expected to shed much light on our notion of progress as applied to the diverse fields of modern learning with which the notion is contemporary, and to show it to be largely misconstrued if only in point of emphasis.

All this, then, is simply another means of pointing to the essentially reflexive or self-referential character of methods of analysis, be they lay or scientific; of indicating, in principle, that resultant accounts are, themselves, so to speak, inextricably part and parcel of the events whose very observable/accountable character is witness to their artful accomplishment and whose ways remain largely unexamined. We will find opportunity to deepen this formulation.

The assertion that the esoteric is everywhere contained 'within' the exoteric – and, more accurately, appears *as* the exoteric – directly indicates that the former is in some sense – in radical contrast to the latter – secret; secret if only insofar as first, its presence is indicated and insisted upon by practitioners but its contents are nowhere specifically revealed (i.e., in so many words), and second, insofar as even its uninterpretable presence is in no way obvious, so that, for the majority of researchers, its presence 'in' their data is merely recorded as the insistence of practitioners and thereafter largely ignored. We will later go on to show first, that the issue of secrecy or esotericism is crucial indeed, and second, that as the practitioners bear often confusing witness, it is a secrecy in two radically different and opposed meanings of the term. It is perhaps useful to anticipate our argument with the following proposal: the esoteric or true hermaneutics of the Occult, is that body of instructions and that body of informed teachings which are secret (fundamentally obscure as opposed to entirely withheld) both by design (in the fashion of the oft-repeated injunction, 'cast ye not pearls before swine') *and* inexorably, irremediably. It is in light of this distinction that we must re-examine our notions concerning the adjectives 'occult' and 'arcane'. It was held – explicitly or by aversion – by the practitioners of the Sacred Sciences not only that '. . . under the sacred histories, allegories, symbols, emblems, figures, and parables, were concealed the elements of a sublime science . . .' (as Manly Hall puts it in describing the Old Testament[1]), but that, in our own terms, for this science to be imparted via the structures of recognizably objective, descriptive, i.e., analytic speech or writing, is itself a special sort of impossibility as perhaps denoted by the term 'ineffable' as applied to the non-dualistic experiences of the mystics; that inherent to and immanent in the structures of natural language formulae is the totality of the dualistic world for and within which they can be seen as adequate formulations; and that, ultimately, the embodied or reflexive character of those formulations must, perforce, conceal their own 'work' whose accomplishment, first and foremost, is the constituting of the occult sciences and their objects precisely as possible subjects of investigation such and only such as they are thus 'given' for those doing the investigating. Thus for those structures – again, be they lay or scientific – formulations of the Occult are holocryptic not only by conscious design, but by necessity. The elaborate symbolism dealing with and pointing to the inexorably veiled character of the Occult Doctrine attests to the contention that 'it can simply be no other way.' So, when Grillot de Givry says,

> Whether through fear of persecution or from that love of secret and hidden things innate in the heart of some men, these thinkers surrounded their doctrine with an illusive mystery, declared it forbidden to the profane, and insisted that knowledge of it was reserved to a very limited number of the elect . . . (from *Witchcraft Magic and Alchemy*)

or when William Leary says, 'Due to the inadequacies of ancient language they [biblical occultists] were compelled to explain their higher teachings in parable and allegory' (from *The Hidden Bible*), they are echoing at best a half-truth, and at worst a common, persistent, and fundamental misunderstanding.

In contrast to what have herein been characterized as the workings of analytic science and its formulations, the occult sciences *may be said* to have as their object *not* the improvement of understanding via improvements in the tools and methods of observation and formulation in and of a world pre-theoretically given, but, instead, the transformation of the very structures of awareness, such that their descriptions are pre-eminently directed not to a world pre-supposed and, in the words of Merleau-Ponty, 'always already there' but to the very pre-suppositional structures of consciousness themselves from and within which such a world can arise. Further, the occult sciences are directed to a *transcendence* of the fundamental structures of awareness within which specific methods of making the world observable and accountable for-all-practical-purposes are employed, relied, and insisted upon. The point to be demonstrated is that this 'transcendence' involves, at least, a practice, a method – understood as a mode of being-in-the-world – within which the essential reflexivity of natural language formulae is of omnipresent relevance. The insistence on the part of Occult practitioners that their appropriate modes of discourse are everywhere and on every occasion those which we recognize as symbol, myth, allegory, and parable, that their doctrine is fundamentally and essentially occult, assures us that, with respect to members of society's methods of making the world observable and reportable for-all-practical-purposes we are in the presence of something interesting. Our first task, then, a task to which the present paper is largely devoted, is to locate a phenomenon which would lend these introductory remarks their sense, and do so where previous efforts have seemingly failed to find anything which would justify our interest.

Available records of alchemy in the West can be traced to

Alexandrian Egypt and date from approximately the third century AD. The influences emerging from Hellenistic Egypt of the 'post-Alexandrian Greek-Oriental synthesis'[2] were dominant until the close of the Middle Ages, that is, approximately 1,500 years. In the development of Hellenistic culture, at a time roughly coincident with the development of Christianity, an oriental influence surfaced in the form of a radically transformed and syncretic paganism which, in combination with Greek secular culture, produced a profoundly religious admixture of Eastern mystery religion and Greek logos.

Its multifarious manifestations displayed a remarkable and thusfar unsatisfactorily explained unity, the more remarkable considering the diversity of cultures there encountered and synthesized.

The result was an indisputably exhalted spiritual philosophy or philosophies, and, with reference to the Greek culture which nurtured and, in a sense, gave birth to it, we may apply Heidegger's observation without hesitation: '[U]nderstanding the most alien cultures and 'synthesizing' them with one's own may lead to Dasein's becoming for the first time thoroughly and genuinely enlightened about itself.'[3] The dominant elements of this synthesis were, according to Jonas, Alexandrian Jewish philosophy, Babylonian astrology and magic, Eastern mystery cults become 'spiritual mystery religions,' Neoplatonism, Neopythagorianism, and 'that group of spiritual movements' known collectively as Gnosticism in which these elements were variously incorporated.[4] Alchemy, at least at that time and place, was intimately connected with Gnostic and related doctrines, and the prominant Greek alchemist, Zosimos, whose records along with those of the other Greek alchemists come to us from Alexandria by way of Byzantium, is named both alchemist and Gnostic. C. A. Burland says:

> it is probably true . . . that there was no real 'school' of alchemists in Ptolemaic Egypt, or even in any part of the Roman Empire. Yet from Alexandria flowed the amalgam of ideas which could later be sorted out from the confused mass to make a unified concept possible. But we must remember that the philosophy which dealt with the nature of man's relationship to the universe was always the basic point from which all experiments took their origin.[5]

The 'orientalization' of Hellenism was concluded, according to Jonas, by AD 300, and the writings of Zosimos are generally dated from the preceding century. Zosimos himself claims that the knowledge of alchemy was a priestly prerogative in Egypt and that its practices and doctrine were secreted within that caste. The

129

claim that the art, in some form, derives from ancient Egypt, while widely offered in some circles, is thus far neither supported by the evidence nor entirely ruled out. Assuming the possibility, Titus Burkhardt writes,

> That no early Egyptian documents remain is not surprising, since it is an essential feature of a sacred art that it is transmitted orally; that it should be committed to writing is usually a first sign of decadence, or of a fear that the oral tradition is going to be lost.[6]

We do have apparently earlier evidence of alchemical activity than that of Zosimos and his age from a Bolos Emocritos or Bolos of Mendes, dated by E. J. Holmyard as having lived about 200 BC.[7] Although this is the date often assigned to him, there is, as in the majority of cases of alchemical authors, a seemingly insoluble mystery concerning just who this Democritos was and when exactly he lived. (For example, the historian of chemistry, J. M. Stillman, dates him from 'a little earlier than the beginning of our era.'[8]) He is thought to be other than Democritos of Abdera (known to us for his notion of the atomic structure of matter), the confusion of identities being attributed to an error in Pliny's history. In most instances, the alchemical writer is referred to as Pseudo-Democritos, reflecting the negative consensus of opinion on at least that much concerning him. At any rate, Bolos Democritos's *Physika* is apparently the earliest extant mention of what are considered specifically alchemical notions on record in the West, and is followed by a hiatus of from 300 to 500 years in the written record, depending on when one chooses to date his work. This gap notwithstanding, Holmyard writes that,

> It cannot be doubted that such early alchemical practice and theorizing went on continuously from the time of Bolos Democritos, but unfortunately scarcely any records of it remain until we reach a period some 500 years later. . . . . It is [otherwise] clear from the writings of Zosimos that, in the interval which had elapsed since Bolos Democritos . . . alchemical speculation ran riot.[9]

We raise the issue of Democritos by way of showing that the historical origins of Alchemy in the West remain thus far opaque and that about all that can be safely concluded is that alchemy emerged in a recognizable form no later than 200 to 300 years after the birth of Christ and that warranted inference, if not the record, places its beginnings considerably earlier.

Alchemy in China developed apace with the Alexandrian school of Democritos and there exists an edict from 144 BC proscribing its practice. Holmyard reasonably argues from the existence of the edict that alchemy in China had 'a fairly lengthy previous history.'[10] In 133 BC an alchemist was said to have been received by the Emperor Wu. Chinese sources are said to indicate that the Royal Art was first practiced by a Dzou (Tsou) Yen, who dates from the fourth century BC, although Arthur Waley attributes the earliest extant treatises to a Pao P'u Tzŭ and concludes that an alchemy of gold, as opposed to that of other substances formerly more highly valued, 'existed in China at least as early as the first century BC.'[11] Our own conclusion, though not a particularly helpful one, is that if we look to China for the sources of alchemy, as in the West, the records fade into remote history, rewarding the search with few positive indications to any effect.

Chinese alchemy displays such a remarkable similarity of terms and doctrine to the Western version that the sharing of traditions can hardly be doubted. Waite observes that, 'There are . . . strong points of identity in the symbolical terminology common to both literatures – for example, "the Radical Principle," the "Green Dragon," the "True Mercury," the "True Lead," and so on.'[12] Granting the certainty of intercourse between China and the West ('Transmission of knowledge and ideas was much more widespread in the ancient world than has sometimes been supposed, so that we might expect to find Chinese alchemical information affecting the practitioners of Persia, Mesopotamia, Arabia, and Egypt, as well as itself being influenced by a stream in the other direction'[13]) and the near certainty of alchemical intercourse between these and other ancient cultures, it appears that although the records favor the East, as between China and Egypt (not to mention other more doubtful claimants) alchemy cannot in total safety be said to have originated in the one place in preference to the other. For our purposes, the controversy is of no particular moment except in so far as these questions of history must be allowed, perforce, to rest: alchemy cannot be dated and its beginnings cannot be located.

From Hellenized Egypt alchemy spread to Constantinople whence, indeed, our first records of Greek alchemy derive. With the Arab conquest of Alexandria in AD 640 it passed into Islamic keeping, became admixed with Syrian influences and flourished with unprecedented vigor. At about the eleventh or twelfth century alchemy was transfused into Europe via Moslem Spain, that is, some time shortly after experimental as opposed to spiritual alchemy begins to fade in China.

The art, as it is generally known, prospered in medieval Europe. Although it was given impetus during the Renaissance with the influx of Greek sources from Byzantium following the Turkish conquest there (1453) and, indeed, reached what may properly be considered a peak, its decline was presaged by the growing humanism and rationalism of the fifteenth century from which it never recovered. It gradually faded from all respectability and thereafter from sight at about the middle of the eighteenth century.

The historical languages of alchemy are thus prominantly Greek, Arabic, Syrian, Latin, and, finally, the various vernaculars of Western Europe. Subsequent to the eighteenth century it is rarely heard from again, that is, from the pens of its practitioners, some of whom are reputed on good evidence to be still about in small numbers but once again entirely secretive.

While the history of alchemy, *per se*, is happily not our direct concern, some points of interest relevant to our purposes are raised with its discussion. The first of these is the inspiration for the alchemical doctrine of the transmutability of matter, specifically, of lesser metals to gold. Most historians of alchemy have stayed well clear of a close look at the question, preferring to mention almost in passing the suppositious evolution of primitive metallurgy under the dominant influence of an equally primitive animism. The perhaps most causally connected argument to this effect is that forwarded by Berthelot.[14] Berthelot reasons from the Leyden Papyrus (dated from about the third century AD) that the doctrine of the transmutation of metals arose, after the fashion of an understandable confusion, from the early Egyptian goldsmith's art of sophisticating or adulterating metals. He argues from the evidence of such attempts at sophistication and from the fact that similar if not identical practices reappear among the Greek alchemists, that it is but a short step from the sophistication of metals to the attempt at their transmutation. A. E. Waite, however, deals with this thesis summarily:

> It is impossible to separate the Theban Papyrus [the Leyden Papyrus was found at Thebes, along with the Stockholm Papyrus] from the context of other Papyri with which it is in close relation, as admitted by Berthelot, who says: 'The history of Magic and of Gnosticism is bound up closely with that of the origin of Alchemy, and the alchemical Papyrus of Leyden connects in every respect with two in the same series which are solely Magical and Gnostic.' The proposition sounds inscrutable, for how in the name of reason can it be affirmed that the note-books of an artisan, containing methods of gilding silver and so forth, stand in any relation to a doctrine of the aeons, not to speak of the invocation of spirits? But if a Sacred Art arose under the name of Alchemy

then . . . there might well be such a connection in that time
and place of the world . . .

It is to be understood that the Greek alchemists are by no
means in the same category as the compiler of the Theban
Papyrus, and that their memorials are not comparable to the
note-books of artisans.[15]

It should be noted that we are not ultimately concerned with
denying a thesis which combines animism and metallurgy for whatever interest it may have. The point at issue is the origin of
alchemy as such and in the form in which it has survived in the
West from at least the third century AD. References to 'mystico-
religious symbolism' in relation to metallurgy gives us no better
indication concerning the origins of alchemy *per se*, and if such
reasoning is to be allowed, it must be extended backwards in time
to 'in the beginning,' that is, to mythic time – as, indeed, it has
been on occasion but by the alchemists themselves – where or
when it ceases to be an historical event or of historical interest.

Berthelot's attempt to derive alchemy from Egyptian metallurgy
takes us to the heart of the issue: for although he recognized the
presence of what he terms 'mystical fancies' in the earliest of
known alchemists, and although it appears from Berthelot's
history that not only was the 'mystical element' present from the
beginning but that it in fact gave rise to Alchemy *per se* and
eventually so-called, the thesis that alchemy is a superimposition
of a version of animism on the body of an emergent science was
so difficult to lay aside – perhaps so self-evident – that Berthelot
committed himself to a thesis which leaves Waite so justifiably
incredulous on its own evidence.

The belief that alchemy is or was merely proto-chemistry and
that the omni-present 'mystical element' could have been and
eventually was exorcized after the fashion of a superfluous
addendum, (to the profound benefit of, if not human knowledge
in general, then certainly scientific knowledge in particular) has
characterized or has been pre-supposed in the vast majority of
accepted research.

From the 'century of enlightenment' up to and including our
own times, it has been customary to regard alchemy as a
primitive precursor of modern chemistry. As a result of this,
almost all the scholars who have concerned themselves with
its literature have had no cause to see in it anything other
than the earliest stages of later chemical discoveries.[16]

We can further briefly examine the status of alchemy qua primitive chemistry, relying here on a work by the historian of chem-

istry, J. M. Stillman, entitled, *The Story of Alchemy and Early Chemistry*. We are looking for indications of the evolution of modern chemistry out of the approximately 2,000-year-old practice of alchemy.

Of the later Greek alchemists Stillman says,

[They] added nothing of importance to the knowledge to be gleaned from the pseudo-Democritus or Zosimos. With the lapse of time, these writings give the impression that their writers lack familiarity with the operations of chemistry and metal working, and are more and more lost in a mystical philosophy.[17]

With respect to the Arabian alchemists, Stillman cites Berthelot and Kopp to the following effect: '[T]he later chemical advances previously attributed to them were of later origin . . .';[18] '[T]heir writings are without interest in the history of the development of chemistry.'[19] Referring to a tenth-century compilation of Arabian chemical knowledge, Stillman continues, 'The practical knowledge as here illustrated is not a great advance over the chemistry as known to Pliny or as shown in the Theban Papri . . .'[20] Moving on to the fourteenth and fifteenth centuries he says elsewhere and simply, 'Of the works of all these writers, there is nothing that advances to any material extent the knowledge of chemical facts or thought, however they may have appealed to those who cultivated the philosophy of alchemy as such.'[21] And Waite says even more simply concerning the 'book aspects' of alchemical history, 'it goes on from century to century, ever saying the same thing, yet ever saying it differently, and at the same time revealing nothing that was intelligible to the unversed mind.'[22]

Thus in light of the notion of the development or evolution of science, we find alchemy – when conceived of as the beginnings of a science – seemingly stagnant precisely where and when, according to expectation, it should by all rights be developing, i.e., in Alexandria, among the Moslem Arabs and in medieval and Renaissance Europe, where otherwise the natural sciences did indeed flourish and evolve. Throughout the possibly 2,000 years of its history, alchemy undergoes no appreciable change and has contributed surprisingly little of worth to the corpus of chemical theory or fact, especially considering the length of its history and the diverse, scientifically rich cultures through which it has passed so largely unaffected. The historians of science are apparently nonplussed where they take cognizance of this fact and Stillman goes so far as to suggest – rather tautologically, given his assessment of the chemistry of the particular period – that,

When we consider how important were the contributions of Arabian scholars in other domains of science as astronomy and mathematics it seems strange that their contributions to chemical science and practice were so unimportant. The inference seems clear that the domain of chemical science of the time, founded on the mystical alchemistry of the Alexandrian schools did not attract the ablest scholars, so that except for the work of artisans in the various trades the field of chemistry occupied the attention of students of inferior acumen and initiative.[23]

Finally, in another time and place he finds alchemy again not behaving according to reasonable expectation.

Considering the intellectual awakening of the thirteenth century, and the revival of interest in the natural sciences, as shown in works of the encyclopedists and other writers, and the influence of new universities, it would seem reasonable to anticipate that the fourteenth and fifteenth centuries should have exhibited a marked advance in chemical thought and discovery. On the contrary these centuries exhibit very little which would justify such expectations.[24]

Alchemy, when assumed to be a primitive chemistry, presents us with an inexplicably contrary nature: it simply emerges into the light of history full-grown. The alchemist Morienus is quoted as saying,

If, therefore, thou shalt rightly consider those things which I shall say unto thee, as also the testimonies of the ancients, well and fully shalt thou know that we agree in all things, and do all of us reveal the same truths.[25]

If alchemy is a precursor of modern chemistry we might again reasonably expect that any culture with a long-standing familiarity with its practice would eventually evolve a recognizable form of modern chemical science. That is, we might expect that its appearance would indicate the presence of at least pre-scientific thought presaging an evolution into more modern forms. Contrary to our common-sense expectations and to the reasonable extension of the historical view of alchemy, both China and India, for example, practiced alchemy and yet never evolved a noteworthy natural science on its basis or any other. Experimental alchemy was practiced in China for at least 1,100 to 1,200 years and yet never evolved into a chemistry proper.

While there can be many *post hoc* explanations for these negative findings, and while the observations themselves are hardly conclusive to any effect, they are nonetheless counter-intuitive and render the historical conception of alchemy as proto-science and the grounds upon which it rests highly suspect. When experimental alchemy disappears (both in China and in the West), it is not because it has in any demonstrable sense 'become' experimental chemistry, but rather that its practitioners have retreated further and further from the laboratory and into a purely speculative or mystical Hermetism. When chemical phenomena ceased to be regarded alchemically, it was because a new intellectual/scientific ethos had appeared and banished its predecessor, not that, for example, Newton and Boyle had succeeded in their attempts to transform alchemy into chemistry.

Alchemy, then, from the point of view of its credible historians, is a primitive form of chemistry retarded in its development and in the rationalization of its methods by a stubborn animization of laboratory fact and a reputed disdain for experiment conformable with the pervasive reverence for and reliance upon ancient authorities. In terms of this view, the alchemist's strange persistence in the ways of his magisterium can be no better than a puzzling aberration or a wilful fraud. We should keep in mind in this connection that some of the more illustrious names in alchemy (such as, Trithemius, Heinrich Khunrath, and Michael Maier) belong to approximately the same age as Tycho Brahe, Galileo, and Copernicus, and that alchemy continued to be practiced into the seventeenth century which was, notwithstanding the persistence of the later alchemists, 'marked by an increase in chemical experimentation and by a still greater independence of thought.'[26] These men come down to us, then, as reactionary vestiges of a dying age, and the entire field has subsequently been left to those for whom the so-called irrational aspects of alchemy have their own fascination.

The objections to the claims of alchemy spanning the last two or three centuries, have rested, for the most part, on the fact that artificially (artfully) produced gold is not readily forthcoming, that the process, if veridical, is not 'colorably' described, and that the claim is contrary to the theories and findings of chemistry and, given the technology of the alchemists, preposterous.

It is *not* that we disbelieve the possibility of transmuting matter; quite likely many men of science would allow it as one of numerous unactualized possibilities. Moreover, were the fact of successful transmutation of base metals to gold to be announced from a modern university laboratory, the proverbial 'average citizen' would likely wonder at the economic consequences, but it is unlikely that the feat would strike him as any more miraculous than countless other scientific marvels which have long since distended the boundaries of our credibility and expectation to encompass the heretofore fantastic, unnatural, other-worldly and impossible.

It is rather that we disallow the structure of rationality underlying the methods of alchemy as manifest in the language whereby that rationality is, on claim, demonstrated and its victories made observable.

Men are not credulous because they believe anything (the man who believes anything is by all standards insane), but because they believe anything *within reason*: a man, that is, will be credulous according to his time. The language of alchemy is, to the modern observer, a transparent nonsense, and, indeed, our word 'gibberish' comes from the name of the Arabian alchemist, Jabir, and the European alchemist who, according to practice, assumed his name (Geber).

This, however, is not equivalent to merely noting that the language of alchemy is unintelligible, for although the language of science is largely unintelligible to the non-scientist, it is not *ipso facto* nonsense. The practice of alchemy was rooted in a deeply sedimented sense of the terms and methods via which a thing's or an event's existence – no less than its rational accountability – was demonstrated and made observable.

The point here is that the naturalistic objections to alchemy stem not so much from a rejection of its claims to transmutation, as from a rejection of the methods and terms by which its claims were advertised, communicated, and, for some, adequately demonstrated. The question as to whether or not the alchemists were, in fact, able to transmute matter is far from our foremost concern, and is, in any case, not answered one way or the other by the 'historical evidence.' There is abundant testimony by 'reliable witnesses' to the effect that such transmutations have taken place 'before their eyes' and without possibility or opportunity for conjuration or fraud. There are likely an equal number of revealed attempts at conjury. We leave such testimony to those who are willing to debate the 'facts' on the merits of such evidence, concluding that the decidability of an issue on the basis of such evidence deserves a study in its own right. Aside from which, the list of eye-witnesses, howsoever long and howsoever dignified its members, would, in the context of the modern view of alchemy, seem more curious than edifying.

Occular demonstration was, for the vast majority of the students of alchemy, the end and not the beginning of their studies, studies which not infrequently demanded the better part of a lifetime, which explicitly promised to be immeasurably difficult, and which offered absolutely no guarantees of ultimate success. An alchemist has written,

> To one who is acquainted with the scope and meaning of this Art, it is not so strange that only few attain to our knowledge; to him the wonder is rather that any man has ever succeeded in discovering its methods.[27]

The view of alchemy, then, as a misguided chemistry or as a vain striving after riches can in no way bring to account the methods by which the quest for the philosopher's stone was accounted a rationally defensible, i.e., reasonable enterprise. The alternative, though presenting us with a more curious phenomenon than the one it explains, is to posit a 2,000-year endemic irrationality, suddenly and mysteriously swept away with the advent of the Enlightenment.

The rejection of alchemical rationality stems from an explicit rejection of occult ontology: the casual contempt and disregard shown it by modern science and philosophy is but the shadow of a former conflict to which the antagonists were then very much alive. At stake in this conflict was no less than the entire ontological orientation of Western civilization the outcome of which was finally and symbolically sealed by the acceptance of the Copernican universe. When we regard alchemy from the point of view of the history of science, we are in rather the same position as those who, by needs, study Gnosticism from the records of the church, and our being alive to the issues is prejudiced by the historicization. History is, in large measure, written by the victors, and for that reason alone is it synonymous with progress; and our notion of progress is the ghost that haunts the hermeneutic enterprise.

At about the middle of the nineteenth century a popular occultism flourished (after the fashion of such minor movements) in Europe and America and is active, indeed is thriving, to this day. This movement – assuming it may be so regarded – is interesting in many respects and deserving of study in its own right. In terms of our inquiry, it reflected the ontological schism which emerged with the Renaissance, broadly viewed, and from the vista of one of its poles attempted to bring alchemy to view in a 'new light.' In 1850 M. A. Atwood's *Hermetic Philosophy and Alchemy* was published anonymously in England. It was followed in 1857 by A. E. Hitchcock's *Remarks on Alchemy and the Alchemists* published in America. At the same time, the often brilliant and often doubtable French occultist, Eliphas Lévi (Alphonse Louis Constant) was forming his own view of many matters including among them alchemy. There is, as Waite observes and as far as we know, no reason to believe that these authors were known to each other, nor, for that matter and at that time, much outside their own countries. Yet, the view was strangely consistent: alchemy emerges from these studies as a mystical science of the soul veiled in the terminology and symbolism of chemistry. Waite, who took it upon himself in *The Secret Tradition in Alchemy* to disabuse others of what he regarded as so much folly, characterized (caricatured) this new light on alchemy as follows:

> Man is for all adepts the one subject that contains all, and he only need be investigated for the discovery of all. Man is the true laboratory of Hermetic Art, his life is the subject, the grand distillery, the thing distilling and the thing distilled, and self-knowledge is at the root of all alchemical tradition.[28]

Writing from within the modern occult movement and to its students, Waite turned his prodigious scholarly energy to the refutation of the view of alchemy as a mystical philosophy 'talking about one thing [mysticism] in terms of another [chemistry].' Although he readily acknowledged the fact of literatures 'written from within and without,' alchemy, he claimed, was not one of them, that is, until about the beginning of the seventeenth century and the tradition which began with Heinrich Khunrath and Jacob Böehme. Prior to the divorce of alchemy from the laboratory (paralleling the rise of modern science) says Waite, the alchemist's concern was chemical transmutation, conducted in a laboratory familiar to us from medieval renderings as crowded with well-used crucibles, furnaces, athanors, stills, alembics, and other such standard and requisite implements. Waite's method consists first, in quoting from alchemical texts, recipes and instructions which, if they were in fact a veiled symbolism would defy recognition as such (not to mention attempts at interpretation) and which, otherwise, are plainly what they appear to be, i.e., recipes and formulae, and second, in unmasking the curious hagiology that had grown up around and had always been an integral and interesting part of the *Lives of the Alchymistical Philosophers*. Waite's point is hardly to be doubted, but by proving his thesis he proves too much; while there cannot be and – outside of a limited circle – never has been any doubt as to the alchemists' laboratory activities and goals, even the most superficial attention to the literature – not excluding the literature Waite has excerpted whereby to make his case – can fail to impress the reader with the height and breadth of its concerns and the pervasive and deep religiosity of what little penetrates the obscurity of its reflections upon the events in a crucible. A somewhat closer look uncovers a remarkable consistency in the whole, remarkable in that such consistency as becomes apparent does so out of a seemingly *nonetheless* unrelieved obscurity, and a methodic approach to the objects and events within its purview (and within this purview, we might add, little of lasting importance is excluded). But, finally, and above all, one is struck by the fact that if this literature is indeed motivated by the practices and results of calcination, sublimation, fusion, crystallization, and distillation,[29] then the whole is transfixed by a spiritual vision – in the sense of a 'seeing' – which scans no less than the development and evolution of spirit in matter, nature, and God, and definitely not least, the soul of man, and which, by way of its explication, calls for more than the no-news assurance that the alchemist was an alchemist by virtue of his being manifestly engaged in what we would unhesitatingly recognize as practical chemistry. René Alleau writes,

> The basis of alchemy is its study of the mineral kingdom, a purely material matter, but its concept of the Philosopher's Stone starts from four fundamental abstract concepts: the desire for release, the idea of a new genesis of metal and a second birth for man, the demiurgic rite of death and resurrection, and the mystic exaltation of matter. The concrete metamorphosis of the Stone would confer analogical illumination on the spirit of the 'artist' who transformed it and gazed upon it.[30]

The nineteenth-century occultists attempted to rescue the alchemists from a reductive science which, in the spirit of its century, had, if not banished the mystery from the universe, then laid siege to it in the church and was not about to credit its survival in alchemy. (The threat to those who continued to feel the presence of the mystery and to value its memorials was real enough;) in 1857, for instance, the distinguished French chemist, Marcellin Berthelot, had flatly decreed, 'From now on there is no mystery about the Universe.'[31] But the occultists were subject as well to the inherited ontological schism and resultant 'negative mythology' which characterized that peculiar age; if a perfection of sorts had been obtained in science by omitting the mystery, then a perfection in mystery could be as easily obtained by omitting the science; in order to save alchemy they turned it 'inside out' such that, with its back now everywhere to its object, it could only reflect upon itself. Alchemy now treated exclusively of what could be ridiculed, but not destroyed, by the stultifying ethos of that time, the quest for spiritual regeneration. And, while this view was closer to the matter than that of the history of science, the inquiry into the structure and nature of the visible was given over by default to those in terms of whose expertise all that remained was to fill in the missing pieces. Intimidated, not to mention likely repulsed, by the science of their time (which had substituted for 'our world of quality and sense perception, the world in which we live, and love, and die, another world – the world of quantity, of reified geometry, a world in which, though there is place for everything, there is no place for man'[32]), nineteenth-century occultists rescued alchemy by removing it from the laboratories which were at the time crowded with practitioners anathema to its spirit, proclaiming its integrity as a spiritual dicipline against a science which they often had neither the training nor perhaps the inclination to rebut. The transmutation of base metals to gold became, *mutatis mutandis*, the transformation of the lower self to spiritual or Christic gold; alchemy became a metaphor. Those who had tried to preserve the presence of the mystery had rendered it impotent: the chemical symbolism of alchemy was, in the case of Hitchcock, decoded with a key which, though it provided an access, revealed underneath a core of spiritual platitude, and in the case of Atwood and Lévi presented a far from convincing and easily caricatured recourse to magnetism and the like.

The ultimate variation on this theme is perhaps that contained in the monumental works on alchemy by C. G. Jung's works, to which he devoted 'decades.' The Jungian thesis reappears frequently in modern research, C. A. Burland, Marie-Louise Von Franz and the translators of *Aurora Consurgens*, and John Joseph Stoudt being examples. It suffices to quote Jung for our present purposes, i.e. to demonstrate the ways in which the alchemist was deprived of his very phenomenon and to note that here, the victories of science are complete and unquestioned:

[T]he alchemists were fascinated by the soul of matter, which, unknown to them, it had received from the human psyche by way of projection. For all their intensive preoccupation with matter as a concrete fact they followed this psychic trail, which was to lead them into a region that, to our way of thinking, had not the remotest connection with chemistry. Their mental labours consisted in a predominantly intuitive apprehension of psychic facts, the intellect playing only the modest role of famulus . . . The misfortune of the alchemists was that they themselves did not know what they were talking about.[33]

Reformulated by Von Franz, who adopts the Jungian perspective, it reads as an emphatic call for the remedies of plain talk and clear thinking.

[We need] assume that the author [of *Aurora Consurgens*] did not express himself in clearly understandable concepts *for the simple reason that he did not possess them*, and that he was giving a stammering description of an *unconscious content which had* irrupted into his consciousness.[34] [Emphasis in the original]

We find contained in this curious statement an explanation for the secrecy of alchemical formulations and for the particular language with which the secret was articulated. An adequate explanation with respect to our subject is, however, not really a 'simple' one as we shall see, and requires more than the Jungian analytic which is, by all standards, an explanation *obscurum per obscurius*, a substitution of one hidden for another by its removal from the world and its relocation in the psyche.

That alchemy is an esoteric or secret science is precisely that which, in effect, must be ignored by the historian's, no less than by the psychologist's, view of the art as either primitive chemistry or primitive psychology: their acknowledgement of the *full* seriousness of the claim would require further the acknowledgement that its purport is lost upon them and that, consequently, that which upon the testimony of practitioners is the whole of the teaching, is to them an unrelieved obscurity. Secrecy, then – the universal insistence of practitioners – is to the modern student, either a wilful obfuscation and withholding of information or an ignorance of the 'facts' whose remedy is, on every occasion, 'plain talk' or, simply, 'saying-in-so-many-words.' This being the case, the psychologist's condescension and the historian's impatience with the literature of alchemy are at once perfectly understandable, and the historian's suspicion that the secret is without specific content fully justified. A. E. Waite, a curious but seemingly nonetheless impeccable scholar of alchemy and the occult, gives voice to the summary view:

If I . . . had such a predisposition and so pursued it that I learned how to transmute metals, I should either make known my process or reserve the fact of its discovery. I should not write mystery theses to announce that I possessed the secret and place it under impassable veils, while affirming that I revealed the whole Art.[35]

The secret of the alchemist is the secret of the production of the philosopher's stone via which base metals are transmuted into purest gold. Possession of the stone consists, first, in its apprehension, and subsequently, in its production, its apprehension being the beginning and most difficult stage of the work.

'There are two orders in this art, that is, beholding by the eye and understanding by the heart . . .'[36] That is, the alchemist speaks both of a 'hidden' stone and a stone manifest. Of the former, Bonus writes,

[It] is not sensuously apprehended, but only known intellectually, by revelation or inspiration. Alexander says: There are two stages in this Art, that which you see with the eye, and that which you apprehend with the mind.[37]

The possession of the stone in the inexorable dual-sense of revel-ation or dis-covery and of bringing forth or manu-facture – of, seemingly, ideal and real – rewards the student with all benefits, correlatively physical/material and intellectual/spiritual. The rewards may be provisionally specified thus as health (a sufficiency of) wealth, gnosis and transcendence.

Our Arts frees not only the body, but also the soul from the snares of servitude and bondage . . . Indeed, it may be said to supply every human want, and to provide a remedy for every form of suffering.[38]

Though the method is secret it is, of course – on claim and in some yet to be examined sense – *nonetheless* 'revealed' in the literature, though under the cover of various veils. The secret, that is, is not one which is entirely withheld. An obvious question arises: if the art and the method are secret, why then an attempt to reveal them publicly at all, the various guises and obfuscations notwithstanding? The answer is given as first, to guide the worthy and serious student who, without aid, would be exposed to specific dangers (both psychic and physical being variously alluded to) and who, in any case, would not otherwise attain to success in an enterprise fraught with fraudulent exponents and nearly insur-mountable difficulties, and second, as a being motivated at the same time or exclusively by (divine) inspiration to communicate and (thereby) perpetuate sacred and fundamental truths. The various circumlocutions are thus designed to accomplish these aims while simultaneously withholding these invaluable and poten-tially dangerous teachings from the foolish, the ignorant, the avar-icious, the wicked, the profane. There are, moreover, intimations going all the way back to the earliest of Greek alchemists, of an oath – whether to God or men – and a proscription, in general, with reference to revealing the method.

Those then worthy of receiving initiation into the secrets of nature and the soul are precisely those who, having undergone an antecedent conversion, are thus enabled to proceed to initiation; i.e., precisely those whom God permits. 'Hence the impure and those living in vice are unworthy of it. Therefore is this Art to be shewn to all God-fearing persons because it cannot be bought with a price.'[39] (Conversion is a logical antecedent if not always a temporal: 'the art is sacred, and all its adepts are sanctified and pure. For "men either discover it because they are holy, or it makes them holy.' "[40])

Noteworthy in this context is the omnipresent assurance that it is not merely the clever man who will attain to the sanctuary, but the sanctified (defects of moral or of character being unsurmountable hindrances in the full attainment of the work): strictly speaking it is thus not attained but received. The stone, in other words, can be and invariably is described as a 'gift of God' to those deserving of his mercy. 'For this art', says Paracelsus, 'is truly a gift of God. Wherefore not everyone can understand it. For this reason God bestows it upon whom He pleases, and it cannot be wrested from Him by force . . .'[41]

The nature of this kind of secret, then, is decidely not that of common meaning, i.e., the matter being simply withheld or helplessly obscured: for if the veils are such as to be exclusively penetrable by the worthy and, conversely, as to be in no way penetrable by their opposites, then a *specific* language is indicated (i.e., which speaks to and is understood by the sanctified and the wise). '[T]he mode of our Art is one,' insists Bonus.[42] And Geber writes,

> I therefore teach it [this Art] in such a way that nothing will remain hidden to the wise man, even though it may strike mediocre minds as quite obscure; the foolish and the ignorant, for their part, will understand none of it at all . . .[43]

That is to say, a maieutic language is indicated which is directly dictated in its features by the nature of its task (i.e., of keeping the profane from the gates of the sanctuary while safely bringing forth the worthy) no less than by the nature of its objects (concerning which more is to be said presently). And as these are, respectively, spiritual and transcendent it is more than merely *honoris causa* that the language and the inspiration to speak are attributed, by the alchemist, to God. There is, in other words, the sense in which it is to God and to God alone that the veils such and only such as they are specifically construed may, phenomenologically speaking, be referred. The alchemist who resorts to a language designed merely to obscure and not to enlighten, i.e., who resorts to a language which in its features does *not* lead the worthy nearer the desired goal, are chastised for their 'envy' (a specific term in the context of alchemical literature).

'[T]he Sages have expressed their knowledge in mysterious terms in order that it might be made known to no person except such as were chosen by God Himself . . . [T]hough the phraseology of the Sages be obscure', says Bonus, 'it must not therefore be supposed that their books contain a single deliberate falsehood . . .'

> Those for whom the knowledge of Alchemy is intended, will be able, in course of time and study, to understand even the most obscure of Alchemistic treatises: for they will be in a position to look at them from the right point of view.[44]

The alchemist, himself sanctified and thus inspired to speak, is the 'voice' of the language of God as well as the instrument of his will, and thus the obscurities of formulation *devolve* upon the alchemist, first as the inherited and assumed form of his *responsibility* for keeping 'knowledge of the mystery from the world,'[45] and, in their expression, as the sign and witness of his *ability* to do so while in those same formulations informing the worthy. While, *at the same time*, the formulations originate with 'the Providence of the Most High'[46] who, ultimately, may be relied upon to 'effectually guard this Arcanum from falling into the hands of covetous gold seekers and knavish pretenders to the Art of Transmutation,'[47] much as He could but does not reveal His secrets with the world. The language via which the Arcanum is paradoxically both 'revealed' and 'withheld' is thus, *in its features* a specific language, a revealed language or a dis-covered language to which the denomination 'secret' – as exoterically understood – lends no clarity whatsoever.

It follows directly upon these assertions that the language of alchemy is secret in a correlative sense: that is, the sense in which it alone, from the pens of the alchemists and as their testimony would have it, is inadequate or insufficient to its task. For if the language is – for its understanding – dependent upon the prior or simultaneous revelation of the objects and the relations to which it applies, then, 'The words of the Sages may mean anything or nothing to one who is not acquainted with the facts which they describe,'[48] such that a continual reference to Nature as the locus of these yet to be dis-covered 'facts' is itself literally indispensable. 'In our glorious Art nothing is more necessary than constant reference to the facts of Nature, which can be ascertained only by actual experiment.'[49] Presaged in these remarks is a radical contrast to the ways of natural language formulae, or of procedure for the accomplished rational accountability of witnessed things and events within which tacit reference to a world pre-supposed and already known in common – to an imperative, not lightly to be dispensed with, what-it-can-have-come-to-when-all-is-said-and-done – is both a characteristic feature of those formulae and the artfully managed guarantee of their cogency, their sense, their very practical accomplishments, i.e., their victories one and all. 'The practice of this great work', says Benedictus Figulus, 'remains our Grand Secret or Arcanum, and unless it be revealed Divinely, or by artificers, or in experiments, it also can never be learnt from books.'[50]

The first sense, then, in which the teachings of the alchemists are secret is one which is only nominally attributable to the wilful practices of the alchemist himself. But, insofar as the instructions refer *nonetheless* or *as well* to 'things' seen and touched, in the 'real' world and recognizable as its objects, i.e., insofar as the instructions result in the chemical operations which have provided the historians of alchemy-*qua*-primitive-science with indubitable material for their speculations, then – with reference to those operations and their objects – we can surely imagine that the alchemist might speak otherwise, that is, might speak 'plainly.' Indeed, as the alchemist says, 'The thing . . . is accessible and known to all men, of much superfluity, to be found everywhere, and by all.'[51] Its dual nature is often referred to with the following kind of paradox:

> They [the Sages] call it [the Stone] the vilest and commonest of all things, which is found among the refuse in the street and on the dunghill; yet they add that it cannot be obtained without considerable expense. They seem to say in the same breath that it is the vilest and that it is the most precious of all substances.[52]

So that, aside from the sense which follows logically from all that has been said above, that 'one who can perform the practical operations of Alchemy is not yet an Alchemist, just as not every one who speaks grammatically is a grammarian,'[53] and that, '"one action does not make an artist"',[54] and the lamented 'blind torturing of metals'[55] (as the alchemist/mystic Thomas Vaughn expresses it), notwithstanding, it remains indicated that, on the exoteric side, there is a secret capable of being otherwise revealed which must be kept from the hands of the unworthy, not lest they become alchemists, but, 'lest the world should be devastated.'[56] Geber writes,

> I hereby declare that in this *Summa* I have not taught our science systematically, but have spread it out here and there in various chapters; for if I had presented it coherently and in logical order, the evil-minded, who might have misused it,

would be able to learn it just as easily as people of good will
. . .[57]

And yet there remains the second and vastly more evocative sense in which the teachings of alchemy, *per se*, are secret; the sense, that is, in which the teachings as provided in the literature are the *best possible* description of their objects and their methods, and in which the seeming obfuscation is an inexorable one. 'How can anyone', asks Bonus, 'discover the truth in regard to any science, if he lacks the sense to distinguish the special province of matter, or the material relations, with which that science deals? Such people need to exercise faith even to become aware of the existence of our Art.'[58] That is, the objects of alchemy, the objects which make up its special gnosis, and the relations appertaining to them are, as intimated, *in and of themselves* hidden to the profane and the unitiated, and all formulations referring to them are, perforce and by definition, irreparably obscure, i.e., occult. '[E]very substantial truth [is] a secret,' according to Thomas Vaughn.[59] The essential obscurity results in the paradox of alchemical formulation no where better summed up than in Geber's *Summa*:

> Whenever I have seemed to speak most clearly and openly about our science, I have in reality expressed myself most obscurely and have hidden the object of my discourse most fully. And yet in spite of all that, I have never clothed the alchemical work in allegories or riddles, but have dealt with it in clear and intelligible words and have described it honestly, just as I know it to be and have myself learnt it by divine inspiration . . .[60]

In terms then of the truth-value of formulations concerning these secrets, the traditional notion of truth as the correspondence of mind and its object appears very problematic indeed. The 'objects' with which the art of alchemy ultimately deals are decidedly not the 'things,' present-at-hand, with which we are familiar and by which we are surrounded in all directions to a distance coincident with the limits of imagination. In fact, properly speaking, they are not objects at all: they are not given with the world, and, as opposed to finding them already there upon every awakening, we may search for them throughout a lifetime or not – the issue having no necessary effect on our ability to conduct our everyday practical affairs in a world of normal and given objects. They are, in a word, hidden, and the first goal of the alchemical pursuit is the discovery of the very 'matter' with which the science deals.

As Thomas Vaughn enjoins, 'learn first what it [the Stone] is before you go to seek it.'[61]

And if, as we can read in Eirenaeus Philalethes, and as, otherwise, all alchemists insist, 'the Philosophical Work is no fiction, but grounded in the possibility of Nature . . .'[62], then it is assuredly not the nature of *our* science, but of the science of the Greeks; i.e., nature not as the plurality of lifeless objects with which we are ontologically coincident, but as *physis*, 'the process', says Martin Heidegger, 'of a-rising, of emerging from the hidden, whereby the hidden is first made to stand.'[63] As one alchemist expresses it, 'the nature, that is to say, which is bestowed upon things and infused into them from heaven.'[64] 'When the goal of the seeking is hidden,' says Paracelsus, 'the manner of seeking is also occult . . .'[65]

The two senses of the word 'secret' now reveal themselves as two stages in the same process or Art: the first is the making visible of that which was formerly hidden and whose proper method is itself 'occult,' and the second is the artful manipulation of the outward sign or symbol – the 'thing' – whereby its occult properties and potentialities might be real-ized. Thus, 'Our Art is partly natural and partly supernatural, or Divine.'[66] The process signified having been revealed in the properties of its sign, then the operations to be performed are themselves the recognizable recipes of chemical operations which 'can be learned in a single hour of one who knows . . .'[67], and are elsewhere described as 'a true woman's or cook's work.'[68] Of the process it is further said that, 'Were it stripped of all figures and parables, it would be possible to compress it into the space of eight or twelve lines.'[69]

> Behold the base thing with which our Sanctuary has been opened! For it is a thing well known by everyone; yet, he who understands it not finds it seldom or never. The wise man keeps it, the fool throws it away, and its reduction is easy to the initiated.[70]

The two senses in which the word 'secret' or 'occult' may be applied to the Art correspond, then, to two realms of being with which it deals inexorably (and whose estrangement – the one from the other – is the modern legacy and the premise of modern research on alchemy); that realm in and of the world and visible, on the one hand, and that realm hidden from the world, though nonetheless hidden in the world, and, as we have intimated, appearing *as* the world, on the other. (This is the emphatic sense in which the literary method of the alchemists, in so far as the two realms correspond, respectively, to the exoteric and the esoteric in language, imitates their view of nature (physis), that is, an elaboration of the sense in which the resultant secrecy of formulation is attributable more to God than to the alchemist himself. 'The Artist in this profession', says Paracelsus, 'ought in all things exactly to imitate Nature.'[71]) To the first realm of being belongs the secret the alchemist could but refuses to reveal, i.e., the secret of the informed manipulation of, largely speaking, objects with which we are either familiar or can readily make ourselves familiar. To this familiar realm of objects belongs the just-this-right-here and the just-that-over-there – the present-at-hand as it were – and the traditional notion of truth as relates to these objects is, as Heidegger deals with it, the gradually accomplished correspondence of mind and thing, of intellect and its object.[72] The notion of truth-as-correspondence makes the world itself out in terms of the sum of its objects of which, we might say, man is but one, with, however, an intimation, if not a promise, of ultimate mastery over the others: the pre-theoretic discovery of the 'worldhood' of the world needs be ignored so that 'the problem' should appear and be presented as an essential plurality whose solution resides in the result of a perpetual search for similarities. Knowledge of such objects aspires – at some ideal future and by way of some ideal conclusion – to specify the nature of the world as an accomplished apprehension of the sum of and relation between its parts. In this sense, it is an infinite program which is incapable of having brought the world to its full accountability as yet and as such, but rather is always on its trail, always and necessarily, at every successive moment, more closely than ever. It is a truth with a marked history, characterized as 'the human enterprise,' and summarily captioned 'the myth of the total explication of the world' by Merleau-Ponty.[73] What remains hidden to this view and in this world awaits the advent of better instruments, of improvements in the methods, angles and technology of observation. Beyond all such conceivable improvements, the rest is presumably silence and darkness. Indeed, the legendary and apocryphal refusal of the churchmen to gaze through Galileo's telescope might be read for a deeper symbolism, with a different moral, than has heretofore been examined.

We see, then, that the notion of truth-as-correspondence, from the point of view of the epistemological considerations raised here, brings us up against a rarely thematized ontology concerning the being of the objects it brings under examination ontically and which it always already has, and as a consequence, the being of the world as such (in its worldhood) about which it is necessarily (i.e., essentially) unreflective.

In strong contrast to truth as relates to the things given with the essential and ever-prior discovery of the world, is truth as relates to things hidden. Its methods are properly phenomenological.

> Now what must be taken into account if the formal conception of phenomenon is to be deformalized into the phenomenological one, and how is this latter to be distinguished from the ordinary conception? What is it [Heidegger continues] that phenomenology is to 'let us see'? What is it that must be called a 'phenomenon' in a distinctive sense? What is it that by its very essence is *necessarily* the theme whenever we exhibit something *explicitly*? Manifestly, it is something that proximally and for the most part does *not* show itself at all: it is something that lies *hidden*, in contrast to that which proximally and for the most part does show itself; but at the same time it is something that belongs to what thus shows itself, and it belongs to it so essentially as to constitute its meaning and its ground.[74] [emphasis in the original]

Heidegger elsewhere characterizes truth as relates to the hidden as an 'event', 'which occurs, so to speak, from without,'[75] as, indeed, the alchemists have always emphasized by attributing illumination with respect to such 'objects' to an agency such as God or the Holy Ghost. Truth as concerns the hidden is thus precisely the moment of its revelation, dis-covery or becoming visible. 'Whatever is hidden from common observation is the province of Art; but as soon as the hidden has become manifest and visible, the task of our Art is accomplished, and all that remains to be done is purely mechanical . . .'[76] So says Basilius Valentinus. And from Bonus, 'In all these matters . . . nothing short of seeing a thing will help you to know it.'[77] 'Find our Art . . . and you will have proved its reality . . .'[78] And elsewhere, 'If we understand the substance of our Stone as it is, there is nothing left to study but the method of treatment, and this method will be suggested by the knowledge we already possess.'[79]

We find an Art, that is, whose truth *is* the event characterized by the revelation of its object 'in the first place' and as *thereby* rendered accountable in precisely the invariable fashion of its coming to be at all; its observability, that is, is necessarily *recognizably* coessential with nothing more and nothing less than the events produced in an order of 'situated practices of looking-and-telling'[80] with which it is primordially coextensive, which observability, as an event, constitutes, as well, its truth. This is to say no less than that the reflexivity of those practices is not only irrecusable, but is *essentially interesting* (in contrast to the otherwise essentially *uninteresting* reflexivity of recognized practices of producing an account for-all-practical-purposes) as often borne witness by the sanctification or morally sanctioned inviolability of accounts as related to the objects of the Sacred Sciences in no lesser degree than the sanctification of the objects themselves with which, in this view, they are regarded as in some sense coextensive. We have an excellent example from the *Zohar*, a classic literature of Kabbalism (from the Jewish Occult tradition). The Torah, in the form of 'a beautiful and stately damsel, who is hidden in a secluded chamber of her palace' who says to her would-be lover, viz., the student,

> [D]o you see now how many mysteries were contained in that sign I gave you on the first day, and what its true meaning is? Then he understands that to those words indeed nothing may be added and nothing taken away.[81]

The language used to describe such objects and their relations, in their hiddenness – keeping in mind that they 'belong' nonetheless and in some sense to what does show itself, are its ground – will inevitably exhibit certain features which lend to the putative attribute of secrecy its distinctive character. The language, in *naming* its objects, at the same time anticipates and participates in their dis-covery, and in naming what does show itself, refers – as the sign to the thing signified – to that which is still to be exhibited and made visible, where literally no alternative is conceivable. It is a language which, in order to be learned, must be known. In the *Theatrum Chemicum Britannicum*, by Elias Ashmole, we read,

> The first Paine is to remember in minde,
> How many seeken, and how few doe finde,
> And yet noe Man may this Science wynn,
> But it be tought him before that he beginn . . .[82]

In John Frederick Helvetius's tale of his encounter with an alchemist and his own quest after the key to Alchemy, we read,

> I besought him [relates Helvetius] that as a stranger had made known to him this priceless mystery, so he would extend the same boon to myself, or give me at least sufficient information to remove the greater difficulties. Were there certitude on one point, its connections would be discovered more easily. But he answered: 'It is not so in our Magistery: if you do not know the whole operation from beginning to end, you know nothing at all. I have indeed told you everything . . .'[83]

In naming a thing which is familiar or can be readily made familiar – after the perhaps no less mysterious fashion of that activity –

the thing named is not the more for having been named, the thing sought. The 'true' name of the philosopher's stone, known only to the alchemist, were it invoked, would bring its object no closer to visibility. And we are assured, on every hand, that, ultimately, it is *one* thing we are seeking though, 'There are as many names for our stone as there are things or designations of things.'[78] Thus a reference to things – names – is not a reference to objects, but a reference to phenomenological attributes, both of the 'thing' sought in itself, and in the process – and herein the role of the alchemist – of its coming to be, that is, in the dual sense of its apprehension and its manu-facture wherein the phenomenal and the phenomenological are resolved and the work completed.

> Our Stone, from its all-comprehensive nature, may be compared to all things in the world. In its origin and sublimation, and in the conjunction of its elements, there are analogies to things heavenly, earthly, and infernal, to the corporeal and the incorporeal, to things corruptible and incorruptible, visible and invisible, to spirit, soul, and body, and their union and separation, to the creation of the world, its elements, and their qualities, to all animals, vegetables, and minerals, to generation and corruption, to life and death, to virtues and vices, to unity and multitude, to actuality and potentiality, to conception and birth, to male and female, to boy and old man, to the vigorous and the weak, to the victor and the vanquished, to peace and war, to white and red, and all colours, to the beauty of Paradise, to the terrors of the infernal abyss . . . [W]e have an infinite variety of names used to describe our precious Stone, every one of which may be said . . . to represent a certain aspect of the truth of our Art.[84]

It follows, thus, that,

> whoever would take literally what the other philosophers . . . have written, will lose himself in the recesses of a laybrinth from which he will never escape, for want of Ariadne's thread to keep him on the right path and bring him safely out . . .[85]

(This feature of Occult formulations is at least as old as Gnosticism itself. G. R. S. Mead writes, 'The Gnostics were ever changing their nomenclature. . . . He who makes a concordance of names merely, in Gnosticism, may think himself lucky to escape a lunatic asylum. . . . If they contradict one another, in the view of the word-hunter, they do not contradict themselves for the follower of ideas.'[86] 'Alas,' says Valentinus, if men only had eyes to see, and ears to hear not merely what I say, but to understand the secret meaning . . .'[87]

In the process, then, of its coming to be, which being made observable is its truth, the names and references given the stone exhibit prominently the following features: their sense is undecidable without knowledge of the purpose of the user and the circumstances of their use; 'descriptions involving them apply on each occasion of use to only one thing, but to different things on different occasions;' they can be used 'to make unequivocal statements that nevertheless seem to change in truth value;' their use refers to something not necessarily named by some replica of the word; '[t]heir denotation is relative to the speaker;' and, ' [t]heir use depends upon the relation of the user to the object with which the word is concerned.'[88] These are some of the features taken up by Garfinkel under the heading of 'indexical expressions' and we find that in strong contrast to the ways of science for which, as Garfinkel obsserves, their substitution by objective or context free expressions is 'both an actual task and an actual achievement'[89] without which its victories are unimaginable, that the language of alchemy is through and through indexical and the preferred use of indexical expressions is insisted upon; i.e., the reflexivity of resultant formulations is an essential feature of alchemy as method, requiring, in the words of one of its practitioners, 'a profound natural faculty for interpreting the significance of those symbols and analogies of the philosophers, which in one place have one meaning and in another a different.'[90]

It might be illustrative to provide an example of the alchemical use of names and attributes.

This Virgin and Blessed Water have philosophers in their books called by a thousand names, as a Heaven, Celestial Water, Heavenly Rain, Heavenly or May Dew, Water of Paradise, Aqua Regia, Corrosive Aqua Fortis, a sharp vinegar and brandy, a Quintessence of Wine, a waxy green juice, a waxy Mercury, a water becoming green, and Green Lion, a Quicksilver, a Menstruum, a Blood and Menstruum, urine and horse-urine, Milk, and Virgin's Milk, white Arsenic, Silver, a moon, a woman and woman's seed, a sulphureous, steamy water and smoke, a fiery burning spirit, a mortal penetrating poison, a basilisk which kills everything, an envenomed worm, a poisonous snake, a dragon, a poisonous serpent which devours its offspring, a strong fire, and a clear, a fire of horse dung and horse dung, a sharp salt and sal armoniac, a saltary and common salt, a sharp soap, lye, and viscous oil, an ostrich-stomach which devours and digests an eagle, a vulture and hermetic bird, a seal and vessel of Hermes, a smelting and calcining stove. Innumerable other names of beasts, birds, vegetables, waters, humours, of milk, of blood, and of men have been given to it . . . [And yet] [t]he receipt consists of only one thing, and with this key all the books of the philosophers are particularly and universally closed, and surrounded and guarded as with a strong wall.[91]

And from the same work we read, 'From these and similar attributes, or circumstances, and in no other way, may this matter be known and prepared . . .'[92] 'It is true', says Bonus, 'that in the books of the Sages the impression is conveyed as if there were many substances and many methods: but they only mean different aspects or stages of the same thing . . . There are many names, but one regimen.'[93] This, indeed, is the universal testimony of the alchemists. So, from the *Turba Philosophorum*, 'Therefore, those names which are found in the books of the Philosophers, and are thought superfluous and vain, are true and yet are fictitious, because they are one thing, one opinion, and one way.'[94] 'How then', Bonus might well ask, 'shall we, by considering their works only superficially, and according to their literal interpretation, fathom the profound knowledge required for the practical operations of this Magistery?'[95] The author of the *Aurora Consurgens* writes, by way of a partial answer to the question in general, 'The letter killeth, but the spirit quickeneth. Be renewed in the spirit of your mind and put on the new man, that is, a subtle understanding. If ye understand in the spirit, ye shall also know the spirit.'[96] Which is perhaps a prescription that alchemy be rediscovered, not as a literature, but as speech, directed to those phenomena on whose behalf it claims to speak, 'for reading is a dead speech, but that which is uttered with the lips the same is living speech.'[97]

The modern views of alchemy treat of it either as an art directed exclusively to a description of the properties and behavior of matter, or, conversely, exclusively to the properties and behavior of psyche; the alchemists, themselves, are respectively either poor chemists or poor psychologists. It hardly need be reiterated that the two schools reflect the two poles of the Great Schism which signalled both their emergence as autonomous modes of description, indeed, seemingly as autonomous modes of being-in-the-world, and the death of alchemy in which, as we have indicated, the two poles represent, structurally, two aspects or stages of one enterprise in which they are indissoluably linked, the nature of that indissolubility being specified. The thesis of the historian of science fails singularly to convince, and that, on the basis of its own methods and its own evidence; the alchemists' preoccupation with the 'transmutation' of self, of the structures of awareness, of 'seeing,' finds no place there. The Jungian thesis, as representing the opposite pole of a radical subject–object dualism, and its most sophisticated and widely adopted expression as concerns alchemy, fails, inevitably, for the opposite reason; the alchemists' insistence that theirs was a science of nature, of matter, is dismissed as little better than a consensually validated hallucination. The two pictures, structurally enantiomorphic, are in and of themselves totally unable to regard the practitioners of the art they attempt to bring to accountability as other than epiphenomena in their own drama. Their resolution resides, ironically enough, in the doctrine acknowledged as the very foundation of the Spagyric Art by all the practitioners to whom it was, *per se*, familiar, and which otherwise is given ample testimony in all the alchemists wrote; that is, the doctrine of the Macrocosmos and the Microcosmos, attributed to the putative patron of Alchemy, the Thrice Great Hermes. It stipulates, in brief, that the Great World, the world of nature (as *physis*) is recapitulated in the Lesser World, that is, man, although their being at a distance from each other is a fundamental feature (alchemy is not to be mistaken for either a modern phenomenology or a true mysticism). Any description of the former, the macrocosmos – in its essence – is, perforce, a description of the latter, the microcosmos. 'Thus the outward world represents and explains the inner one. The former is the sign, the latter the thing indicated.'[98] The ' discovery' is hardly as modern as we might believe. Alchemy thus reveals itself as a unique phenomenology which can be encountered in the methods via which it brings its world to observability, no less than to accountability, and, via which, after its own lights, it presents itself as a rationally defensible enterprise. The methods developed by Harold Garfinkel, it is believed, are singularly suited to provide access to the ways of that accountability in general, and indeed, wherever they are found and on every occasion of their use.

It is with respect to the methods of ethnomethodology, their central recommendation and the specific features of members' practices they uncover, that the practices of the occult sciences may be, at least in some sense, recovered on behalf of its practitioners, via, that is, an examination of the radical contrast between their methods, and the methods of 'recognizably ordinary talk' in terms of which they are recognized specifically. That alchemy defines the human enterprise and man's function in the world as that of 'making visible,' assures us that with respect to the findings of ethnomethodology, we are in the presence of something interesting. 'For the "firmament"', says Paracelsus, 'needs an agent through which to work, and this agent is man and

155

man alone. Man has been so created that through him the miracles of nature are made visible and given form.'[99]

It is proposed that further study will reveal – again, with respect to the methods and findings of ethnomethodology and much after the fashion of their attempted application here as 'guide' – that, in terms of the experiential (phenomenological) radical dualism of subject and object (the self and the world at a distance) and its history and fate as the history and fate of consciousness itself, two essential languages, both as, in their features, conceivable, and as evidenced in history, corresponding to two ontologies, mark the trail of our being-in-the-world: the first, a language for which the reflexivity of accounts is relied upon that the cogency, reproducibility, objectivity and good sense of its descriptions be accomplished for-all-practical-purposes and in no other fashion, in which, that is, the reflexivity of accounts is essentially uninteresting; and second, a language which 'points beyond itself,' whose reference is transcendent; a prescriptive as opposed to a descriptive language for which the disengagement of the activities of the observer is unimaginable (whose accomplishment is always some particular somebody's doing on some particular occasion of use) and in terms of which the inexorable reflexivity of being-in-the-world is of omnirelevance (is essentially interesting) as method. Of the two languages, the essential analysis of the former will show itself to be the unique possibility of the latter, which is the proper method of its discovery, indeed, of the dis-covery of all occult properties wherever they are to be found.

Notes

1 Cf. Manly P. Hall, *Old Testament Wisdom*, The Philosophical Research Society, Inc., Los Angeles, 1957.
2 Hans Jonas, *The Gnostic Religion*, Beacon Press, Boston , 1967, p. 12.
3 Martin Heidegger, *Being and Time*, Harper & Row, New York, 1962, p. 222.
4 Hans Jonas, *op. cit.***, cf. Introduction.
5 C. A. Burland, *The Arts of the Alchemists*, The Macmillan Company, New York, 1968, p. 17.
6 Titus Burckhardt, *Alchemy*, Stuart & Watkins, London, 1967, p. 16.
7 E. J. Holmyard, *Alchemy*, Penguin Books, 1957, Baltimore, pp. 23–6.
8 John Maxson Stillman, *The Story of Alchemy and Early Chemistry*, Dover Publications, Inc., New York, 1960, p. 25.
9 E. J. Holmyard, *op. cit.*, p. 25.
10 *Ibid.*, p. 31.

11 Arthur Waley, *The Travels of an Alchemist*, Routledge & Kegan Paul Ltd, London, 1931, p. 12.
12 A. E. Waite, *The Secret Tradition in Alchemy*, Alfred A. Knopf, New York, 1926 , p. 57.
13 E. J. Holmyard, *op. cit.*, pp. 38–9.
14 Cf. Marcellin Berthelot, *La Chimie au moyan âge*, Paris, 1893. (Our reference is, however, to A. E. Waite, *op. cit.*)
15 A. E. Waite, *op. cit.*, pp. 65 and 68.
16 Titus Burckhardt, *op. cit.*, p. 7.
17 John Maxson Stillman, *op. cit.*, p. 169.
18 *Ibid.*, p. 182.
19 *Ibid.*, p. 183.
20 *Ibid.*, p. 217.
21 *Ibid.*, p. 297.
22 A. E. Waite, *op. cit.*, p. xix.
23 John Maxson Stillman, *op. cit.*, pp. 218–19.
24 *Ibid.*, p. 273.
25 Bonus of Ferrara, *The New Pearl of Great Price*, Vincent Stuart Ltd, London, 1963, p. 79.
26 John Maxson Stillman, *op. cit.*, p. 379.
27 Bonus of Ferrara, *op. cit.*, p. 109.
28 A. E. Waite, *op. cit.*, p. 20.
29 Cf. E. J. Holmyard, *op. cit.*, p. 43.
30 René Alleau, *History of Occult Sciences*, Leisure Arts Limited, London, p. 73.
31 Louis Pauwels and Jacques Bergier, *The Morning of the Magicians*, Stein & Day, New York, 1964, p. 10.
32 Alexandre Koyré, *Newtonian Studies*, Harvard University Press, Cambridge, 1965, p. 23.
33 C. G. Jung, *Mysterium Coniunctionis*, Bollingen Foundation, New York, 1963, pp. 124–5.
34 Trans. R. F. C. Hull and A. S. B. Glover, *Aurora Consurgens*, Routledge & Kegan Paul, London, 1966, p. 153.
35 A. E. Waite, *op. cit.*, p. 286.
36 Trans. R. F. C. Hull and A. S. B. Glover, *op. cit.*, p. 117.
37 Bonus of Ferrara, *op. cit.*, p. 124.
38 *Ibid.*, p. 139.
39 Benedictus Figulus, *A Golden and Blessed Casket of Natures Marvels*, Vincent Stuart Ltd, London, 1963, p. 48.
40 Bonus of Ferrara, *op. cit.*, p. 11.
41 Trans. Norbert Guterman, *Paracelsus Selected Writings*, Bollingen Foundation Inc., New York, 19 58, p. 149.
42 Bonus of Ferrara, *op. cit.*, p. 119.
43 Titus Burckhardt, *op. cit.*, p. 29'.
44 Bonus of Ferrara, *op. cit,*., pp. 129–30.
45 Eirenaeus Philalethes and Others, *Collectanea Chemica*, Vincent Stuart Ltd, London, 1963, p. 79.
46 *Ibid.*, p. 79.
47 *Ibid.*

48 Bonus of Ferrara, *op. cit.*, p. 134.
49 *Ibid.*, pp. 132–3.
50 Benedictus Figulus, *op. cit.*, p. 278.
51 *Ibid.*, p. 84.*
52 Bonus of Ferrara, *op. cit.*, pp. 111–12.
53 *Ibid,.*, p. 138.
54 *Ibid.*, p. 13.
55 A. E. Waite, *op. cit.*, p. 16.
56 Trans. A. E. Waite, *The Turba Philosophorum*, Stuart & Watkins, London, 1970, p. 188.
57 Titus Burckhardt, *op. cit.*, p. 31.
58 Bonus of Ferrara, *op. cit.*, p. 85.
59 Trans. A. E. Waite, *The Works of T homas Vaughn Mystic and Alchemist*, University Press, New Hyde Park, 1968, p. 96.
60 Titus Burckhardt, *op. cit.*, p. 30.
61 Trans. A. E. Waite, *The Works of Thomas Vaughn*, *op. cit.*, p. 103.
62 Eirenaeus Philalethes, *op. cit.*, p. 63.
63 Martin Heidegger, *An Introduction to Metaphysics*, Anchor Books Doubleday & Company, Inc., Garden City, 1961, p. 12.
64 Trans. R. F. C. Hull and A. S. B. Glover, *op. cit.*, p. 111.
65 Trans. Norbert Guterman, *op. cit.*, p. 111.
66 Bonus of Ferrara, *op. cit.*, p. 123.
67 *Ibid.*, p. 137.
68 Benedictus Figulus, *op. cit.*, p. 242.
69 Bonus of Ferrara, *op. cit.*, p. 140.
70 Benedictus Figulus, *op. cit.*, p. 316.
71 Trans. A. E. Waite, *The Hermetic and Alchemical Writings of Paracelsus*, vol. I, University Books Inc., New Hyde Park, 1967, p. 113.
72 Cf. W. B. Macomber, *The Anatomy of Disillusion*, Northwestern University Press, Evanston, 1968.
73 Cf. Maurice Merleau-Ponty, *The Visible and the Invisible*, Northwestern University Press, Evanston, 1968.
74 Martin Heidegger, *Being and Time*, *op. cit.*, p. 59.
75 W. B. Macomber, *op. cit.*, p. 61–2.
76 Basilius Valentinus, *The Triumphal Chariot of Antimony*, Vincent Stuart Ltd, London, 1962, p. 66.
77 Bonus of Ferrara, *op. cit.*, p. 86.
78 *Ibid.*, p. 88.
79 *Ibid.*, p. 245.
80 Harold Garfinkel, *Studies in Ethnomethodology*, Prentice-Hall, Inc., Englewood Cliffs, 2967, p. 1.
81 Gersholm G. Scholem, *On The Kabbalah and its Symbolsim*, Routledge & Kegan Paul, London, 1965, pp. 55–6.
82 Elias Ashmole, Esq., *Theatrum Chemicum Britannicum*, Johnson Reprint Corporation, New York, 1967, p. 29.
83 A. E. Waite, *op. cit.*, p. 312.
84 Bonus of Ferrara, *op. cit.*, pp. 146–7.
85 Titus Burckhardt, *op. cit.*, p. 28.

86 G. R. S. Mead, *Fragments of a Faith Forgotten*, Theosophical Publishing Society, London, 1900, pp. 309–10.
87 Basilius Valentinus, *op. cit.*, pp. 32–3.
88 Harold Garfinkel, *op. cit.*, p. 4–5.
89 *Ibid.*, p. 5.
90 Bonus of Ferrara, *op. cit.*, pp. 134–5.
91 Benedictus Figulus, *op. cit.*, pp. 320–1.
92 *Ibid.*, p. 85.
93 Bonus of Ferrara, *op. cit.*, pp. 122–3.
94 Trans. A. E. Waite, *The Turba Philosophorum*, *op. cit.*, pp. 157–8.
95 Bonus of Ferrara, *op. cit.*, p. 112.
96 Trans. R. F. C. Hull and A. S. B. Glover, *op. cit.*, p. 117.
97 Trans. A. E. Waite, *The Turba Philosophorum*, *op. cit.*, p. 131.
98 Benedictus Figulus, *op. cit.*, p. 185.
99 Trans. Norbert Guterman, *op. cit.*, p. 112.

6 On formal structures of practical actions*

Harold Garfinkel and Harvey Sacks

The point of the paper

The fact that natural language serves persons doing sociology, laymen or professionals, as circumstances, as topics, and as resources of their inquiries, furnishes to the technology of their inquiries and to their practical sociological reasoning *its* circumstances, *its* topics, and *its* resources. That reflexivity is encountered by sociologists in the actual occasions of their inquiries as indexical properties of natural language. These properties are sometimes characterized by summarily observing that a description, for example, in the ways it may be a constituent part of the circumstances it describes, in endlesss ways and unavoidably, 'elaborates' those circumstances and is 'elaborated' by them. That reflexivity assures to natural language characteristic indexical properties such as the following: The definiteness of expressions resides in their consequences; definitions can be used to assure a definite collection of 'considerations' without providing a boundary; the definiteness of a collection is assured by circumstantial possibilities of indefinite elaboration.[1]

'Indexical' features are not particular to laymen's accounts. They are familiar in the accounts of professionals as well. For example, the natural language 'formula,' 'the objective reality of social facts is sociology's fundamental principle,'[2] is heard by professionals according to occasion as a definition of Association members' activities, as their slogan, their task, aim, achievement, brag, sales pitch, justification, discovery, social phenomenon, or research constraint. Like any other indexical expression the tran-

*Reprinted from *Theoretical Sociology: Perspectives and Developments*, John C. McKinney and Edward Tiryakian (eds.), Appleton-Century-Crofts; 1969.

sient circumstances of its use assure it a definiteness of sense as definition or task or aim, etc., to someone who knows how to hear it.[3] Further, as Helmer and Rescher[4] showed, in no occasion is the formula assured a definiteness that exhibits structures other than those that are exhibited by pointed references. This is to say, when the definiteness of the expression is analyzed with prevailing methods of logic and linguistics it exhibits few or no structures that available methods can handle or make interesting. Sociology's methods of formal analysis are differently disappointed by these expressions: their definiteness of sense is without structures that can be demonstrated in the *actual* expressions with the use of available mathematical methods, to specify a sense, definitely. In a search for rigor the ingenious practice is followed whereby such expressions are first transformed into ideal expressions. Structures are then analyzed as properties of the ideals, and the results are assigned to actual expressions as their properties, though with disclaimers of 'appropriate scientific modesty.'

The indexical properties of natural language assures to the technology of sociological inquiries, lay and professional, the following unavoidable and irremediable practice as its earmark: Wherever and by whosoever practical sociological reasoning is done it seeks to remedy the indexical properties of practical discourse; it does so in the interests of demonstrating the rational accountability of everyday activities; and it does so in order that its assessments be warranted by methodic observation and report of situated, socially organized particulars of everyday activities, which of course include particulars of natural language.

The remedial practices of practical sociological reasoning are aimed at accomplishing a thoroughgoing distinction between objective and indexical expresssions with which to make possible the substitution of objective for indexical expressions. At present that distinction and substitutability provides professional sociology with its infinite task.[5]

These motives and recommendations are easily observed in most of the conference papers, though they are perhaps liveliest in those of Blalock,[6] Douglas,[7] Inkeles,[8] Lazarsfeld,[9] Levy,[10] Moore,[11] Parsons,[12] and Spengler[13] who use them to locate needed tasks for sociological theorizing, to cite achievements, and to take note of available methods and results as professional stock in trade. The remedial program of practical sociological reasoning is specified in such characteristic practices of professional sociological inquiry as the elaboration and defense of unified sociological theory, model building, cost-benefit analysis, the use of natural metaphors to collect wider settings under the experience of a locally known setting, the use of laboratory arrangements as experimental schemes of inference, schematic reporting, and statistical evaluations of frequency, reproducibility, effectiveness, etc., of natural language practices and of various social arrangements that entail their use, and so on. For convenience we shall collect such practices of professional sociology's practical technology with the term 'constructive analysis.'

Irreconcilable interests exist between constructive analysis and ethnomethodology in the phenomena of the rational accountability of everyday activities and its accompanying practical technology of practical sociological reasoning. Those differences have one of their foci in indexical expressions: in contrasting conceptions of the ties between objective and indexical expressions, and in contrasting conceptions of the relevance of indexicals to the tasks of clarifying the connections between routine and rationality in everyday activities. Extensive phenomena that constructive analysis has missed entirely are detailed in the ethnomethodological studies of Bittner,[14] Churchill,[15] Cicourel,[16] Garfinkel,[17] MacAndrew,[18] Moerman,[19] Pollner,[20] Rose,[21] Sacks,[22] Schegloff,[23] Sudnow,[24] Wieder,[25] and Zimmerman.[26] Their studies have shown in demonstrable specifics (1) that the properties of indexical expressions are ordered properties,[27] and (2) *that* they are ordered properties is an ongoing, practical accomplishment of every actual occasion of commonplace speech and conduct. The results of their studies furnish an alternative to the repair of indexical expressions as a central task of general theory building in professional sociology.

The alternative task of general theory building is to describe that achievement in specifics in its organizational variety. The purposes of this paper are to locate that achievement as a phenomenon and to specify some of its features; to describe some structures in the practices which make up that achievement; and to take notice of the obviousness, enormous interest, and pervasiveness which that achievement has for members, be they lay or professional analysts of ordinary activities. We do so with the aim of recommending an alternative account of formal structures in practical actions to those accounts that make up the work and achievements of practical sociological reasoning wherever it occurs: among laymen, of course, but with overwhelming prevalence in contemporary professional sociology and other social sciences as well, and in all cases without serious competitors.

Members' methods of sociological inquiry

Alfred Schutz[28] made available, for sociological study, the practices of commonsense knowledge of social structures of everyday activities, practical circumstances, practical activities, and practical sociological reasoning. It is his original achievement to have shown that these phenomena have characteristic properties of their own and that thereby they constitute a legitimate area of inquiry in themselves. Schutz's writings furnished us with endless directives in our studies of the circumstances and practices of practical sociological inquiry. The results of these studies are detailed in other publications.[29] They furnish empirical justification for a research policy that is distinctive to ethnomethodological studies. That policy provides that the practices of sociological inquiry and theorizing, the topics for those practices, the findings from those practices, the circumstances of those practices, the availability of those practices as research methodology, and the rest, are through and through *members' methods* of sociological inquiry and theorizing. Unavoidably and without hope of remedy the practices consist of *members' methods* for assembling sets of alternatives, *members' methods* for assembling, testing, and verifying the factual character of information, *members' methods* for giving an account of circumstances of choice and choices, *members' methods* for assessing, producing, recognizing, insuring, and enforcing consistency, coherence, effectiveness, efficiency, planfulness, and other rational properties of individual and concerted actions.

The notion of 'member' is the heart of the matter. We do not use the term 'member' to refer to a person. It refers instead to mastery of natural language, which we understand in the following way.

We offer the observation that persons, in that they are heard to be speaking a natural language, *somehow* are heard to be engaged in the objective production and objective display of commonsense knowledge of everyday activities as observable and reportable phenomena. We ask what it is about natural language that permits speakers and auditors to hear, and in other ways to witness, the objective production and objective display of commonsense knowledge, and of practical circumstances, practical actions, and practical sociological reasoning as well? What is it about natural language that makes these phenomena observable–reportable, i.e., *account-able* phenomena? For speakers and auditors the practices of natural language somehow exhibit these phenomena in the particulars of speaking, and *that* these phenomena are exhibited is itself, and thereby, made exhibitable in further description, remark, questions, and in other ways for the telling.

The interests of ethnomethodological research are directed to provide, through detailed analyses, that account-able phenomena are through and through practical accomplishments. We shall speak of 'the work' of that accomplishment in order to gain the emphasis for it of an ongoing course of action. 'The work' is done as assemblages of practices whereby speakers in the situated particulars of speech mean differently than they can say in just so many words, i.e., as 'glossing practices.' An understanding of glossing practices is critical to our arguments, and further discussion will be found in the Appendix.

I. A. Richards[30] has provided a thematic example. He suggests the use of question marks to bracket some piece of talk or text, for example, ?empirical social research?, ?theoretical systems?, ?systems of sequences?, ?social psychological variables?, ?glossing practices?, as a way of instructing a reader to proceed as follows: How the bracketed phrase is to be comprehended is at the outset specifically undecided. How it is to be comprehended is the task of a reading whereby some unknown procedure will be used to make the text comprehensible. Since nothing about the text or procedure needs to be decided for the while, we will wait for the while, for whatever the while. When and if we have read and talked abbout the text we will review what might be made of it. Thus we can have used the text not as undefined terms but as a gloss over a lively context whose ways, as a sense assembly procedure, we found no need[31] to specify.

Richards's gloss consists of practices of talking with the use of particular texts in a fashion such that how their comprehended character will have worked out in the end remains unstated throughout, although the course of talk may be so directed as to compose a context which embeds the text and thereby provides the text's replicas with noticed, changing, but unremarked functional characters such as 'a text in the beginning,' 'a text as an end result,' 'an intervening flow of conversation to link the two,'[32] and so on.

Apparently speakers can, will, could, ought, and do proceed in the fashion for which Richards's gloss of a text is a thematic example, to accomplish recognizably sensible definiteness, clarity, identification, substitution, or relevance of the notational particulars of natural language. And apparently speakers can proceed by glossing, and do the immense work that they do with natural language, even though over the course of their talk it is not known and is never, not even 'in the end,' available for saying in so many words just what they are talking about. Emphatically, that does not mean that speakers do not know what they are talking about, *but instead they know what they are talking about in that way.*

Richards's gloss is merely one of these ways.[33] Glossing practices exist in empirical multitude. In endless, but particular, analyzable ways glossing practices *are* methods for producing observable and reportable understanding, with, in, and of natural language. As a multitude of ways for exhibiting-*in*-speaking and exhibiting-*for*-the-telling that and how speaking is understood, glossing practices *are* 'members,' *are* 'mastery of natural language,' *are* 'talking reasonably,' *are* 'plain speech,' *are* 'speaking English' (or French, or whatever), *are* 'clear, consistent, cogent speech, i.e., rational speech.'

We understand mastery of natural language to consist in this: In the particulars of his speech a speaker, in concert with others, is able to gloss those particulars and is thereby meaning differently than he can say in so many words; he is doing so over unknown contingencies in the actual occasions of interaction; and in so doing, the recognition *that* he is speaking and *how* he is speaking are specifically not matters for competent remarks. That is to say, the particulars of his speaking do not provide occasions for stories about his speaking that are worth telling; nor do they elicit questions that are worth asking, and so on.

The idea of 'meaning differently than he can say in so many words' requires comment. It is not so much 'differently than what he says' as that *whatever* he says provides the very materials to be used in *making out* what he says. However extensive or however explicit what a speaker says may be, it does not by its extensiveness or its explicitness pose a task of deciding the correspondence between what he says and what he means that is resolved by citing his talk *in verbatim*.[34] Instead, his talk itself, in that it becomes[35] a part of the selfsame occasion of interaction becomes another contingency of that interaction. It extends and elaborates indefinitely the circumstances it glosses and in this way contributes to its own accountably sensible character. The thing that is said assures to speaking's accountably sensible character its variable fortunes. In sum, the mastery of natural language is throughout and without relief an occasioned accomplishment.

Ethnomethodology's interest in formal structures of practical actions

Ethnomethodology's interests, like those of constructive analysis, insistently focus on the formal structures of everyday activities. However, the two understand formal structures differently and in incompatible ways.

We call attention to the phenomenon that formal structures are available in the accounts of professional sociology where they are recognized by professionals and claimed by them as professional sociology's singular achievement. These accounts of formal structures are done via sociologists' mastery of natural language, and require that mastery as the *sine qua non* of adequate professional readership. This assures to professional sociologists' accounts of formal structures its character as a phenomenon for ethnomethodology's interest, not different from any other members' phenomenon where the mastery of natural language is similarly involved. Ethnomethodological studies of formal structures are directed to the study of such phenomena, seeking to describe members' accounts of formal structures wherever and by whomever they are done, while abstaining from all judgements of their adequacy, value, importance, necessity, practicality, success, or consequentiality. We refer to this procedural policy as 'ethnomethodological indifference.'

Ethnomethodological 'indifference' cannot be viewed as a position which would claim that no matter how extensive a volume like Berelson's might become, problems yet could be found. Nor in that regard, would it be that in so far as the predictive efficacy of professional sociology had an asymptotic form, one could count on a margin of error as a stable property within which research could proceed. Counting on the fact that given the statistical orientations of professional sociology one would always have 'unexplained variance' is not our way of locating yet unexplained phenomena. Our work does not stand then in any modifying, elaborating, contributing, detailing, subdividing, explicating, foundation building relationship to professional sociological reasoning, nor is our 'indifference' to those orders of tasks. Rather, our 'indifference' is to the whole of practical sociological reasoning, and *that* reasoning involves for us, in whatever form of development, with whatever error or adequacy, in whatever forms, inseparably and unavoidably, the mastery of natural language. Professional sociological reasoning is in no way singled out as a phenomenon for our research attention. Persons doing ethnomethodological studies can 'care' no more or less about professional sociological reasoning than they can 'care' about the practices of legal reasoning, conversational reasoning, divinational reasoning, psychiatric reasoning, and the rest.

Given ethnomethodology's procedure of 'indifference,' by formal structures we understand everyday activities (a) in that they exhibit upon analysis the properties of uniformity, reproducibility, repetitiveness, standardization, typicality and so on; (b) in that these properties are independent of particular production cohorts; (c) in that particular cohort independence is a phenomenon for members' recognition; and (d) in that the phenomena (a), (b), and (c) are every particular cohort's practical, situated accomplishment.

The above development of formal structures contrasts with that which prevails in sociology and the social sciences in that the ethnomethodological procedure of 'indifference' provides for the specifications (c) and (d) by studying everyday activities as practical ongoing achievements.

A further contrast between ethnomethodology's treatment of formal structures and that of constructive analysis is specified by the characteristic that it is as masters of natural language that constructive analysts recommend and understand that their accounts of formal structures provide aims and singular achievements of their technology of research and theory. It is as masters of natural language that constructive analysts understand the accomplishment of that recommendation to be constructive analysis' infinite task. Constructive analytic accounts of formal structures are thus practical achievements, through and through. Natural language provides to constructive analysis its topics, circumstances, resources , and results as natural language *formulations* of ordered particulars of members' talk and members' conduct, of territorial movements and distributions, of relationships of interaction, and the rest.

Ethnomethodologically, such practices whereby accounts of formal structures are done comprise the phenomena of practical sociological reasoning. Obviously those practices are not the monopoly of Association members. The remainder of the paper takes that phenomenon under scrutiny. The paper reviews members' methods for producing and recognizing formal structures of everyday activities by examining members' practices of *formulating*.

The phenomenon

In that inquiries are done that make use of or are about members' talk, an inquirer will invariably exhibit a concern to clarify that talk in the interests of the inquiry. So, for example, an interviewee's remark, 'She didn't like it here so we moved,' may provide a researcher occasion to do such things as give that utterance a name, tell who 'she' is, where 'here' is, who the 'we' covers. In the large literature in logic and linguistics such terms have been called indicators, egocentric particulars, indexical expressions, occasional expressions, indices, shifters, pronominals, and token reflexives. A list of such terms would start with 'here,' 'now,' 'this,' 'that,' 'it,' 'I,' 'he,' 'you,' 'there,' 'then,' 'soon,' 'today,' 'tomorrow.'

We begin with the observations about these phenomena that

everyone regularly treats such utterances as occasions for reparative practices; that such practices are native not only to research
but to all users of the natural language; that without knowing
what a particular research dealt with one could list the terms that
would need to be clarified, or translated, or replaced, or otherwise
remedied, and that the terms could be located and their remedies
proposed and demonstrated for all practical purposes, with or
without research and with or without knowing how extensive are
similar concerns of others. The large and ancient literature in logic
and linguistics that bears on researchers' work is a minor tributary
in the rush of that omniprevalent work.

We treat as fact that researchers, *any* researchers, lay or
professional researchers, naive or not to logic and linguistics, who
start with a text, find themselves engaged in clarifying such terms
that occur in it. What should be made of that sort of fact? What
do we, in this article, want to make of that fact?

If, whenever housewives were let into a room, each one, on
her own, went to some same spot and started to clean it, one
might conclude that the spot surely needed cleaning. On the other
hand, one might conclude that there is something about the spot
and about the housewives that makes the encounter of one by the
other an occasion for cleaning, in which case the fact of the
cleaning, instead of being evidence of dirt, would be itself a
phenomenon.

Indexical expressions have been 'studied' and have been dealt
with in identical fashion times without end, not only in naivety, but
more interestingly, in apparently required disregard of previous
achievements. The academic literature furnishes evidence of how
ancient is that reparative work. The Dissoi Logii,[36] a fragment of
text from approximately 300 BC, gives attention to the sentence 'I
am an initiate' because it presents difficulties. The issue is that of
the truth or falsity of a sentence when, if said by A it was true,
but if said by B it was false; if said by A at one time it was true,
but if said by A at another time it was false; if said by A from
one status of A it was true, but if said by A from another it was
false.

To the problems that sentences like this one pose, programmatic
solutions have long been available. One would begin by replacing
'I' with a proper name; would add a date; would specify a status
with respect to which the speaker was 'an initiate.' A stupendous
amount of work has been devoted to such phenomena. In the
next section that work is briefly characterized.

A characterization of indexical expressions

Not only does an awareness of indexical expressions occur in the earliest writing, it occurs in the work of major authors over the entire history of logic. Every major philosopher has commented on them. Consider for example Charles S. Peirce[37] and Ludwig Wittgenstein:[38] Peirce because he is usually cited to mark the beginning of modern logicians' and linguists' interest in indexicals, and Wittgenstein because when his later studies are read to see that he is examining philosophers' talk as indexical phenomena, and is describing these phenomena without thought of remedy, his studies will be found to consist of a sustained, extensive, and penetrating corpus of observations of indexical phenomena.

We borrow from the remarks by logicians and linguists to characterize indexical expressions. Edmund Husserl[39] spoke of expressions (1) whose sense cannot be decided by an auditor without his necessarily knowing or assuming something about the biography and purposes of the user of the expression, the circumstances of the utterance, the previous course of discourse, or the particular relationship of actual or potential interaction that exists between the user and the auditor. (2) Bertrand Russell[40] pointed out that descriptions involving them apply on each occasion of use to only one thing, but to different things on different occasions. (3) Such expressions, he said, are used to make unequivocal statements that nevertheless seem to change in truth value. (4) Nelson Goodman[41] wrote that each of their 'utterances' constitutes a word and refers to a certain person, time, or place but names something not named by some replica of the word. (5) Their denotation is relative to the user. (6) Their use depends upon the relation of the use to the object with which the word is concerned. (7) Time for a 'temporal indexical expression' is relevant to what it names. (8) Similarly, just what region a spatial indexical expression' names depends upon the location of its utterance. (9) Indexical expressions and statements containing them are not freely repeatable in a given discourse in that not all their replicas therein are also translations of them.[42]

Logicians and linguists in their explicit attempts to recover commonplace talk in its structural particulars encounter these expressions as obstinate nuisances.[43] The nuisances of indexicals are dramatic wherever inquiries are directed to achieve for practical talk the formulation and decideability of alternatives of sense, or fact, or methodic procedure, or agreement among 'cultural colleagues.' Features of indexical expressions have motivated among professionals endless methodological studies directed to their remedy. Indeed, the work by practitioners to rid the practices of *a* science, of *any* science, of these nuisances, because, and in the ways such work occurs in all sciences,[44] furnishes each science its distinctive character of preoccupation and productivity with methodological issues. Whatever the science, actual situations of practical investigative activities afford researchers endless occasions and motives for attempts to remedy indexical expressions. Thus, virtually without exceptions, methodological studies, wherever they occur, lay and professional, have been concerned to remedy indexical expressions while insistently holding as aims of their studies a programmatically relevant distinction between objective and indexical expressions, and a programmatically relevant substitutability of objective for indexical expressions. In these programmatic studies of the formal properties of natural languages and practical reasoning, the properties of indexicals, while furnishing investigators motivating occasions for remedial actions, remain obstinately unavoidable and irremediable.

Such 'methodological' concerns are not confined to the sciences. One finds ubiquitous concern among conversationalists with faults of natural language. Faults are assigned by members to usage by others about whom it is said that they have small vocabularies. Such concerns are accompanied by a prevalent recommendation that terms, utterances, and discourse may be clarified, and other shortcomings that consist in the properties of indexical expressions may be remedied by referring them to 'their setting' (i.e., the familiar recommendations about the 'decisive relevance of context').

More pointedly, we call particular attention to a conversational practice which has frank methodological intent. One finds conversationalists, in the course of a conversation, and as a recognized feature of that conversation, *formulating* their conversation. Formulating, in conversation, is discussed at length in the following sections.

Naming, identifying, defining, describing, explaining, etc., a conversation i.e., formulating a conversation, as a feature of that conversation

Among conversationalists it is an immensely commonplace feature of conversations that a conversation exhibits *for its parties* its own familiar features of a 'self-explicating colloquy.' A member may treat some part of the conversation as an occasion to describe that conversation, to explain it, or characterize it, or explicate, or translate, or summarize, or furnish the gist of it, or take note of its accordance with rules, or remark on its departure from rules. That is to say, a member may use some part of the conversation as an occasion to *formulate* the conversation, as in the following colloquies.

A: Do you think the federal government can go in and try that man for murder?

B: No.

B: It's a matter of state.

A: [Now let me ask you this.]

B: You would not be critical at all.

A: Of Westmoreland.

B: Of the military, – of the – of this recent operation.

A: Of course I'd be critical.

B: [Well you certainly don't show it!]

JH: Isn't it nice that there's such a crowd of you in the office?

SM: [You're asking us to leave, not telling us to leave, right?]

HG: I need some exhibits of persons evading questions. Will you do me a favor and evade some questions for me?

NW: [Oh dear, I'm not very good at evading questions.]

(In fatigued excitement a psychiatric resident pauses in telling a supervising faculty member about his discovery of Harry Stack Sullivan's writings.)
Faculty member: [How long have you been feeling like this?]

Boston policeman to a motorist: [You asked me where Sparks Street is, didn't you? Well, I just told you.]

These excerpts illustrate the point that along with whatever else may be happening in conversation it may be a feature of the conversation for the conversationalists that they are doing something else, namely, what they are doing is saying-in-so-many-words-what-we-are-doing (or what we are talking about, or who is talking, or who we are, or where we are, etc.)

We shall speak of conversationalists' practices of saying-in-so-many-words-what-we-are-doing as doing formulating. Instead of hyphens we shall use square brackets to designate about the text they enclose that it is a formulation. In the preceding colloquies the formulating that one of the conversationalists is doing appears in brackets.

Two phenomena are of particular interest for us. (1) We offer as observations about practices of formulating that not only are they done, but they are also recognized by conversationalists as constituent features of the conversation in which they are done. We shall speak of this by saying *that* formulating is being done is, for conversationalists, 'exhibited *in* the speaking.' (2) We offer the further observation that formulating, as a witnessed feature of conversation, is available to conversationalists' report, or remark, or comment and the like. To have a way of speaking of this we shall say *that* formulating is done is 'exhibitable *for* the telling.'

Each of the colloquies provides an example of the first phenomenon. An example of the second phenomenon is found in the fact that we report these colloquies and call attention, with the use of brackets, to the work of formulating being done in each. The square brackets are used to designate the following features of formulating:

(1) Above all, formulating is an account-able phenomenon. This is to say (a) it is a phenomenon that members make happen; that members perform. (b) It is observable by members. (c) In that members can do the phenomenon and observe it, it is report-able.[45] (d) The phenomenon is done and reportable by members with texts such as those that are bracketed. It is done as well with script, utterances, or graphics, i.e., with circumstantially particular, notational displays. (e) The bracketed text is a phase of an interactional enterprise. And (f) the text is meaning differently than the speaker can say in so many words.

(2) All of the foregoing features are practical accomplishments over the exigencies of actual interaction.

(3) The expression, [ ], is prefaced with 'doing' in order to emphasize that accountable-conversation-as-a-practical-accomplishment consists only and entirely in and of its work. The prefix 'doing' is also used to emphasize about this work of accountable conversation that it is members' work. That is to say, this work has essential ties to mastery of natural language.

Our illustrations have so far been chosen from laymen's work. The bracketing, and its effects, is relevant as well to the work of social scientists. If we place brackets on topicalized practices in the social sciences with which its practitioners speak of techniques of data collection, of research designs, of descriptive adequacy, of rules of evidence, and the like, we then ask what is the work for which these topics are its accountable texts. For example, linguists speak of 'parsing a sentence with the use of phrase markers.' By bracketing that text with gloss marks [parsing a sentence with the use of phrase markers], we understand that we

172

are now addressed to the question: What is the work for which 'parsing a sentence with the use of phrase markers' is that work's accountable text? The bracketing has similar relevance to the above case as it has to the case where we ask: What is the work for which [playing a game of chess according to the rules of Chess] is that work's accountable text?

If we speak of work's accountable text as a 'proper gloss' we may ask: What is the work for which [speaking without interruption at a cocktail party] is its proper gloss? What is the work for which [The equilibrium size distribution of freely forming groups] is its proper gloss? Figure 6.1 displays these relationships.

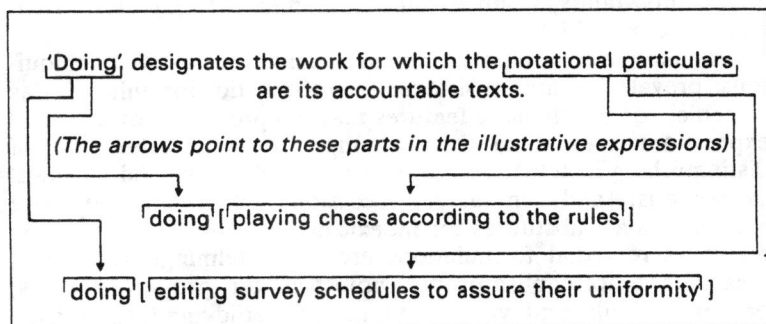

'Doing' designates the work for which the notational particulars are its accountable texts.

(The arrows point to these parts in the illustrative expressions)

'doing' ['playing chess according to the rules']

'doing' ['editing survey schedules to assure their uniformity']

FIGURE 6.1

A final remark about brackets: Their use reminds us that glossing practices are phases of interactional enterprises. Enterprises of intelligible, particular appearances of organized everyday activities are done unavoidably, only, and exclusively by competent speakers, who can do them only and entirely through the particulars of notational displays in natural language. Gloss enterprises are practical accomplishments. They are immensely varied phenomena, for they differ in ways dictated by a world of 'social fact,' albeit a world of social fact that is members' achievements. As practical achievements gloss enterprises are as immensely varied as are organizational arrangements, for organizational arrangements are such achievements.

According to occasion, doing formulating may be members' undertakings, aims, rules, obligated behaviors, achievements, passing episodes, or standing circumstances. The work is not restricted to special circumstances. To the contrary, it occurs routinely, and on a massive scale. Members are particularly knowledgeable of, sensitive to, and skillful with this work; with doing it, assuring it, remedying it, and the like.

Doing accountably definite talk

We used the metaphor of housewives and spots to characterize the prevalence and insistence by members upon the work of doing formulations as remedies for the properties of indexical expressions. But, as we have noticed, in that formulations consist of glosses, and in that the properties that formulations exhibit as notational displays – properties that are used by speakers to accomplish rational speech – are properties of indexical expressions, the very resources of natural language assure that doing formulating is itself for members a routine source of complaints, faults, troubles, and recommended remedies, *essentially* (see pp. 177–8).

We take the critical phenomenon to consist in this: With ubiquitous prevalence and insistence members do formulations as remedies for problematic features that the properties of indexical expressions present to their attempts to satisfy the aims of distinguishing in actual occasions between objective and indexical expressions, and, in actual occasions, providing objective expressions as substitutes for indexicals. We observe that among members remedial formulations are overwhelmingly advocated measures to accomplish proper subject matter, proper problems, proper methods, and warranted findings in studying formal structures of practical talk and practical reasoning. We observe that their advocacy of remedial formulations is accompanied by practices with which members are just as overwhelmingly knowledgeable and skilled, practices whereby speakers guarantee and are guaranteed that formulations are *not* the machinery whereby accountably sensible, clear, definite talk is done. Such practices are seen in the following phenomena.

(1) There are innumerable conversational activities in doing which multitudes of names are available for naming them as conversational phenomena; people know the names, they can mention the names, summarize with the names, and so on, and yet in the course of the activities the names are not much used. Indeed, a commonplace but little understood phenomenon consists of cases where in doing [saying in so many words what one is doing] the activity is recognizedly incongruous, or boring, or furnishes evidence of incompetence, or devious motivation, and so forth.

(2) There is a tremendous topical coherence in ordinary conversations, and yet conversationalists' formulation of topics is a very special thing: it is rarely done; in any particular case it is not only probably disputable but is perhaps irremediably disputable; and though one gets talk that is topical, topical names are not inserted.

(3) There occurs as a commonplace achievement in ordinary conversations, and for conversationalists furnishes commonplace evidence of conversational competence, that conversationalists title relevant texts, search for, remember, recognize, or offer relevant texts without those texts being topicalized; where the success of search, recall, offer, recognition, and the rest depends upon vagueness of topic, aim, rule of search, rule of relevance, and the rest, and where the work of storage and retrieval of relevant texts incorporates this vagueness as an essential feature in its design.

(4) Another phenomenon was described in a previous study.[46] Students were asked to write what the parties to an ordinary conversation were overheard to have said, and then to write alongside, what the parties actually were talking about. The phenomenon is this: The students, having been set the task of saying in just so many words what the parties were actually talking about, immediately saw that the work of satisfying the task hopelessly elaborated the task's features. Somehow they saw immediately that the very task that had been set – 'Tell me as if I didn't know, what the parties were literally talking about' – was faulted, not in the sense that the auditor would not know, or could not or would not understand, or that there was not enough time or paper or stamina or vocabulary or words in English for a writer to tell it, but that

> I had required them to take on the impossible task of 'repairing' the essential incompleteness of *any* set instructions no matter how carefully or elaborately written they might be. I had required them to formulate the method that the parties had used in speaking, as rules of procedure to follow in order to say what the parties said, rules that would withstand every exigency of situation, imagination, and development . . . [This was the task] that required them to write 'more,' that they found increasingly difficult and finally impossible, and that became elaborated in its features by the very procedures for doing it.

We take as the critical import of these phenomena that they furnish specifics for the observation that *for the member it is not in the work of doing formulations for conversation that the member is doing [the fact that our conversational activities are accountably rational].* The two activities are neither identical nor interchangeable.

We notice also that doing formulating is 'occasioned.' By this we mean that cited times, places, and personnel whereby formulating is done – that concrete, definite, clear, determinate specifications of where? when? who? what? how many? – are unavoidably and without remedy done as accountable phenomena. Also, it is not only that members may use particular rules to provide for the occasioned character of a formulation, but the failure to use particular rules is usable by a member to find what it is that formulating is doing in a conversation, where the fact of formulating does not mean to those doing it that doing it is definitive of its work, but instead, doing it can be found to be joking, or being obstinate, and the like.

In short, doing formulating for conversation itself exhibits for conversationalists an orientation to [the fact that our conversational activities are accountably rational]. Doing formulating is not the definitive means whereby the fact is itself done or established. The question of what one who is doing formulating is doing – which is a members' question – is not solved by members by consulting what the formulation proposes, but by engaging in practices that make up the *essentially* contexted character of the action of formulating. Even the briefest consideration of doing formulating in conversation returns us – naive speaker or social scientist – to the phenomenon in conversation of doing [the fact that our conversational activities are accountably rational].

What are we proposing when we propose that the question of what one is doing who is doing formulating is solved by members by engaging in practices that make up the *essentially* contexted character of the action of formulating? What kind of work is it for which [the fact that our conversational activities are accountably rational] is its proper gloss?

Formal structures in accountably rational discourse: the 'machinery'

We learn to ask from the work of conversationalists: What kind of 'machinery' makes up the practices of doing [accountably rational conversation]? Are there practices for doing and recognizing [the fact that our activities are accountably rational] without, for example, making a formulation of the setting that the practices are 'contexted' in? What is the work for which [the fact that our activities are accountably rational] is an accountable text? What is the work for which [definiteness, univocality, disambiguation, and uniqueness of conversational particulars is assured by conversationalists' competence with speech in context] is a proper gloss?

We ask such questions because we learn from the phenomena that are problematic for conversationalists that 'times,' 'places,' or 'personnel' for example, with which conversationalists say in so many words who, or where, or when, or since when, or how long since, or how much more, or with whom, or what, are contexted phenomena. More accurately, they are *essentially* contexted phenomena.

By 'contexted phenomena' we mean that there exist specific practices such that: (1) they make up what a member is doing when he does and recognizes [the fact of relevant time, place, personnel, etc.]; (2) they are done with or without formulating *which* now, or which where, or with whom, or since when, or how much longer, and the like; (3) they make up members' work for which [practices of objective, clear, consistent, cogent – i.e., rational – language] is a proper gloss; and (4) they meet the first three criteria by satisfying the following constraints (to which we refer with the adjective, 'essential'):

(1) They are cause for members' complaints; they are faulted; they are nuisances; troubles; proper grounds for corrective, i.e., remedial action.

(2) They are without remedy in the sense that every measure that is taken to achieve a remedy preserves in specifics the features for which the remedy was sought.

(3) They are unavoidable, they are inescapable; there is no hiding place from their use; no moratorium; no time out; no room in the world for relief.

(4) Programmatic ideals characterized their workings.

(5) The ideals are available as 'plain spoken rules' to provide accounts of adequate description for all practical purposes, or adequate explanation, adequate identity, adequate characterization, adequate translation, gist, analysis, rule, etc.

(6) Provision is made 'in studies by practicing logicians' for each ideal's 'poor relatives,' as indexical expressions are the poor relatives of objective expressions; as commonsense knowledge is a poor relative of scientific knowledge; as natives' practices and natives' knowledge are poor relatives for professional practices and professional knowledge of natives' affairs, practices, and knowledge; as Calvin N. Mooers's descriptors are poor relatives of sets, categories, classes, or collections in formal logic; or, as formal structures in natural language are poor relatives of formal structures in invented languages. For 'poor relatives' we understand 'embarrassing but necessary nuisances,' 'lesser versions,' 'non-phenomena,' 'no causes for celebration,' 'ugly doubles' that are relied on by members to assure the claims of the relatives that went to college and came back educated. Ideals are not the monopoly of academies, and neither are their poor relatives confined to the streets. Always in each other's company, they are available in immense varieties for they are as common as talk.

Being theorized out of existence by members' ironic contrast between commonsense knowledge and scientific knowledge, they are also difficult to locate and report with the use of that contrast.

(7) Members are unanimous in their recognition of the foregoing six characteristics of specific practices. Members are also unanimous in their use of these characteristics to detect, sense, identify, locate, name – i.e., to formulate – one or another 'sense' of practical activities as an 'invariant structure of appearances.'

Speaking practices, in that they satisfy such constraints, are inescapably tied to particulars of talk, and thereby speaking practices are, inescapably, exhibited and witnessed as ordered particulars of talk. Speaking practices, in that they satisfy such constraints, exhibit the features of 'production cohort independence,' or 'invariant to in and out migrations of system personnel,' or 'invariant to transformations of context,' or 'universals.' They exhibit features of invariance by providing members' methods with their accountable character as *unavoidably* used methods with which particulars are recovered, produced, identified, and recognized as connected particulars; as particulars in relationships of entailment, relevance, inference, allusion, reference, evidence; which is to say as collections of particulars, or classes, or sets, or families, or groups, or swarms.

Members use these to detect various ways of doing [invariance] in members' practices. Because members do so, we shall use them in the same way; namely as constraints that speaking practices must satisfy if we are to count those practices as members' resources for doing and recognizing [rational adequacy for practical purposes of natural language]. They provide characteristics of the practices with which members accomplish and recognize rational discourse in its indexical particulars, i.e., 'practical talk.'

What are those practices?[47]

We learn some if we ask about a *list* of indexical expressions, how long the list might be. To answer this question we need a procedure that will get us a list of indexical terms. Such a procedure is easily available, for we notice that any 'one' of the properties of indexical expressions cited on pp. 169–70, and any combination of them, may be read as a prescription with which to search an *actual* occasion of discourse, an *actual* utterance, or an *actual* text.

When this is done, we observe the following.

Any actual occasion may be searched for indexical terms, and any actual occasion will furnish indexical terms. Whatever is the number of terms in an actual text, that text will furnish members.[48] An actual occasion with *no* text will furnish members. Any member of the list of indexical terms can be used as a prescription to locate replicas. Listing any replica of a member of the list is an adequate procedure for locating another member. Any procedure for finding *a* member is adequate for finding for *all* terms of a language that they are members, which includes 'all' – which is to say that in finding for all terms of a language that they are members we are exploring and using the members' use of 'all.' 'A one,' 'any one,' and 'all' lists of indexical terms exhibit the same properties as the particular members of 'a one,' 'any one,' and 'all' lists. Any text without exception that is searched with the use of any one or combination of properties from a list of *properties* of indexical terms will furnish members to the list. Any list of indexical terms can be indefinitely extended, as can any list of properties of indexical terms. Every procedure for finding and adding more members to the list of properties exhibits the same properties as the members it finds. Every list of properties of indexical expressions can be extended indefinitely. Whatever holds above for 'terms' holds equally for 'expressions' and 'utterances.' Finally, the preceding properties remain invariant to such operations as search for, recognition of, collection, counting, forming sentences with, translating, identifying, or performing consistency proofs or computations upon list members.

Consequences

We have seen what and how members do [the fact that our activities are accountably rational]. We have seen that the work is done without having to do formulations; that the terms that have to be clarified are not to be replaced by formulations that would not do what they do; that they are organizable as a 'machinery' for doing [accountably rational activities]; and that the abstract phenomenon of [accountable rationality] is available to natives, to ethnomethodologists, and to social scientists since the 'machinery,' because it is members' 'machinery,' in the way it is specifically used to do [accountably rational activities] is thereby part of the phenomenon as its production and recognition apparatus. We have given that work some structure. We tried to exhibit the obviousness of it, and to exhibit its enormous interest and pervasiveness for members.

(1) It seems that there is no room in the world to definitively propose formulations of activities, identifications, and contexts. Persons cannot be non-consequentially, non-methodically, non-alternatively, etc., involved in doing [saying in so many words what we are doing]. They cannot be engaged in non-consequentially, non-methodically, non-alternatively saying, say, 'This is

after all a group therapy session' or 'With respect to managerial roles, the size and complexity of organizations is increasing, and hence the requirements necessary for their successful management also.'

That there is no room in the world for formulations as serious solutions to the problem of social order has to do with the prevailing recommendation in the social sciences that formulations can be done for practical purposes to accomplish empirical description, to achieve the justification and test of hypotheses, and the rest. Formulations are recommended thereby as resources with which the social sciences may accomplish rigorous analyses of practical actions that are adequate for all practical purposes.

We are *not* saying that it is a specific trouble in the world that one cannot find out what somebody means – what any given person means in any next thing they say, or in any last thing they said – by using a procedure of requesting a formulation for each piece of talk. But we *are* saying that in so far as formulations are recommended to be definitive of 'meaningful talk' something is amiss because 'meaningful talk' cannot have that sense. Which is either to say that talk is not meaningful unless we construct a language which is subject to such procedures, or *that* could not be what 'meaningful talk' is, or 'meaningful actions' either. We *are* saying that we ought not to suppose that in order for persons in the course of their conversations and other ordinary activities to behave in an orderly fashion, one set of things that has to be involved is that they are always able, say, to formulate their role relationships and systematically invoke their consequences. For if it is the case that there is no room in the world for that, then either orderly activity is impossible, or *that* requirement for orderly activity is in any actual case relevant, irrelevant, cogent, absurd, wrong, right, etc., that requirement being formulatable in any actual case as any of these or others, separately or combined, for no more than for all practical purposes.

(2) We took notice to begin with of the notion that formulating could save the difficulties with indexicals.[49] We saw that formulating could not do that and, furthermore, that indexicals would not need saving from difficulties. We have seen that the allegedly to-be-remedied features of terms are omnipervasive. And so one must entertain the fact that *none* of them need saving.

(3) Professional sociology's achievement is to have formulated rational accountability of social structures of practical activities as precepts of constructive analysis. The social structures of everyday activities, as we remarked before, are understood by the formulations of constructive analysis to consist of such properties as uniformity, social standardization, repetition, reproducibility,

typicality, categorizeability, reportability of ordinary conduct, of talk, of territorial distributions, of beliefs about one thing or another that are invariant to changes of production cohorts. The practical technology of constructive analytic theorizing is available, in apotheosis, in the work of Talcott Parsons, Paul Lazarsfeld, and RAND techniques of systems analysis. We observe that its practitioners insist that the practices of constructive analysis are *members'* achievements. We learn from practitioners that, and how, adequate application of its precepts to demonstrations of formal structures in actual occasions demands *members'* competence. We observe, too, that particulars in procedures and results of constructive analysis furnish to members perspicuous exhibits of vaguely known 'settings.'[50] In every actual occasion of their use, particulars in procedures and particulars in results provide *members* with the combination of unavoidable, irremediable vagueness with equally unavoidable, irremediable relevance. From practitioners we understand that the combination of essential vagueness and relevance is available to *members* only, for *members'* production, evaluation, and recognition. In short, we learn from practitioners of constructive analysis that our findings about formulating are extendable to constructive analysis.

Formulating does not extend to constructive analysis as its gloss, nor is formulating a generalization of the experience of analysis. Least of all is formulating a generalization of the practices of professional sociologists. It is extendable in the ways that doing [constructive analysis] is what *members* do; like [saying specifically in so many words just what we are doing], or [saying what is meant and meaning what is said in a few well chosen words], or [removing from cell titles the nuisances of indexical expressions], or [mapping the system of real numbers on collections of indexical expressions], or [abstracting methodological paradigms from the work of ESR], or [thinking sequentially]. Because doing [constructive analysis] is what members do, what we observe about formulating is observed as well in the practices of professional sociologists doing [constructive analysis]. In that work we see *members* being careful to build context-free descriptions, relevant instructions, perspicuous anecdotes, cogent proverbs, precise definitions of ordinary activities, and context-free formalizations of natural language practices, and using members' competence with natural language practices to assure the doing and recognition of [adequate evidence], [objective description], [definite procedure], [clear, consistent, cogent, relevant instructions], [computable conversations], and the rest. In that work we see professional sociologists' insistence on members' competence to assure these glosses as concerted accomplishments.

181

The machinery of professionals' gloss achievements is described only in barest part by the practices that were described on pp. 174–9 as members' machinery for doing [rational talk for practical purposes]. How such glosses are done has not been elucidated beyond ethnographic remarks furnished by sociological practitioners, lay and professional. What various kinds of enterprises [objective sociological formulations], [definite instructions] and the rest are as conversational accomplishments is not known.

(4) From an inspection of the work of constructive analysis we learn that rational accountability of everyday activities as practical accomplishments is accounted by members to consist of the practices of constructive analysis. From that work we learn, too, that such accounts are themselves warranted features of that practical accomplishment. From their practices we learn that formal structures in the practices of constructive analysis, which, in the sense described on pp. 176–9 are *formal structures in members' natural language practices*, are *not* available to the methods of constructive analysis. We are not proposing an 'impossibility' argument in the sense of a logical proof, nor are we offering an in-principle account of constructive analysis. Nor are we recommending 'an attitude toward,' 'a position on,' or 'an approach to' constructive analysis. Nor are we saying that formal structures are not available to constructive analysis because of 'trained incapacity,' 'habitual preferences,' 'vested interests' and the like. Most emphatically, we are not offering advice, praise, or criticism.

Instead, we are taking notice of that unavailability as a phenomenon. We offer the observation about that unavailability that it is invariant to the practices of constructive analysis. This is not to say that the phenomenon somehow 'defies' the efforts of constructive analysis. The unavailability of formal structures is assured by the practices of constructive analysis for *it consists of its practices*. The unavailability of formal structures is an invariant feature of every actual occasion of constructive analysis, without exception, without time out, without relief or remedy, no actual occasion being excepted no matter how transient or enduring, the unavailability being reportable, assured, done, and recognized not only unanimously, but with required unanimity by whosoever does sociology – or, equivalently, by whosoever knows how to talk.

That formal structures in members' natural language practices are not available to the methods of constructive analysis establishes the study of practical sociological reasoning. Ethnomethodological studies have been using that unavailability to locate one or another 'piece' of constructive analysis and bring under scrutiny how its achievement is for members an accountable phenomenon. The availability of these studies establishes the *de facto* existence of an alternative to the prospects and perspectives of this conference, for although formal structures of constructive analysis are not available to constructive analysis, they are not otherwise unavailable; they are available to ethnomethodology. That this is so is less interesting than the question of whether they are available to ethnomethodology uniquely.

Appendix

Notes on glossing

The following are examples of different methods for doing observable–reportable understanding, i.e., account-able understanding. They were selected from a collection of reports of ordinary occasions in which persons who, in the same ways that they recognize or understand each other as knowing how to speak, are engaged in concertedly meaning differently than they can say in just so many words.

The examples are intended to specify 'glossing practices' as a topic. The foregoing definition is used as a weak rule to serve our interests of extending and organizing the collection: of search, detection, exclusion, titling, and so on. Is it to be read as a weak rule for the time being? It occurred to us, of course, that a more exact definition is an aim in collecting them. That aim is familiar to those who want their studies of natural language to be taken seriously. Of course we, too, entertain such an aim, but where glosses are concerned we do not entertain it too seriously because we learn when glosses are being studied, and from what we learn about glossing practices, that such an aim is not interesting. It *is* interesting instead that that aim cannot be satisfied. We shall see this from some of the examples. Further, *that* a weak definition is used to formulate as a goal a strong definition that is aimed at with the use of a weak definition, and for the accomplishment of which the weak definition is a resource, is another hope that cannot be satisfied. Or better, it is a hope that is satisfied in this way: One acquires a skill that counts as a recognized mastery of natural language. And that, too, is interesting. Further features are provided by particular and definite ways that that aim cannot be satisfied, and seem to add up to this: definiteness of glossing practices is available to study without it making any difference that definitions are lacking, are weak, loose, etc. We find that to be a repeating 'logical' feature. We are fascinated by it, and are seeking it out wherever we can.

Perhaps glossing practices can be person-specific. We are undecided. In any case the examples were selected to illustrate several differing ways in which their production is organized as a concerted, practical accomplishment. For example, Richard's gloss consists of a method whereby yet-to-be-comprehended texts are glossed over unknown ways of arriving at definite sense, where no account of a way of arriving at whatever definite sense the process comes to is called for by those doing it, or needs by them to be provided. Two variations on this thematic characteristic are provided in the case of 'mock-ups' and where definitions are used in first approximation to stronger ones.

Mock-ups. It is possible to buy a plastic engine in a hobby shop that will tell something about how auto engines work. The plastic engine preserves certain properties of the auto engine. For example, it will show how the pistons move with respect to the crankshaft: show with winking lights how the pistons are timed to a firing sequence, and so on. As we shall see it is also interesting and relevant that to make the pistons work the user has to turn the fly-wheel with his finger.

Call that plastic engine an account of an observable state of affairs. We offer the following observations of that account's features. First, in the very way that it provides for an accurate representation of features in the actual situation, and in the very way it provides for an accurate representation of *some* relationships and *some* features in the observable situation, it also makes specifically and deliberately false provision for some of the *essential* features of that situation. Second, in making this deliberately false provision it provides that the deliberately false provisions must be there if the account is to be treated as an account of that situation. Third, by reason of this false provision the account is said by the user of the account to be a 'something like,' to 'resemble' the situation he wants to use it to represent. Fourth, the knowledge of the ways in which the account – for example, the plastic engine – makes false provision is for the user a controlling consideration in permitting it to be used as an account of the actual situation. Fifth, the mock-up, for example, the plastic engine, in the entirety of its particular, actual features, whatever they are, and for whatever uses they might be put to, is understood throughout by the user to have the status of a guide to practical actions in the actual situation, whatever as an actual occasion it may consist of, when the user must come to terms with an actual engine. Sixth, this intended use is exclusively the matter of the user's choice when deciding for himself the adequacy of the mock-up and the mock-up's correct use. Finally, its use is accompanied by the user's willingness, upon whatever occasion he might encounter a feature in the actual situation that the mock-up falsely provides for, to pay full authority to the actual situation, and to let the mock-up stand without the necessary impulse of having to correct it.

A definition used in first approximation resembles Richards's gloss and mock-ups in that it furnishes still another way to accomplish recognized definiteness of talk without ever specifying how that definiteness is done.

Definitions used in first approximation occur in articles where an author at the beginning of an article may furnish a definition which he accompanies with the request that its looseness be forgiven for the time being; that for whatever reasons he will not define it more closely then and there, but if the reader will permit its provisional character he will proceed with his arguments and at a later point provide a second definition which can then be substituted.

The following example of such a definition adds still another feature. It was chosen because it provides an exhibit that the reader can use to see a case for himself in which definiteness of talk is achieved although how definiteness of talk is done is essentially unspecifiable.

Consider the following as a definition in first approximation of 'glossing:'

I want to speak about persons who know how to talk –
speakers of a language – engaged in multitudinous practices
of meaning differently than they can say in so many words
over actual occasions of interaction. I want to collect their
practices with the term 'glossing.' I want to use this definition
for the time being as a rule with which to locate relevant actual
occasions that might be searched for exhibits, and with which
exhibits might be compared, described, grouped, titled,
captioned, and so on. A more exact definition will be treated
as the aim of our inquiries. As we come, in the course of our
collecting enterprise, to learn more about what I am using the
term 'glossing' to speak about, and as we are able to furnish
the matter of our concern with greater definiteness, we shall
rewrite the definition so as to formulate from the exhibits, and
from the reflections that they motivate, their essential features
and the essential connections between these features.

We notice that with any candidate actual occasion to examine, the definition is used to an indefinitely specified depth of self-embeddedness. Even so no antinomies block or stifle its sense; nor are we confounded by the 'depth' of its recursiveness.

Anthropological quotes. An anthropologist returns from the field with his notebooks to the company of professional colleagues.

Having spent time in the field he has the task of turning his texts into a professionally acceptable report. For example, Manning Nash[51] reminds graduate students in his seminars about the tandem features of criticism and field-work: One day, each one in his turn will return from a strange society and will have to report his findings in coherent, declarative sentences. The anthropologist is going to have to write in detail what he learned from the natives to whom he is likely to have been a stranger in the critical sense that for months, and perhaps for his entire stay, their language was apt not to have been under his control. He need give no account of how his field-notes were collected. Only rarely do anthropologists tie their notes and how they were collected, expanded, analyzed, revised, and otherwise used, to their field circumstances as constituent features of those circumstances. Even less frequently do they report how the notes were turned into a report intended to be read by co-professionals. Nevertheless, 'the ways this is done' is treated by all – by writer and colleagues – as contingently accountable over the occasions in which the 'writing' is done and over the occasions in which the report is read and discussed. It is with respect to such circumstances of professional work that the use of anthropological quotes are interesting and relevant glossing practices.

The procedure of reporting in anthropological quotes is as follows. The anthropologist proceeds to rewrite the texts as a report using a procedure that he calls 'writing.' A prevailing task that is done by 'writing' is to propose an account of what his natives, in the language *they* talked, will be treated as actually and not supposedly having been talking about, given that the anthropologist cannot and will not say finally and in only so many words what they were really talking about. In this fashion he reports to colleagues that *they* talked in this way, definitely. So, for example, he cites the natives in their native terms and treats those terms with the device of a 'glossary.' That is to say, he recommends to colleagues that *he* will mean by *his* translations of natives' terms what the natives were really talking about, that he will treat the natives and their practices as final authority for, although what those might consist of beyond what he has written he cannot say and says so. The writer means what the native really means, given that the writer elects to be cautious in specifying in just so many words 'what the native really means.' This further 'what the native really means,' which is incorporated into the report as the professional's paraphrase of native informants' reportage, is glossed over the report as it is available in an actual occasion through work of professionally unspecified methods of authorship and readership.

As far as professionals are concerned, practices of anthropological glossing provide anthropologists with practices and circumstances that distinguish them from other professionals. The professional association consists of the availability of competent readers and unexplicated circumstances over which that kind of writing gets glossed. Via association membership, definiteness of sense and facticity of the report is intimately tied to conversational settings, conversation devices, conversational 'machinery' in which, and with which what is actually and not supposedly reported will have been 'seen for the saying' to have been written in so many words.

Certifying an event that you did not bid for illustrates a practice whereby a definiteness is discovered within a conversational schedule, the point of interest being that definiteness is discovered by exploiting the differences between time ordering in the event's production and the accountable time ordering of the produced event. The practice is as follows: You are conversing with another person: the person laughs. You are momentarily surprised for you had not meant to make a joke. In that you hear the person laugh you smile so as to assign to the other person's laugh its feature that his laugh detected your wit, but you conceal the fact that the other person, when he laughed, furnished you an opportunity to 'claim a credit' you did not seek.

Rose's gloss. Professor Edward Rose, a colleague at the University of Colorado, reports a practice that makes deliberate use of the property that definiteness of circumstantial particulars *consists* of their consequences. He uses that property as follows, to find out definitely what he *has* been doing.

On a visit to a city he has never seen before Rose is met at the airport by his host. They are driving home when Rose [looks] out the window – which is to say, Rose, after doing [looking ahead] then does [watching something go by] by turning his head to accord with the passage of the auto. Rose's problem is to get his partner to provide him with what he has been looking at. Doing the notable particulars [looking ahead] and [watching something go by] and their serial arrangement are the crux of the matter and make up Rose's artfulness. Continuing to do [lookinng out the window] Rose remarks, 'It certainly has changed.' His host may say something like, 'It was ten years before they rebuilt the block after the fire.' Rose, by having said, 'It certainly has changed' finds in the reply, and with the use of the reply, what he, Rose, was talking about in the first place. Picking that up, he formulates further the concerted, sensible matter that the two parties are making happen as the recognizable, actual, plainly heard specifics in a course of conversation: 'You don't say. What did it cost?', etc.

Notes

The work for this paper was supported in part by the Air Force Office of Scientific Research, grant AF-AFOSR-757-67. A version of this paper, 'On "Setting" in Conversation,' was read at the annual meetings of the American Sociological Association in San Francisco, August 31 1967, at the session on Sociolinguistics, chaired by Dr. Joshua Fishman. Hubert L. Dreyfus, Elliot G. Mishler, Melvin Pollner, Emanual Schegloff, Edward A. Tiryakian, Lawrence Wieder, and Don H. Zimmerman commented on the paper. Particular thanks are due to David Sudnow and Joan Sacks for their generosity with editorial tasks. An exceptional undergraduate term paper, 'Gloss Achievements of Enterprises' by Nancy McArthur motivated many of the paper's reflections.

1 On pp. 169–70 the properties of indexical expressions are discussed at length.
2 Emile Durkheim, *The Rules of Sociological Method*, Chicago, University of Chicago Press, 1938.
3 This property is elucidated in Don H. Zimmerman and Melvin Pollner, 'Making sense of making sense: explorations of members' methods for sustaining a sense of social order,' unpublished manuscript.
4 Olaf Helmer and Nicholas Rescher, *The Epistemology of the Inexact Sciences*, Santa Monica, RAND Corporation, October 13 1958.
5 We mean by 'infinite task' that the difference and substitutability motivates inquiries whose results are recognized and treated by members as grounds for further inferences and inquiries. It is with respect to the difference and substitutability as aims of inquiry that 'infinite task' is understood by members to refer to the 'open' character of sociological fact, to the 'self-cleansing' body of social scientific knowledge, to the 'present state of a problem,' to cumulative results, to 'progress' and the rest.
6 Hubert M. Blalock, Jr., 'The Formalization of Sociological Theory' in *Theoretical Sociology, Perspectives and Developments*, edited by John C. McKinney and Edward A. Tiryakian, Appleton Century Crofts, New York, 1970.
7 Jack Douglas, 'The general theoretical implications of the sociology of deviance,' in John C. McKinney and Edward A. Tiryakian (eds), op. cit..
8 Alex Inkeles, 'Sociological theory in relation to social psychological variables,' in John C. McKinney and Edward A. Tiryakian (eds), op. cit..
9 Paul Lazarsfeld, 'The place of empirical social research in the map

of contemporary sociology,' in John C. McKinney and Edward A. Tiryakian (eds), op. cit..

10 Marion J. Levy, Jr., 'Theory of comparative analysis,' in John C. McKinney and Edward A. Tiryakian (eds), op. cit..

11 Wilbert E. Moore, 'Toward a system of sequences', in John C. McKinney and Edward A. Tiryakian (eds), op. cit..

12 Talcott Parsons, 'General sociological theory,' in John C. McKinney and Edward A. Tiryakian (eds), op. cit..

13 Joseph Spengler, 'Articulation of economic and sociological theory,' in John C. McKinney and Edward A. Tiryakian (eds), op. cit..

14 Egon Bittner, 'Police discretion in emergency apprehension of mentally ill persons,' *Social Problems*, vol. 14, Winter 1967, pp. 278–92; 'The police on skid-row: a study of peace keeping,' *American Sociological Review*, vol. 32, October 1967, pp. 699–715.

15 Lindsey Churchill, 'Types of formalization in small-group research,' Review Article, *Sociometry*, vol. 26, September 1963; 'The economic theory of choice as a method of theorizing,' paper delivered at the American Sociological Association Meetings, August 31 1964; 'Notes on everyday quantitative practices,' in Harold Garfinkel and Harvey Sacks, eds. *Contributions to Ethnomethodology*, Indiana University Press (in press).

16 Aaron Cicourel, *Method and Measurement in Sociology*, Glencoe, The Free Press, 1964; *The Social Organization of Juvenile Justice*, New York, John Wiley and Sons, 1968.

17 Harold Garfinkel, *Studies in Ethnomethodology*, Englewood Cliffs, Prentice-Hall, Inc., 1967.

18 Craig MacAndrew, 'The role of "knowledge at hand" in the practical management of institutionalized idiots,' in Harold Garfinkel and Harvey Sacks, eds., *Contributions to Ethnomethodology*, Indiana University Press, (in press); with Robert Edgerton, *Time Out: A Social Theory of Drunken Comportment*, Aldine Publishing Co. (in press, 1968).

19 Michael Moerman, 'Ethnic identification in a complex civilization: who are the Lue?,' *American Anthropologist*, vol. 65, 1965, pp. 1215–30; 'Kinship and commerce in a Thai-Lue village,' *Ethnology*, vol. 5, 1966, pp. 360–4; 'Reply to Naroll,' *American Anthropologist*, vol. 69, 1967, pp. 512–13; 'Being Lue: uses and abuses of ethnic identification,' American Ethnological Society, *Proceedings of the 1967 Spring Meeting*, pp. 153–69, Seattle, University of Washington Press, 1968.

20 Don H. Zimmerman and Melvin Pollner, *op. cit.*

21 Edward Rose, 'Small languages,' in Harold Garfinkel and Harvey Sacks, eds., *Contributions to Ethnomethodology*, unpublished manuscript; *A Looking Glass Conversation in the Rare Languages of Sez and Pique*, Program on Cognitive Processes Report No. 102, Boulder, Institute of Behavioral Science, University of Colorado, 1967; *Small Languages: The Making of Sez*, Part 1, Bureau of Sociological Research, Report no. 16, Part 1, Boulder, Institute of Behavioral Science, University of Colorado, June, 1966.

189

22 Harvey Sacks, *Social Aspects of Language: The Organization of Sequencing in Conversation*, unpublished manuscript.
23 Emanuel Schegloff, 'Sequencing in conversational openings,' *American Anthropologist* volume 70, pp. 1075–95, 1968. 'The First Five Seconds,' Ph.D. dissertation, Department of Sociology and Social Institutions, University of California, Berkeley, 1967.
24 David Sudnow, *Passing On: The Social Organization of Dying*, Englewood Cliffs, Prentice-Hall, Inc., 1967; 'Normal crimes: sociological features of a penal code in a public defender's office,' *Social Problems*, Winter 1965, pp. 255–76.
25 D. Lawrence Wieder, 'Theories of signs in structural semantics,' in Harold Garfinkel and Harvey Sacks, ed., *Contributions to Ethnomethodology*, unpublished manuscript.
26 Don H. Zimmerman and Melvin Pollner, *op. cit.*; Don H. Zimmerman, 'Bureaucratic fact finding in a public assistance agency,' in Stanton Wheeler, ed., *The Dossier in American Society* (in press); 'The practicalities of rule use,' in Harold Garfinkel and Harvey Sacks, eds., *Contributions to Ethnomethodology*, unpublished manuscript; 'Paper Work and People Work: A Study of a Public Assistance Agency,' Ph.D. dissertation, Department of Sociology, University of California, Los Angeles, 1966.
27 i.e., socially organized in the sense in which this paper is talking of formal structures as accomplishments.
28 Alfred Schutz, *Collected Papers I: The Problem of Social Reality*, 1962; *Collected Papers II: Studies in Social Theory*, 1964; *Collected Papers III: Studies in Phenomenological Philosophy*, 1966, The Hague, Martinus Nijhoff; *The Phenomenology of the Social World*, Chicago, Northwestern University Press, 1967.
29 See footnotes 16 through 26.
30 I. A. Richards, *Speculative Instruments*, Chicago, University of Chicago Press, 1955, pp. 17–56.
31 We mean that none was called for, and that in other glossing practices something else could be the case.
32 These remarks are adapted from suggestions that we took from Samuel Todes, 'Comparative phenomenology of perception and imagination: Part I: Perception,' *The Journal of Existentialism*, vol. VI, Spring 1966, pp. 257–60.
33 This cannot be emphasized too strongly. Because we used the present perfect tense to report Richard's gloss there is the risk that our description may be read as though we were recommending that Richards's gloss defines *the* way that clear, definite speaking is done. Richards's gloss is only *one* way that clear, definite speaking is done. There are others. The others also consist of glossing practices, which are different than Richards's gloss. Richards's gloss is used as a perspicuous example, not as a definition.
34 The following excerpt provides two structurally distinct examples. (1) Not only is the speaker making out from what was said, what was meant, by the person whose talk is being quoted by the speaker, but (2) the whole body of talk is introduced by the speaker as

showing that its speaker knows what is meant by the talk of a just-prior speaker, i.e., it is delivered with 'I know what you mean' as its initial part.

> T: I know just what you mean. We, we go through this thing every year. My father said, 'No gifts.' And we tried to analyze what –
> B: Does no gifts mean no gifts or does it mean more gifts?
> T: No, he he gave us one reason why 'no gifts.' And I was questioning the reason. I didn't think it was his, a legitimate reason. I didn't think it was his real reason. He said, 'Well, you know how the Christmas, all the stores, uh, well, make such a big killing over Christmas, killing, and Christmas is becoming commercialized, and therefore, I don't wanna be sucked into this thing. I'm not giving gifts this year.'
> J: 'You spend your money and buy something you really want, and I'll spend my money and buy something I really want.'
> T: But we figured there must be something deeper, because if a guy is aware of, that Christmas is becoming very commercialized, uh, must he submit to this idea and reject it entirely, and end up giving no gifts, or is it because he really doesn't, he's not a person that likes to give anyway?
> B: Yeah.
> T: And this is just a phony excuse for not giving. And finally, I think we figured out it must be some kind of a, a combination, and he really isn't that stingy.

35 The developmental sense of 'becomes' is intended; not its sense of a development in the past that is now finished. To emphasize 'process' the sentence might be read as follows: 'Instead, his talk itself, in that it is in becoming a part of the selfsame occasion of interaction is in becoming another contingency of that interaction.' Similar remarks might be made about 'another.'

36 William Kneale and Martha Kneale, *The Development of Logic*, London, Oxford University Press, 1962, p. 16.

37 Charles S. Peirce, *Collected Papers*, vol. 2, Cambridge, Mass., Harvard University Press, 1932, paras 248, 265, 283, 305.

38 Ludwig Wittgenstein, *Philosophical Investigations*, Oxford, Basil Blackwell, 1953.

39 Occasional expressions are discussed in Marvin Farber, *Foundation of Phenomenology*, Cambridge, Mass., Harvard University Press, 1943, pp. 237–8; and C. N. Mohanty, *Edmund Husserl's Theory of Meaning*, The Hague, Martinus Nijhoff, 1964, pp. 77–80.

40 Bertrand Russell, *Inquiry into Meaning and Truth*, London, Allen and Unwin, 1940, chapter 7, pp. 102–9.

41 Nelson Goodman, *The Structure of Appearance*, Cambridge, Mass., Harvard University Press, 1951, pp. 290ff.

42 A review of indexical expressions is found in Yehoshua Bar-Hillel, 'Indexical expressions,' *Mind*, vol. 63, (ns), 1954, pp. 359–79.

43 Hubert L. Dreyfus, 'Philosophical issues in artificial intelligence,' *Publications in the Humanities*, no. 80, Department of Humanities, Massachusetts Institute of Technology, Cambridge, Mass., 1967; Hubert L. Dreyfus, *Alchemy and Artificial Intelligence*, P-3244, Santa Monica, RAND Corporation, December, 1965.

44 The reader is asked to read for 'all sciences' any inquiries whatsoever that are directed to the detection and assessment of effectiveness of practical activities and to the production of members' accounts of that effectiveness. In addition to the academically taught sciences of the Western world, we include the 'ethno' sciences that anthropologists have described, e.g., ethnomedicine, ethnobotany, and the rest; as well as the enormous number of empirical disciplines that have their effectiveness in and as practical activities as their abiding phenomenon: Azande witchcraft, Yaqui shamanism, waterwitching, astrology, alchemy, operations research, and the rest.

45 It is not only because members can *do* formulating and observe it that formulating is reportable. In that members are *doing* and *observing* formulating being done, it is reportable; or in that members do formulating and observe that it *was* done, it is reportable; or in that members when doing it observe it *will have been done*, it is reportable; in that members when doing it observe it can have been done, etc. The criterial consideration is not the availability of 'tensed' verbs but the temporal structures of such enterprises. Temporal structures of formulating enterprises include of course the availability to members of time references in natural language.

The clumsiness of sentence structure may be something of a benefit if it earmarks the relevance and availability of the extensive, developed, and deep temporal 'parameters' of members doing formulations as accountable enterprises. Particular attention is called to the work that David Sudnow is doing on the temporal parameters of accountable glances.

46 Garfinkel, *op. cit.*, pp. 29–30.

47 Because we are required to learn what these practices are by consulting members, we must require of the methods that we use to locate these practices, and of the practices that such methods locate that they satisfy the same constraints. The arguments to justify this assertion and to show that the method we use is adequate with respect to these requirements are detailed in Harold Garfinkel, 'Practices and structures of practical sociological reasoning and methods for their elucidation,' in *Contributions to Ethnomethodology*, Indiana University Press (in press).

48 'Member' of the list has the conventional meaning of item of the list.

49 We take notice of how practices of practical sociological reasoning seek to remedy the indexical properties of talk: they seek essentially to do so.

50 We have borrowed from remarks made by Hubert L. Dreyfus about

Wittgenstein and Merleau-Ponty during his informal seminar, Harvard University, March 1968.

51 Personal communication.

Index

For Product Safety Concerns and Information please contact our EU
representative GPSR@taylorandfrancis.com
Taylor & Francis Verlag GmbH, Kaufingerstraße 24, 80331 München, Germany

www.ingramcontent.com/pod-product-compliance
Lightning Source LLC
Chambersburg PA
CBHW050707280326
41926CB00088B/2861